INTERTEMPORALITY AND THE LAW

Margarita ...

INTERTEMPORALITY AND THE LAW OF TREATIES

D.W. Greig

BIICL
British Institute of
International and
Comparative Law

Published and Distributed by
The British Institute of International and Comparative Law
Charles Clore House, 17 Russell Square, London WC1B 5JP

British Library Cataloguing in Publication Data
A Catalogue record of this book is available from the British Library

ISBN 0–903067–71–4

Typeset by Cambrian Typesetters
Frimley, Surrey
Printed in Great Britain by Biddles Ltd.,
Guildford and King's Lynn

ACKNOWLEDGEMENTS

This small book was commenced while I was a Visiting Professor at the London School of Economics and Political Science and at King's College, London, in the academic year 1999–2000, working as a Visiting Scholar at the British Institute of International and Comparative Law. I completed it on my return to the Faculty of Law at the Australian National University as a Visiting Fellow in 2000–2001. I am grateful to both the Institute and the ANU for making their research facilities available to me. I should also like to express my warmest appreciation of the invaluable efforts of Ms Susan Hunt of the Law Department at LSE and Ms Jennifer Braid of the Centre for International and Public Law at the ANU in producing a text of the work suitable for submission for publication.

Intertemporality and the Law of Treaties

The significance of temporal elements in relation to the law of treaties has not been addressed to any appreciable extent either in the literature of international law,[1] or in the jurisprudence of international tribunals. This is surprising given that temporal issues arise on the very wording of a number of provisions of the Vienna Convention on the Law of Treaties 1969 and that the relationship between the provisions of that Convention and the development of rules of customary international law inevitably involves a consideration of the time scale over which a particular rule may have emerged.

In legal terminology, temporal matters manifest themselves as questions of law or as issues of fact. As international lawyers, we tend to be more familiar with and to concentrate upon the former and even to disguise the relevancy of fact in legal garb. The very concept of intertemporality would seem to suggest that a legal issue should be assessed in light of all the circumstances, whether of law or fact, contemporaneous with it. In practice, the tendency has been to emphasise the law contemporaneous with a matter as the principal factor against which it has to be assessed. We are most aware of the concept of the intertemporal law from its application to territorial disputes and especially from the words of Huber, the arbitrator, in the *Island of Palmas* case:[2]

> Both parties are also agreed that a juridical fact must be appreciated in the light of the law contemporary with it, and not of the law in force at the time when a dispute arises or falls to be settled.

[1] Bindschedler-Robert, 'De la Rétroactivité en Droit International Public' in *Recueil d'Etudes de Droit International en homage à Paul Guggenheim* (1968), 184; Tavernier P, *Recherches sur l'application dans le temps des actes et des règles en droit international public (problèmes de droit intertemporel ou de droit transitoire)* (1970), a work concentrating on the principle of non-retroactivity, though including, in Part Two, chapters on acquired rights and the distinction between the creation and maintenance of rights drawn by Huber in the *Island of Palmas* case, below nn. 2 and 3; Rosenne, 'The Temporal Application of the Vienna Convention on the Law of Treaties' (1970) 4 Cornell Int LJ 1; Yasseen, 'L'interpretation des traités d'après la convention de Vienne sur le droit des traités' (1976-III) 151 Hag Rec 1 at 64–67; Nascimento e Silva, 'Le facteur temps et les traités' (1977-I) 154 Hag Rec 213 at 265–271; Higgins, 'Some Observations on the Inter-Temporal Rule in International Law', in Makarczyk J (ed.), *Theory of International Law at the Threshold of the Twenty-first Century: Essays in Honour of Krzysztof Skubiszewski* (1996), 173; Higgins, 'Time and the Law: International Perspectives on an Old Problem' (1997) 46 ICLQ 501.

[2] (1928) 2 UNRIAA 829 at 839.

Taken out of context, as it is easy to do, the inference can be drawn from this pronouncement that the given is a (juridical) fact and that this fact has to be understood in the light of the law, rather than in relation to the circumstances surrounding, or giving rise to, the disputed issue. Taken in context, however, the passage cannot be interpreted in this way. The juridical fact to which the arbitrator was referring was the act of discovery so that the question was whether, at the time of the alleged discovery of the island by Spain in the early part of the 16th century, discovery alone created territorial sovereignty over the island.

The limited scope of the above passage is also borne out by the arbitrator's subsequent pronouncement in which he made clear that changes in the law were not excluded from consideration:[3]

> As regards the question which of different legal systems prevailing at successive periods is to be applied in a particular case (the so-called intertemporal law), a distinction must be made between the creation of rights and the existence of rights. The same principle which subjects the act creative of a right to the law in force at the time the right arises, demands that the existence of the right, in other words its continued manifestation, shall follow the conditions required by the evolution of the law.

Whereas the former passage was limited to the juridical fact of discovery, this latter pronouncement is broader in compass. While it refers back at the beginning to 'the act creative of a right' (that is, the act of discovery), the subsequent existence of the right is not dependent upon a single act, but upon the 'continued manifestation' of the right. This manifestation comprised the multiple facts of connection and control which demonstrated the degree of authority exercised (on the evidence, by the Netherlands, rather than by Spain) over the island.

There seemed to be a sufficient connection between the intertemporal law as described in the *Palmas* case and the law of treaties for Waldock, as Special Rapporteur, to incorporate the concept in the form of draft article 56 in his Third Report on the Law of Treaties as follows:[4]

[3] (1928) 2 UNRIAA 829 at 839.

[4] Yb ILC 1964, vol II, 8–9. Elias certainly regarded the 'doctrine . . . as having general applicability in various fields of customary international law', 'The Doctrine of Intertemporal Law' (1980) 74 AJIL 285, including (at 296–302) the interpretation of reservations to international instruments, as in the *Aegean Sea* case, ICJ Rep 1978, 3. Intertemporality can also be a significant issue in a domestic setting. In *Kruger v Commonwealth* (1997) 190 CLR 1, the High Court of Australia had to consider the constitutional legality of the Northern Territory legislation which authorised a government official to undertake the care, custody or control of any Aboriginal or half-caste if, in his opinion, it was necessary or desirable for him to do so. One of the grounds advanced on behalf of the appellants was that the removals which had taken place between 1925 and 1949 under this legislation of members of the so-called 'stolen generation' had been discriminatory. However, as Toohey J commented (ibid, at 97): 'When the Ordinance is analysed and placed in its historical setting, is it reasonably capable of being seen as providing a rational and relevant basis for discriminatory treatment

1. A treaty is to be interpreted in the light of the law in force at the time when the treaty was drawn up.
2. Subject to paragraph 1, the application of a treaty shall be governed by the rules of international law in force at the time when the treaty is applied.

This proposal elicited a range of reactions from members of the Commission. Some were favourable;[5] others were to the effect that paragraph 1 was really a rule of interpretation and should be considered in that context;[6] some took the line that the two paragraphs were unhelpful as they were mutually inconsistent;[7] others treated the issues raised by the draft article as being determinable by reference to the will of the parties.[8] The proposal was then dropped.

Waldock's approach has been criticised on two further grounds. In the first place, it is difficult to regard interpretation and application as such distinct features of the operation of treaties.[9] How a treaty might be applied if interpreted in a particular way is relevant to how it should be

of persons answering the description of 'Aboriginal or half-caste'? No such basis would survive analysis today. But, for the reasons advanced earlier in this judgment, the Ordinance must be assessed by reference to what was reasonably capable of being seen by the legislature at the time as a rational and relevant means of protecting Aboriginal people against the inroads of European settlement.'

In contrast, in *Mabo v Queensland* (1992) 175 CLR 1, the High Court held that native title to land survived the acquisition of sovereignty over Australia by the British Crown. As Brennan J said in the course of his judgment (ibid, at 41–42): 'If it were permissible in past centuries to keep the common law in step with international law, it is imperative in today's world that the common law should neither be nor be seen to be frozen in an age of racial discrimination.

The fiction by which the rights and interests of indigenous inhabitants in land were treated as non-existent was justified by a policy which has no place in the contemporary law of this country . . . Whatever the justification advanced in earlier days for refusing to recognise the rights and interests in land of the indigenous inhabitants of settled colonies, an unjust and discriminatory doctrine of that kind can no longer be accepted. The expectations of the international community accord in this respect with the contemporary values of the Australian people.'

[5] Rosenne (Israel), Yb ILC 1964, vol I, 35, para 11; Bartos (Yugoslavia) ibid, 36, para 20; Tsuruoka (Japan), ibid, 37, para 26; Briggs (USA), ibid, 38, para 38.

[6] Castren (Finland), ibid, 35, para 3; Tabibi (Afghanistan), ibid, 35, para 6; Amado (Brazil), ibid, 38, para 47.

[7] Paredes (Ecuador), ibid, 34, para 13; Castren, ibid, 35, para 2; Tabibi, ibid, 36, para 7; a view rejected by Briggs, ibid, 38, para 40; see also Lachs (Poland), 39, para 54. As Judge Shahabuddeen said in the *Maritime Delimitation in the Area between Greenland and Jan Mayan* case, ICJ Rep 1993, 38 at 134, in relation to the 'extent to which the interpretation and application of a treaty must take account of the subsequent evolution of the law', a matter which 'has been much debated', 'the same facts cannot at one and the same time be subject to two contradictory rules', citing *inter alios* Judge Anzilotti in the *Electricity Company of Sofia and Bulgaria* case (1939) PCIJ Ser A/B, No 77, 64 at 90, and Judge Urrutia, ibid, at 105.

[8] Tsuruoka, ibid, 36–7, para 24; Yasseen (Iraq), ibid, 37, para 33.

[9] See Verdross (Austria), ibid, 33, para 6.

interpreted.[10] Secondly, even if interpretation and application can be identified as separate steps, they do not really match with the 'appreciation' and 'continued manifestation' which formed the basis of the *Palmas* ruling.[11] Overall temporal elements are relevant to the operation of treaties, but not necessarily in the ways indicated by Waldock, particularly with their emphasis on the law rather than on both the law and the facts.

Before proceeding to deal with those elements in more detail, it is instructive to consider a matter mentioned earlier, and that is the lawyer's tendency to dress up issues of fact in legal form. This is probably the explanation for the appearance of Waldock's draft Article 56(1) and also for the attention paid to the notion of a critical date in the *Palmas* case.

With regard to that provision, it has already been pointed out that it was criticised *inter alia* on the ground that it related primarily to the interpretation of treaties and was better dealt with in that context. In its final Commentary, the Commission reported that it had decided to 'omit the temporal element', opting instead for the inclusion of what became Article 31(3)(c) in the Convention as part of its 'general rule of interpretation', in the form of a reference to 'any relevant rules of international law applicable in the relations between the parties' which were to be 'taken into account, together with the context'.[12] However, there was a degree of ambiguity in the Commentary's presentation of the position. The text of Article 31(3)(c), and the reference at the start of the Commentary's consideration of that provision to draft Article 56(1), suggest that it is only the rules at the time the treaty is made which are to be taken into consideration, thus excluding the operation of what appeared in draft Article 56(2) concerning the rules in force at the time when the treaty is applied. Yet the Commentary went on to suggest that the rules of international law referred to in Article 31(3)(c) are not limited to those existing at the time the treaty was made:[13]

[10] The application of this principle is to be seen in cases where an international tribunal has rejected an interpretation of a treaty, preferring another, because the result of choosing the former would be to deprive the treaty of effect, or to render it incompatible with its object and purpose: for the Court, see the *Settlers of German Origin* case (1923) PCIJ Ser B, No 6, 25–26; *Acquisition of Polish Nationality* case (1923) PCIJ Ser B, No 7, 16–17; *Free Zones* case (1927) PCIJ Ser A, No 22, 13; applied *Corfu Channel* case, ICJ Rep 1949, 4 at 24; for other tribunals, see the *Cayuga Indians* claim (1926) 6 UNRIAA 173 at 184; cited in *Asian Agricultural Products Ltd. v Republic of Sri Lanka* (1990) 106 ILR 416 at 440. See also the International Law Commission's final report on the law of treaties, Yb ILC 1966, vol II, 219, para (6).

[11] Higgins, 'Some observations . . .', n. 1 above, at 178 observing that, in her view, 'whether appreciation and continued manifestation . . . are at all the same as interpretation and application is doubtful'.

[12] Yb ILC 1966, vol II, 222, para (16).

[13] Ibid.

the Commission . . . also considered that, in any event, the relevance of rules of international law for the interpretation of treaties in any given case was dependent on the intentions of the parties, and that to attempt to formulate a rule covering comprehensively the temporal element would present difficulties.

The suggestion in this passage may not be explicit, but it seems to be implicit in the wording employed by the Commission, partly in the reference to the difficulties in drafting a comprehensive rule, and partly in the reference to the intentions of the parties. Certainly at the time draft Article 56 was under discussion in the Commission, several members alluded to the significance of the parties' intentions in determining whether the law in force at the time of the drawing up of a treaty or the law in force at the time of application was more important to the interpretation of the instrument.[14] Moreover, as in relation to the time of the conclusion of a treaty, the circumstances existing at the time of its application cannot be excluded from the factors to which the principle of intertemporality requires reference to be made.

As to the situation to which draft Article 56(1) related, that is to say the rules of international law extant at the time of the making of a treaty, it seems rather artificial to regard them as distinct from the context of the treaty. Yet this was clearly the Commission's intention.[15] Nevertheless, the principle of intertemporality would seem to require that the parties to a treaty would expect it to be understood, and therefore interpreted, in light of all relevant circumstances surrounding its making, including the rules of international law contemporaneous with it. Indeed it is possible to interpret the various cases employed by Waldock in his Third Report in justification of draft Article 56(1),[16] as equally supporting the above view of intertemporality. These matters and the cases in question will be dealt with in more detail later.[17]

The other notion that lawyers can employ to dress up factual issues as matters of law is that of the critical date. As with the concept of the intertemporal law, we tend to be familiar with it from cases concerning

[14] De Arechaga (Uruguay), Yb ILC 1964, vol I, 34, para 11; Tsuruoka (Japan), ibid, 36–37, para 24; Yasseen (Iraq), ibid, 37, para 33. This perception of the Commission's thinking is further borne out by the sentence following the passage quoted in the text at n. 13 which reads (Yb ILC 1966, vol II, 222, para (16)): the Commission 'further considered that correct application of the temporal element would normally be indicated by interpretation of the term in good faith', which would seem to require that the intentions of the parties should not be ignored.

[15] Thus, according to the last sentence of the Commentary on paragraph (3)(c) of what became Article 31 of the Convention: the Commission 'decided to transfer this element of interpretation to paragraph 3 as being an element which is extrinsic both to the text and to the "context" as defined in paragraph 2' (ibid), that paragraph providing an exceedingly narrow definition of 'context ', see below p 22.

[16] Ibid.

[17] Below pp 46–49.

territorial disputes, though it is one of the objects of this volume to demonstrate that it can be helpful in relation to treaty law.

Sometimes the date associated with a particular event will be of crucial importance. To take a simple example, in the *Eastern Greenland* case,[18] Norway purported to claim the disputed area on 10 July 1931. Clearly that date was of determinative significance. If, as the Permanent Court held to be the position, Denmark had established its sovereignty over the area in question by that date, the territory would not have been *terra nullius* and Norway's declaration would have been ineffective. Two questions need to be asked, however: how critical, and how specific, is the date?

With regard to the first issue, the *Eastern Greenland* case centred upon a particular date which was both determinative and specific. The same is true with respect to the *Island of Palmas* case.[19] The date of the alleged cession of the island by Spain to the United States in the Treaty of Paris 1898 was 'critical' because it was on that date that the rights of Spain (and therefore of the United States) as against the Netherlands had to be determined. As the arbitrator asserted:[20]

> If a dispute arises as to the sovereignty over a portion of territory, it is customary to examine which of the States claiming sovereignty possesses a title—cession, conquest, occupation, etc.—superior to that which the other State might possibly bring forward against it. However, if the contestation is based on the fact that the other Party has actually displayed sovereignty, it cannot be sufficient to establish the title by which territorial sovereignty was validly acquired at a certain moment; it must also be shown that the territorial sovereignty has continued to exist and did exist at the moment which for the decision of the dispute must be considered as critical.

Too much should not be read into such pronouncements. The selection of a critical date may be important in enabling the tribunal to exclude evidence from consideration rather than the date necessarily, on its own, being in some way determinative of the dispute. In the *Minquiers and Ecrehos* case,[21] France and the United Kingdom apparently accepted that the identification of such a date was all important because acts performed after that date would be disregarded by the Court. Hence, in an attempt to deprive the United Kingdom of the benefit of various acts of administration performed in more recent times, France contended that the critical date was that of a fisheries convention of 1839 between the two countries. Not surprisingly, in order to avoid this outcome, the United Kingdom argued that the only plausible date was that provided by the Special Agreement of 1950 between the two States whereby the dispute had been

[18] (1933) PCIJ Ser A/B, No 53, 45.
[19] (1928) 2 UNRIAA 829.
[20] At 838–839.
[21] ICJ Rep 1953, 47.

submitted to the Court, the reason being that the dispute had 'not become "crystallised" ' before that date.[22]

The Court was reluctant to identify any particular date as critical, in the sense of being determinative of the dispute. It did specifically reject the French preference for the date of the Convention of 1839 on the ground that 'no dispute as to the sovereignty over the Ecrehos and Minquiers groups had yet arisen'.[23] Such a dispute 'did not arise before the years 1886 and 1888, when France for the first time claimed sovereignty over the Ecrehos and Minquiers respectively'.[24] However, the Court seemed to acknowledge that these dates did carry a degree of criticality in that, although events occurring after the dates could 'also be considered by the Court', they would be excluded from consideration if 'the measure in question was taken with a view to improving the legal position of the Party concerned'.[25]

The notion of a critical date is essentially an evidentiary tool available to a tribunal should it wish to employ it and if the circumstances identify an appropriate one.[26] In the *Minquiers and Ecrehos* case, the Court treated the years 1886 and 1888 when the dispute over sovereignty first emerged as being significant, but it did not identify them as critical because of the fact that they did not exclude all evidence of subsequent events, but only limited the scope of the evidence in question. In the more recent *Land, Island and Frontier Dispute*[27] between El Salvador and Honduras, a Chamber of the Court emphasised that, though the principle of *uti possidetis* underlined the importance of the date of independence in boundary adjudication, this did not mean that subsequent evidence of the

[22] Ibid at 59. The United Kingdom defined its view of the critical date in what at first appears to be inflexible terms. Thus Heald had this to say (ICJ Pleadings, vol 2, 48): 'By the term "critical date" is meant the date by reference to which—or rather, by reference to the legal and factual position existing at which—the respective rights of the parties are to be determined.'; and Fitzmaurice (ibid, 61): 'it can be defined by saying that the critical date in a dispute about sovereignty over territory is the date by reference to which—by reference, that is to say, to the situation existing at which—the merits of the parties' claims should be adjudged. It is, in fact, the date on which the situation is deemed to have become crystallised or, as it were, in modern language, frozen. The acts of the parties after that date cannot alter the legal position, so as either to improve or prejudice the claim of either party.' But see below nn. 25 and 26.

[23] Ibid.

[24] Ibid.

[25] Ibid. Despite the Court's reluctance to specify any particular date as critical in the sense advocated on behalf of the United Kingdom, Fitzmaurice continued to maintain this view as the correct one of the critical date in 'The Law and Procedure of the International Court of Justice, 1951–4: Points of Substantive Law: Part II' (1955–6) 32 BYIL 20 at 23.

[26] Hence the tribunal's rather dismissive attitude in the *Argentine-Chile Frontier Award* case (1966) 38 ILR 10 at 80 that 'the notion of the critical date' was 'of little value in the present litigation'.

[27] ICJ Rep 1992, 351.

parties' understanding of the position at that date was excluded.[28] Moreover, the Chamber went on to explain that, even though *uti possidetis* was a cardinal principle, this did not mean that 'the position at the date of independence is always determinative; in short, that no other critical date can arise', for a 'later critical date may arise, for example, either from adjudication or from a boundary treaty'. And, if the *uti possidetis* position could be qualified by adjudication or by treaty, there 'seems to be no reason in principle why [acquiescence or recognition] should not operate, where there is sufficient evidence to show that the parties have in effect clearly accepted a variation, or at least an interpretation, of the *uti possidetis juris* position.'[29]

Looked at from a different perspective, the role of a critical date is to highlight or explain the significance of events occurring within particular periods of time. Viewed in this way, it may be more the period or periods thus identified which are critical.[30] In the *Minquiers and Ecrehos* case,[31] the two periods thus distinguished were that up to 1886 and 1888 in which all evidence of relevant acts was admissible, and the period after those dates when the Court considered that it should ignore any acts of the parties carried out with the specific intention of improving their respective claims.

Despite the contentions of the parties in the *Minquiers and Ecrehos* case, the flexibility of the critical date is apparent from the approach adopted by the Court in that case and by the Chamber in the *Dispute* case between El Salvador and Honduras. In fact, on closer examination, the arguments of the United Kingdom in the former came close to admitting that the concept was not so rigid as that State appeared to be maintaining. In the course of his address to the Court, Fitzmaurice enjoined that the

[28] As the Court explained (ibid at 395): 'There is one further problem . . . and how far that is "republican titles", grants made after independence, in the time of the Federal Republic of Central America, 1821–1839, and thereafter, may be considered as evidence of the 1821 boundary . . . There seems to the Chamber to be no sensible reason to reject the whole category of these grants as evidence just because they are subsequent to 1821. Such republican titles, particularly those granted in the years immediately following independence, may well provide some evidence of what the position was in 1821, and both Parties have offered them as such.' Similarly, the Chamber held (at 399) that it could 'have regard also, in certain circumstances, to documentary evidence of post-independence *effectivités* when it considers that they afford indications in respect of the 1821 *uti possidetis juris* boundary, providing a relationship exists between the *effectivités* concerned and the determination of that boundary.'

[29] Ibid at 401.

[30] See the use of a 'critical period' in the *Taba Award* (1998) 80 ILR 224 at 284, 291, 299 and 324. This is in line with Goldie's asertion in 'The Critical Date' (1963) 12 ICLQ 1251 at 1264 that 'the critical date doctrine . . . is more than a rule excluding evidence in a dispute before an international tribunal . . . It is a rule which sets a term to the span of time during which, in a given case, right-creating facts can be availed of in order to perfect a title.'

[31] ICJ Rep 1953, 47.

'fundamental object' of establishing a critical date was 'to ensure that the dispute is determined on the basis that seems most just and equitable, having regard to all the circumstances of the case.'[32] The invocation of equity in this fashion was designed solely as a basis for selecting what that date should be, because 'serious injustice may result if it is not selected with the most careful regard to all the factors involved'.[33] However, the involvement of what is equitable cannot be limited to the selection of the date. It is equally relevant to other issues such as the purposes and consequences of making such a selection, including the extent to which that selection might be determinative of a particular matter. This is, in effect, what occurred in the *Minquiers and Ecrehos* case and the *Dispute* case, both of which illustrate the value of a critical date as an evidentiary tool in the hands of the interpreter.

In whatever way one explains concepts like the intertemporal law or the critical date, it will be seen that they can also play a part in relation to the law of treaties. Intertemporality may suggest or even require that the evidence existing, or the law prevailing, at a particular time, should be applied to determine, or should even be disregarded from consideration with respect to, the matters in issue between the parties. Intertemporality can thus identify a critical or significant date with regard to a particular dispute or, in some cases, aspect of the dispute, as different dates or periods may be more important to different matters in contention.

As a framework for discussion, the starting point will be the first critical date identified by the intertemporal law, that is the date on which the treaty was concluded. The second major section will deal with the relatively familiar matter of how the law of treaties manages the consequences of changing circumstances over the life of a treaty and may suggest an alternative or additional critical date by reference to the date of application of the treaty. At this time not only will the inevitable consequence be a retrospective view of what has transpired in relation to the treaty, but it may also be necessary to consider prospectively how the treaty might need to be applied in the future (a possibility of particular significance if the treaty is the constitution of an international organisation). A third section will address the part played by the time scale of a treaty's history in the selection of the appropriate rules to govern its termination or suspension. Finally, there will be a discussion of the retrospectivity of the rules contained in Articles 31 and 32 of the Vienna Convention. Though this involves a somewhat unchronological approach, it is this aspect which has been raised by the facts of the *Kasikili/Sedudu Island* case[34] between

[32] ICJ Pleadings, vol 2, 67–68, a point he later reiterated, ibid, 69: 'the conception of a critical date is intended to do justice to the real merits of each country's case'.

[33] Ibid, 69.

[34] Judgment of 13 December 1999; text in (2000) 39 ILM 310.

Botswana and Namibia and it is with a consideration of that case that this monograph will conclude.

I. THE FIRST CRITICAL DATE: THE TIME WHEN A TREATY IS MADE

As already pointed out, the basic principle of the intertemporal law is that, in the words of the *Island of Palmas* award,[35] 'a juridical fact must be appreciated in the light of the law contemporary with it', so that 'the act creative of a right' must be tested against 'the law in force at the time the right arises'. Certainly a treaty constitutes 'a juridical fact' and this aspect of the intertemporal law is readily applicable to the making of a treaty.

It must be admitted that there is a degree of ambiguity in employing a word like 'made', or 'concluded' (the term used most frequently in the Vienna Convention), in relation to a treaty. The making of a treaty is a process, commencing with its negotiation and culminating in the step or steps whereby it is adopted and consented to by the States involved. For some purposes, it may be necessary to examine evidence from the entire process, in which case it would be the period that would be critical if the period is delineated by the date of adoption of, or consent to, the treaty. For other purposes, they are the circumstances at a specific date which are all important, though a second issue can arise as to which of the possible dates is critical, the adoption of the text or the giving of consent by a particular State.

According to Article 11 of the Vienna Convention, acceptance of the obligations of a treaty is dependent upon 'the consent of a State' which 'may be expressed by signature, exchange of instruments constituting a treaty, ratification, acceptance, approval or accession, or by any other means if so agreed'. If the two steps are closely related in time (for example, the exchange of instruments referred to in Article 11, or the adoption of the text of a treaty referred to in Article 9 of the Vienna Convention,[36] followed by its speedy ratification or acceptance), there might be no reason for differentiating between them as far as establishing a critical date is concerned. On the other hand, if a lengthy period elapses between the date of adoption and the date of ratification or acceptance or entry into force of a treaty,[37] it might be necessary to take more than one date into account

[35] (1928) 2 UNRIAA 829 at 839.

[36] By Article 9:

> 1. The adoption of the text of a treaty takes place by the consent of all the States participating in its drawing up except as provided in paragraph 2.
> 2. The adoption of the text of a treaty at an international conference takes place by the vote of two-thirds of the States present and voting, unless by the same majority they shall decide to apply a different rule.

[37] It is only rarely that the date of entry into force will constitute a critical date; for examples see *Lighthouses Arbitration between France and Greece* (1956) 23 ILR 659 at 664–666,

as far as the effects of a treaty are concerned, if indeed the later date does not entirely replace the date of adoption as far as assessing those effects are concerned.

II. WHEN IS A TREATY CONCLUDED IN RELATION TO THE INVALIDITY PROVISIONS OF THE VIENNA CONVENTION?

As already suggested the significance of the critical date or dates or period is not limited to enabling an interpreter to take account of the law in force at the relevant time(s): it equally brings into play the factual circumstances surrounding the event or events by which that date is, or those dates are, identified, or within a period demarcated by such dates. The uncertainties inherent in the 'conclusion' of a treaty as well as the possibility that there might be more than one critical date, as well as periods of time, involved, are well illustrated by various provisions of the Vienna Convention dealing with the grounds for invalidity.

A. *Error*

Take, for example, Article 48(1):

> A State may invoke an error in a treaty as invalidating its consent to be bound by the treaty if the error relates to a fact or situation which was assumed by that State to exist at the time when the treaty was concluded and formed an essential basis of its consent to be bound by the treaty.

The word conclusion appears in the title to Part II of the Vienna Convention, 'Conclusion and Entry into Force of Treaties', where it would seem to signify the date of adoption of a treaty as representing its date of conclusion[38] when that is a separate step from the giving of consent to be bound.

when that date was of critical importance as designating when territory was detached from the Ottoman Empire and therefore available for allocation to Greece; and the *Arbitral Award by the King of Spain* case, ICJ Rep 1960, 192 at 207–9, when the treaty upon which the award was based was to 'be in force for a period of ten years', so that when it determined in accordance with that provision depended upon the ascertainment of the date when the treaty came into force. Support for the use of a critical date in such a context is provided by the way it was employed in the *Electricity Company of Sofia and Bulgaria* case (1939) PCIJ No 77, 64, when the Permanent Court held that the facts constituting the sources of the dispute between Belgium and Bulgaria had all occurred 'subsequent to the material date' (postérieurs á la date critique') (p 82), which was 'the date of the establishment of the juridical bond between the two States under Article 36 of the Court's Statute' (at p 81); applied by the International Court in the *Right of Passage* case, ICJ Rep 1960, 6 at 33–36.

[38] This would be in accordance with the statement in Whiteman M, *Digest of International Law*, vol 14 (1970), 19: 'Conclusion is used to refer to the successful outcome of the negotiations and agreement upon the terms of the accord reached, even though the

The use of the clause 'at the time when the treaty was concluded' in Article 48(1) is more problematic. It can be given a similar interpretation to that just suggested. At the time the treaty was adopted, the State must have erroneously assumed that a fact or situation existed, and that fact or situation must have formed an essential basis of the State's consent to be bound whenever that was given. The difficulty with this interpretation is in a situation where the State only considers becoming a party to a treaty long after it was adopted, and it can only be at that stage that it formed an erroneous assumption as to the existence of the fact or situation so crucial to the giving of its consent to the treaty. To cover that situation Article 48(1) should have been drafted along the following lines:

A State may invoke an error in a treaty as invalidating its consent to be bound by a treaty if the error relates to a fact or situation which was assumed by that State to exist at the time when it gave its consent to be bound by the treaty and formed an essential basis of the giving of that consent.

It is doubtful whether the text of the existing Article 48(1) can be interpreted to cover such a situation.[39] Nevertheless, it should he pointed out that, in Waldock's Second Report on the law of treaties,[40] no such difficulty would have arisen. Article 8 dealt with a 'mutual error', that is where the parties were all labouring under the same mistake regarding the substance of the treaty when they 'entered into' it.[41] Article 9 covered a

agreement reached is subject to ratification or other subsequent approval.' With regard to the Vienna Convention, its text was adopted on 22 May 1969, but the Final Act was 'Done at Vienna' on 23 May 1969, and it is the latter date which the UN gave as when it was 'concluded' (see 1155 UNTS 331, No 18232). For a consideration of differing opinions as to whether conclusion of a treaty goes further than adoption of its text and includes its subsequent ratification (which in the case of most multilateral treaties would produce a range of different dates of conclusion for the various participating States), see McDade, 'The Effect of Article 4 of the Vienna Convention on the Law of Treaties 1969' (1986) 35 ICLQ 499 at 507–510.

39 Vierdag, 'The Time of the "Conclusion" of a Multilateral Treaty: Article 30 of the Vienna Convention on the Law of Treaties and Related Provisions' (1988) 59 BYIL 75 at 89, saw no temporal difficulties with his assertion about Article 48 that: 'The structure of the provision points to an early error, made by representatives in the stage of adoption of the text, or of signature subject to ratification. The consent to be bound, which comes later, is supposed in Article 48 to have been expressed already, and now appears to rest on an erroneous basis. So the time of the conclusion of the treaty in Article 48 is the moment the text of the treaty is adopted.' It is true that, at one time, the effect of an accession clause, if accepted, was 'to result in a new treaty albeit identical with the old one [—] between the original contracting parties and the acceding State' (Lauterpacht's First Report on the Law of Treaties, Yb ILC 1953, vol II, 121, n. 3), but as Vierdag's comments suggest, this perception of what is encompassed by conclusion is not in accordance with contemporary analysis.

40 Yb ILC 1963, vol II, 36

41 Ibid, 48. As Vierdag pointed out (59 BYIL at 80): 'Another expression used extensively in international treaty practice but nowhere defined is to "enter into" a treaty. This term normally appears to refer to expressing consent to be bound.'

situation of 'unilateral error', where 'only one or some of the parties to a treaty has or have entered into it under an error', and specifically provided in paragraph 3 that, 'in the case of a State acceding to a treaty in the conclusion of which it did not take part, it may invoke an error as invalidating its consent to be bound by the treaty'.[42] Not only was it apparent that the error must coincide with the giving of consent, that is the act of entering into the treaty, but also that this principle was to operate even in the case of a State which had not participated in negotiating the treaty and only subsequently acceded to the instrument. Following criticism of the attempt to differentiate between the two types of fraud,[43] the provisions were redrafted to form a single article. It is not altogether clear whether this revised version would have produced a similar result to that achieved by what ultimately became Article 48.1.[44]

It is difficult to understand why the shift to the Article 48 version took place as far as the requirements are concerned that the error must have related to a fact or situation assumed by the State to have existed when the treaty was concluded and must also have 'formed an essential basis of its consent to be bound by the treaty' at the time that consent was given. It is particularly illogical given that the Commentary to draft Article 34 asserted that it was to apply 'no less to an error made by only one party than to a mutual error made by both or all of the parties'.[45] Perhaps the reason why the position of a State was ignored which had satisfied the second criterion by being in error at the time it gave its consent to the treaty, but, having not been involved in the original negotiations, would not have made the qualifying assumption of the first requirement, was the

42 Yb ILC 1963, vol II, 48.

43 See Paredes (Ecuador), Yb ILC 1963, vol I, 38, para 68; Rosenne (Israel), ibid, 39, para 75; Briggs (USA), ibid, 40, para 8; Elias, ibid, para 13; Tunkin (USSR), ibid, 41, para 25; specific objection was also made to the limitation of unilateral error to cases of 'innocent misrepresentation, negligence or fraud of the other party or parties': see Tunkin, ibid, para 27; Ago (Italy) agreeing, ibid, para 28: 'If an error was intentionally induced by the other party, that was, in practice, the case referred to by article 7, i.e. fraud; but in the case of an error in the true sense of the word, it mattered little whether it had been caused unintentionally by the other party or was due to other circumstances, so long as the error had been the deciding reason for consent and consent was thus vitiated.'

44 According to the new draft Article 34(1) (Yb ILC 1963, vol II, 195): 'A State may invoke an error respecting the substance of a treaty as invalidating its consent to be bound by the treaty where the error related to a fact or state of facts assumed by that State to exist at the time when the treaty was entered into and forming an essential basis of its consent to be bound by the treaty.' For it to retain the meaning of the earlier draft, it would have to be interpreted as if it read '. . . assumed by that State to exist at the time when it entered into the treaty and forming an essential basis. . .'; the use of 'when the treaty was entered into' without the addition of the words 'by that State' suggests that draft Article 34(1) was already intended to have the meaning subsequently adopted in the wording of Article 48.

45 Yb ILC 1963, vol II, 196, para (6); the same assertion was made in the Commentary to the Commission's final text, Yb ILC 1966, vol II, 244, para (5).

tendency of members of the Commission to treat error as of primary significance in relation to bilateral treaties or multilateral treaties with a limited number of parties.[46]

Article 48 is open to the objection that it does not provide a satisfactory or principled resolution to the effects of error on a treaty. The concept of the critical date provides a valuable means for assessing and explaining the provision's shortcomings. Article 48 gives rise to the possibility that two such dates might be required. If the date of conclusion of, and the date of consent to, the treaty are not sufficiently proximate, it will be necessary for the victim State to demonstrate that it satisfied the relevant standard of error required at each of the dates. Yet principle would seem to dictate that it is only the act of consent that should be linked to the requisite degree of error and that therefore the only relevant critical date should be the time at which that consent was given.

B. Fraud

Despite some similarity, at least in theory, between error and fraud (after all an error might well be caused by the conduct of another party, which, if done deceitfully, would amount to fraud), Article 49 deals with the latter in a different way:

> If a State has been induced to conclude a treaty by the fraudulent conduct of another negotiating State, the State may invoke the fraud as invalidating its consent to be bound by the treaty.

Vierdag suggested that 'conclude' in this context must 'refer to conclude in the sense of "adopt the text", as the fraud occurs through the conduct of "another negotiating State" . . . [which] is, according to Article 2(1)(e), a State which "took part in the drawing up and adoption of the text of a treaty".'[47]

The drafting of Article 49 is defective for a number of reasons, particularly if Vierdag's view is accepted. In the first place, if it is only the conclusion of a treaty by a negotiating State which can be tainted by the fraud of another negotiating State, it would leave the subsequent adherent to the

[46] Waldock (UK) Yb ILC 1963, vol I, 43, para (59); Amado (Brazil), ibid, para (53); Bartos (Yugoslavia), ibid, 35, para (26), though speaking of fraud; Ago (Italy), ibid, 31, para (51), also in the context of fraud; Verdross, ibid, 32, para (64), ditto; Gros (France) ibid, 34, para (17). There were some warnings of the need to differentiate, e.g. by Tunkin (USS), ibid, 41, para 26; Bartos certainly raised the question, ibid, 30, para (34), and above. The most surprising manifestation of this proclivity was the statement in the 1963 Commentary, vol II, 196, para (8), that, if 'the party whose consent to the treaty was induced by the error . . . does invoke the error as invalidating its consent, the effect will be to make the treaty void *ab initio*.' The same mistaken approach was avoided in the final Commentary, Yb ILC 1966, vol II, 244, para (7).

[47] 59 BYIL at 87.

treaty who did not participate in the original negotiations unprotected by Article 49.[48] Secondly, although this objection exists whatever meaning of conclude is adopted, the provision is limited to fraud perpetrated by a negotiating State and does not grant relief in a situation where the victim State was influenced by the fraudulent conduct of a non-negotiating State or of a non-State actor. Thirdly, if Vierdag's view is adopted, the wording of Article 49 could be interpreted as signifying that, as long as a negotiating State was misled by the fraud of another negotiating State in the period up to the conclusion of the treaty, it could, on later acceptance of the treaty, rely upon the earlier fraudulent conduct to escape from the treaty, even if its consent was no longer influenced by the deception.

This third possibility would be totally inconsistent with the general principles of law upon which Article 49 could be said to be based.[49] If the fraud is no longer operative (that is, affecting the judgement of the consenting State), there would be no grounds for its avoiding the treaty. To make sense of Article 49, the concluding of the treaty must be equated with entering into it. This interpretation would be consonant with the earlier version of the provision in draft Article 7 of Waldock's Second Report:[50]

1. Where one party to a treaty has been induced to enter into it by the fraud of another, the former shall be entitled after discovering the fraud—
   (a) to declare that the fraud nullifies its consent to be bound by the treaty ab initio; . . .

. . .

2. Para 1 of this article shall not, however, apply where—
   the adoption of the text of a treaty, which is subject to ratification, acceptance or approval, has been procured by fraud but, after discovering the fraud, the State nevertheless proceeds to ratify, accept or approve the treaty . . .

The interpretation of conclude in this sense would go some way to avoiding the first of the problems indicated above.

Admittedly, there would remain the difficulties associated with the reference to the fraudulent conduct of 'another negotiating State'. For example, it would be an absurd consequence if a non-negotiating, subsequently deceived, adherent to the treaty was denied the protection of Article 49 by virtue of this reference, suggesting as it does that the State influenced by the conduct must be the first negotiating State. There are two possibilities for dealing with the situation. The less satisfactory way would be to regard such a situation as covered by general principles of law outside the Convention. There are two obstacles to such a solution. The preamble affirms only that 'questions not regulated by the provisions of

[48] Nor might such a party be able to seek relief under Article 48, see above p 12.

[49] See the Chairman (de Arechaga)'s comment, Yb ILC 1963, vol I, 41.

[50] Yb ILC 1963, vol II, 36 at 47: see also draft Article 53(1) of the 1963 Report to the General Assembly, ibid, 187 at 194.

the present Convention' can be governed by rules of customary international law, and it is doubtful whether this can be interpreted as meaning that, if a provision of the present Convention dealing with a specific matter is deficient, then an issue which it fails to cover, or deal with adequately, can be resolved by reference to general principles of law. The second difficulty is that, in any case, Article 42(1) prescribes that 'the consent of a State to be bound by a treaty may be impeached only through the application of the present Convention'. A more satisfactory approach would be to emphasise the objective of the provision which is presumably to protect any State from being fraudulently induced to enter into a treaty and that there is no reason to restrict that protection to a negotiating State, that limitation not being specifically stated in, but at most being possibly implied from, Article 49.

The second problem with the reference to 'another negotiating State' is associated with the perpetrator of the fraud. The change from the earlier version which required the fraud to be that of 'another' party had one beneficial effect. In the early years of a treaty's existence, only a limited number of States might have ratified it. Under that version, therefore, a State misled by fraud on the part of a State which had not yet become a party would not have been able to rely upon the fraud to escape from the treaty, presumably until the State in question did become a party. At least the use of the expression 'negotiating State' in Article 49 enables the deceived State to invoke the fraudulent conduct of any of the negotiating States, even those not yet parties to the treaty, as a ground for invalidating its consent. But what is the position where the fraud was perpetrated by a State which was not involved in the negotiations leading to the adoption of the treaty? On the face of it, Article 49 does not cover such a situation. However, if one can regard the 'conclude' as constituting entry into the treaty in question, in order to protect a State which had not participated in the negotiation of the treaty, can one extend the meaning of 'negotiating State' from that specified in Article 2(1)(e) of the Vienna Convention as limited to 'a State which took part in the drawing up and adoption of the text of the treaty'? It would not seem implausible to regard State Y, which was not involved in those negotiations, but with an interest in the treaty, or at least in State X, the victim of Y's fraudulent conduct, becoming a party because of that fraud, to be in effect negotiating with that State in order to induce it to become a party to the original treaty.

Two possible outcomes would seem to flow from this scenario. If the negotiations are regarded as producing a separate arrangement between the two States, the result might be that State X would be entitled to avoid its obligations *vis-à-vis* State Y, even under the original treaty if State Y also became a party to it. This is a somewhat artificial way of viewing the situation as States X and Y would still be regarded as parties to the original treaty in their relations with all other parties. This might not be acceptable to State X once the fraud is revealed. The preferable alternative would be to regard the negotiations as sufficiently linked to the original treaty to enable State X to employ the fraudulent conduct of State Y in its capacity as 'another negotiating State' as a ground for avoiding its acceptance of the treaty altogether.[51] Of course, this interpretation of the wording still would not cover the situation where the fraud was perpetrated by a non-State actor, an issue which seemed to be of no concern either to the Commission or to States represented at the Vienna Conference.[52]

As with the case of error, the identification of a critical date can underscore some of the problems associated with Article 49. Application of the word conclude in its narrower meaning as equivalent to adoption of the treaty would result in that act determining the critical date. This would have the unsatisfactory consequence, outlined above, of preventing subsequent adherents, which had not been involved in the negotiating process, from relying upon Article 49 for protection against fraud. It is difficult to imagine that the Commission really intended their redrafting of the earlier Waldock text to have this result. The suggestion made in this volume at least has the advantage of linking the critical date to the date upon which the victim State gave its consent to the instrument in question.

C. *Corruption or coercion of a State's representative*

The problems stemming from the use of conclude or conclusion in the various provisions concerning invalidity do not arise with regard to

[51] It may be that the remaining parties would not be happy with State Y's continued participation in the treaty, a problem which could arise equally with regard to a fraudulent original negotiating State. It is doubtful, however, whether State Y's conduct, even if it had at the time been a party to the treaty, would constitute a ground for the other parties, acting under Article 60(2)(b) of the Vienna Convention, to suspend or terminate their relationship with State Y under the treaty. In the first place, such a right would require State Y to have committed a material breach of the treaty, that is a breach of 'a provision essential to the accomplishment of the object and purpose' of the treaty in the words of Article 60(3)(b). Article 60(3) does not include a serious breach of a less important provision in its definition of a material breach. Secondly, in any case, it is not certain that such fraudulent conduct in inducing another State to adhere to a treaty constitutes a breach of a treaty obligation owed to the existing parties. Article 26 requires all parties to a treaty to perform it 'in good faith'. Not only may the fraud not constitute a failure to perform that requirement, but it is far from clear what the status of that requirement is between the parties to a treaty. In this situation, of course, the conduct in question was directed towards a State not yet a party to the treaty.

[52] The matter was not raised in the discussions at the 678th and 679th Meetings of the Commission, Yb ILC 1963, vol II, 27–38; and it was only raised at the Vienna Conference in relation to the Corruption of the Representative of a State (that is, what became Article 50 of the Convention): see the comment of Matine-Daftary (Iran), UN Conf, First Session, 264, 47th Mtg, Cttee of the Whole, para 10: 'In some cases, . . . corruption could be imputable not to the contracting State, but to beneficiaries of certain provisions of a treaty, who might be individuals or large companies.'

Articles 50 and 51 which both employ the unambiguous wording the 'expression of a State's consent' if 'procured' by the conduct regarded as sufficiently reprehensible (corruption of a State's representatives or coercion of them) to enable the victim State to avoid the act of consent in question. Whereas the use of conclude or conclusion gives rise to various difficulties, some of a temporal nature, the only temporal matter of any significance in relation to Article 50 or 51 is the critical period leading up to, and the giving of, the prospectively invalid or ineffective act of consent. It is during that period that the subsequently impugned corruptive or coercive conduct will have occurred.

D. Threat or use of force

In contrast, Article 52 reverts to more ambiguous language:

> A treaty is void if its conclusion has been procured by the threat or use of force in violation of the principles of international law embodied in the Charter of the United Nations.

This provision raises obvious issues of retrospectivity which will not be considered here. The Charter predated the Vienna Convention by more than 20 years and embodied some rules of international law which had emerged in the years between the two world wars.[53] However, our concern is what is to be made of the use of 'conclusion' in this context.

At first sight, there would seem to be no reason for departing from the primary meaning of conclusion as denoting the finalising of the negotiations and the adoption of the treaty's text. If the treaty at that stage is void, then it is not possible to ratify it, adhere to it, or bring it into force. The treaty remains a nullity.[54]

However, it is possible to envisage circumstances which differ significantly from the situation concentrated upon by the International Law

[53] The words 'international law embodied in' were inserted in the original ILC draft Aarticle as a result of amendment A/CONF.39/C.1/L.289 and Add 1, UN Conf Docs, 172; see the comments of Smejkal (Czechoslovakia, one of the co-sponsors of the amendment), First Session, 271, 48th Mtg, Cttee of the Whole, paras 39–40.

[54] This would seem to be the position with regard to a void act under Anglo-Australian law: see *Brook v Hook* (1871) LR 6 Exch 89; *Rowe v B & R Nominees Pty Ltd.* [1964] VR 477; *Bedford Insurance Co. Ltd. v Instituto de Resseguros do Brasil* [1985] QB 966 at 986. There did appear to be some difference of opinion amongst members of the International Law Commission on this point in relation to treaties: compare the comments of Paredes (Ecuador), Yb ILC 1963, vol I, 52, para 73 ('For technical reasons of law, it should not be provided that a treaty concluded as a result of the illegal use or threat of force was non-existent, for that would be going too far. It would suffice to say that such a treaty was void *ab initio*, not voidable') with those of Rosenne (Israel), ibid, 55, para 25 ('It was important to realise that the consequence of voidance *ab initio* was simply that there was no treaty; it was not "opposable" in any way . . .').

Commission, namely of a treaty being forcibly imposed upon a single State by another State (or perhaps a group of States) where the provisions of the treaty are those dictated for its personal advantage by the stronger side. What is the legal position where the treaty to which the coerced State accedes is one that already exists as a valid and effective instrument? Suppose States A and B had entered into a local resource-sharing agreement and later, by the threat to use force, secured State C's adherence to the agreement. If 'conclusion' is given the meaning attributed to it in the previous paragraph, Article 51 would not apply to protect State C. To avoid this result, the conclusion of the treaty, and therefore the critical date, would have to be extended to cover the act of acceptance by a later adherent to the treaty, which would then be considered the conclusion of the treaty as far as each of those States was concerned. The outcome of applying Article 52 on that basis would, however, be that the treaty would be void as far as all three States are concerned.

Where A and/or B were involved in the threat or use of force against C, this outcome would not be entirely unmeritorious. It would not be satisfactory, however, if the reason for State C's accession to the resources treaty between A and B was a threat or use of force emanating from State X. Nor would it be an acceptable outcome if a multilateral treaty having a large number of parties were rendered void by State C's forced participation in the treaty, whether the threat or use of force came from without, or even from a single State within, the treaty regime.

No such difficulty would have arisen if the Convention had followed more closely draft Article 12(1)(a) of Waldock's Second Report on the Law of Treaties, which said:[55]

> If a State is coerced into entering into treaty through an act of force, or threat of force employed against it in violation of the principles of the Charter of the United Nations, the State in question should be entitled—
> (a) to declare that the coercion nullifies its consent to be bound by the treaty *ab initio* . . .

The principal objection to this version related to the fact that, under draft Article 12(1)(c) and 12(2), a State could affirm such a treaty or waive its right to avoid the treaty. The reaction was to contend that, since 'the use of force against a State was illegal, except in the case of self-defence covered by Article 51 of the Charter, it followed that a treaty imposed by the use or threat of force must be null and void.'[56]

The reason for adopting this view, at least implicit in the comments made by members of the Commission, was that they were considering the

[55] Yb ILC 1963, vol II, 51.

[56] Tunkin (USSR), Yb ILC 1963, vol I, 57, para 52; Ago (Italy), ibid, 56, para 39; Gros (France) agreeing, ibid, 57, para 45; Yasseen (Iraq), ibid, 56, para 37; Rosenne (Israel), ibid, 55, paras.25–27; Chairman (de Arechaga (Uruguay)), ibid, 54, para 73.

law from the perspective of a particular type of treaty, one where obligations were imposed upon a State by the wrongful conduct of the other party to a bilateral treaty, or of the remaining parties to a multilateral instrument. On the basis of the principle of *ex turpis causa*, such a treaty should be regarded as void, so that there was no question of the victim State having to seek to escape from the consequences of its act of consent. Indeed, despite his advocacy of draft Article 12 entitling the coerced State to declare that its consent was thereby nullified, Waldock stressed that 'treaties resulting from an illegal use or threat of force are lacking essential validity.'[57]

The rule of invalidity is appropriate where the treaty itself is tainted by the coercive conduct of those, the coerced State apart, involved in its making. The rule expressed in Article 52 of the Vienna Convention is satisfactory in those limited circumstances, but it is singularly inappropriate in situations where the act of coercion does not relate to the conclusion of the treaty among the parties, the coerced State apart, themselves, or where that State becomes a party as a result of a later act of coercion so that its position does not appear to be covered by Article 52 at all. The only way of making sense of Article 52 as part of a rational legal order is to regard it as limited solely to treaties tainted by the illegality of the coercion as outlined above. Treaties where the coercion came from outside the treaty, or from only one among a large number of parties, would not be tainted by the coercive act. Nor of course would a subsequent accession to a treaty in such circumstances. In such cases it would not be the treaty, but only the act of consent of the coerced State, which would be a nullity. In terms of the critical date, Article 52 would be limited to the date of the treaty's conclusion, whereas, in the case of a treaty unaffected by the act of coercion, the critical date would be that of the act of consent the validity of which is being called in question.

E. Jus cogens

The provisions in the Vienna Convention dealing with the effects of the *jus cogens* fit comfortably into the scheme of the intertemporal law as explained in the *Island of Palmas* case.[58] The principle that a juridical fact must be appreciated in the light of the law contemporary with it is to be seen in both Article 53 and Article 64 of the Convention.

The former is tied to the date when a treaty is made. As Article 53 in part provides:

> A treaty is void if, at the time of its conclusion, it conflicts with a peremptory norm of general international law.

[57] Commentary to draft Article 12, Yb ILC 1963, vol II, 52, para 7.
[58] (1928) 2 UNRIAA 829.

The use of 'conclusion' in this context must signify the adoption of the treaty for two reasons. In the first place, it is at this stage that the text of the treaty as adopted presents to the world the final intentions of the negotiating States. Thus, it is the contents of the treaty which has to be tested against the requirements of the *jus cogens* as they exist at this time. If Article 53 does apply, the treaty is void and therefore incapable of being brought into effect by the consent of the parties. Secondly, there is no reason for giving the word 'conclusion' a more extensive interpretation because, if the prohibitive rule of the *jus cogens* should develop subsequently, the treaty would be brought to an end in accordance with Article 64 of the Convention:

> If a new peremptory norm of general international law emerges, any existing treaty which is in conflict with that norm becomes void and terminates.

This is in keeping with the second aspect of the intertemporal law, namely that 'the existence of the right', in this case the treaty, 'in other words, its continued . . . [validity] shall follow the conditions required by the evolution of the law.'[59]

As to the critical date, it is the date of emergence of the new peremptory norm that sets the date of termination for the treaty in question. From a practical point of view, the criticality of that date depends upon whether there is any need to show more than that, at the date a dispute over the application of the treaty arose, the norm already existed which rendered that instrument void. However, the significance of the date of application or of adjudication for the law of treaties is a matter which will be considered at greater length in a subsequent section of this volume.[60]

III. CRITICAL FOR THE PURPOSES OF INTERPRETATION

In the interpretation of a treaty, the initial point of departure is that the interpreter should examine the circumstances as they existed at the time the treaty was made. While this requirement, based as much upon common sense as upon general principles of law, identifies the date when the treaty was concluded as critical for the purposes of the interpretative process, it is less clear how broad the circumstances are which can be employed in this process.

The provisions of the Vienna Convention have regularly been cited by the International Court as representing contemporary customary international law governing the interpretation of treaties.[61] It has to be said, however, that those provisions do not provide a satisfactory guide on the particular point under discussion.

[59] Ibid at 845.

[60] Below p 50.

[61] *Territorial Dispute (Libya/Chad)*, ICJ Rep 1994, 6 at 21–22; *Maritime Delimitation and Territorial Questions* case, ICJ Rep 1995, 6 at 18.

A. The context, preparatory work of a treaty and the circumstances surrounding its conclusion

According to Article 31(1) of the Convention, the 'ordinary meaning' is to be given to the terms of a treaty 'in their context'. Context would seem to suggest that the interpreter has to take account of the circumstances surrounding the making of the treaty, without which it might be difficult to understand what the parties had in mind in employing the terminology of the text of the treaty. However, the meaning attributed to context in Article 31(2) of the Convention is extremely narrow:

> The context for the purpose of the interpretation of a treaty shall comprise in addition to the text, including its preamble and annexes:
> (a) any agreement relating to the treaty which was made between all the parties in connexion with the conclusion of the treaty;
> (b) any instrument which was made by one or more parties in connection with the conclusion of the treaty and accepted by the other parties as an instrument related to the treaty.

This provision is open to the criticism that it is textual and not in any sense contextual. Surrounding circumstances are only available to the interpreter automatically:

1. in that very narrow sense;
2. where the evidence is necessary to establish the object and purpose of the treaty to which Article 31(1) also requires reference to be made; or
3. where the information is required to demonstrate the existence of 'any relevant rules of international law applicable in the relations between the parties' within Article 31(3)(a);[62]

any further reference 'to the preparatory work of the treaty or the circumstances of its conclusion' being excluded except, in the words of Article 32, 'to confirm the meaning resulting from the application of Article 31, or to determine the meaning when the interpretation according to Article 31:

(a) leaves the meaning ambiguous or obscure; or
(b) leads to a result which is manifestly absurd or unreasonable.'

Although the balance between context on the one hand, and preparatory work or surrounding circumstances on the other, such evidence being available principally as an aid to resolving an ambiguity, seems, on the wording of Articles 31 and 32 of the Vienna Convention, to be heavily weighted towards the limited role for surrounding circumstances in the latter provision, this view of the two provisions may be misleading. The possible significance of preparatory work as part of the context is obscured by its availability under Article 32 either to confirm the ordinary

[62] Above pp 4–5.

meaning, or to provide a meaning in cases of ambiguity, absurdity or unreasonableness. There is little reason for the Court to admit that the *travaux préparatoires* are in conflict with the apparent meaning of the text.[63]Where there might be a possibility of this occurring, the way out of the dilemma is to treat the text as ambiguous in order to allow recourse to the evidence provided by the *travaux* to resolve the ambiguity in favour of the interpretation which the *travaux* suggest. As for the 'circumstances' of a treaty's conclusion referred to in Article 32, which, on the wording of the provision, must signify something distinct from preparatory work, it is difficult to see how they, unlike the preparatory work, can fulfil the role apparently assigned to them by Article 32. Admittedly much depends upon the scope of the evidence which is included in this category. As long as the category itself is placed exclusively within the hierarchical order of subordination indicated by Article 32, the scope of the category is unimportant. However, if the category is reclassified *de facto* as part of the general rule of interpretation in Article 31, the change could make a significant difference. Indeed, there are a number of examples of cases where the *travaux*/circumstances have been employed, not in that capacity, but more in the guise of context as part of Article 31, notwithstanding that such evidence demonstrates a wider 'context' than that defined in Article 31.

In the *Convention concerning the Employment of Women during the Night* case,[64] the Permanent Court was called upon by the Council of the League of Nations to answer the question whether the Convention applied 'to women who hold positions of supervision or management and are not ordinarily engaged in manual work?' The crucial provision was Article 3 which stipulated that women 'without distinction of age shall not be employed during the night in any public or private industrial undertaking, . . . other than an undertaking in which only members of the same family are employed.' The Court's opinion is usually cited[65] only for its affirmation of the rule years later included in Article 32 of the Vienna Convention that the preparatory work could be relied upon in this case because it 'confirms the conclusion reached on a study of the text of the Convention that there is no good reason for interpreting Article 3 otherwise than in accordance with the natural meaning of the words'[66] as extending to women in positions of supervision or management.

[63] As Judge Schwebel said of the work of the Commission and of the Vienna Conference in response to his own question—'What happens when the *travaux préparatoires* turn out not to confirm but to contradict the meaning arrived at by application of the general rule of interpretation?'—'surprisingly little attention was paid to this critical question' (*Maritime Delimitation and Territorial Questions* case, ICJ Rep 1995, 6 at 31); see further below pp 30–31.

[64] (1932) PCIJ Ser A/B, No 50.

[65] See the Commission's final report on the law of treaties, Yb ILC 1966, vol II, 223, para (18).

[66] Ser A/B, No 50 at 380.

It has to be said that to read the Court's opinion so narrowly would be to disregard its significance in relation to the range of material which it took into account. Although the Court started from the ordinary meaning which it attributed to Article 3 of the Convention,[67] it is apparent, from its subsequent endorsement of the limited role played by preparatory work, that its consideration of the rest of the material must have been justifiable on some other ground,[68] and that ground could only have been the context of, or surrounding or background circumstances to, Article 3.

This view of the case is demonstrated by the way in which the Court dealt with various aspects of the evidence. It started with the proposition that Article 3 was 'in no respect inconsistent either with the title, or with the Preamble, or with any other provisions of the Convention',[69] matters which, even on the Vienna Convention's narrow approach to context, would qualify. The Court then considered, but rejected, the contention that, as the ILO Constitution was aimed principally at ameliorating the lot of manual workers, the Employment of Women at Night Convention must be interpreted as intended to apply only to manual workers.[70] Finally, the Court referred to the business of the Washington Conference, as indicated in its agenda, at which the Convention was to be drafted as a replacement for the earlier Berne Convention. As the latter had been restricted to workers in industry, the Washington Convention should be regarded as similarly limited. The Court did not accept this argument,[71] but it did make it clear that it did not regard such a contention as being 'based on the "preparatory work" . . . of the Convention', but on the context in which the Convention was made, that is to say 'the programme of the Conference . . . and . . . the contents of that programme'.[72] Moreover, it was because they took the opposite view of what could be deduced from 'the agenda, documents and minutes of the Washington Conference which refer to the Berne Convention' that four members of the Court appended a declaration that they could not 'subscribe to the grounds and conclusion of the present opinion'.[73]

67 Ser A/B, No 50 at 373.

68 As the Court stated (ibid): 'If . . . Article 3 . . . is to be interpreted in such a way as not to apply to women holding posts of supervision and management and not ordinarily engaged in manual work, it is necessary to find some valid ground for interpreting the provision otherwise than in accordance with the natural sense of the words.'

69 Ibid.

70 Ibid at 374.

71 Ibid at 376–377.

72 Ibid at 376.

73 Ibid at 382. The four members of the Court were Baron Rolin-Jaequemyns, Count Rostworowski and Judges Fromageot and Schücking. Judge Anzilotti also dissented, but justified his division between evidence which could automatically be used and preparatory work on the basis that the former was necessary to enable an interpreter to ascertain 'the subject and aim' of a treaty (ibid at 383 ff.). Of course, Article 31(1) of the Vienna Convention also enables the surrounding circumstances to be ascertained to the extent necessary to give the terms of a treaty their 'ordinary meaning . . . in light of its object and purpose'.

In light of this case, and the freedom with which the judges made use of evidence that could just as well have been excluded on the ground that it formed part of the preparatory work, the narrow attitude displayed by the International Law Commission and the Vienna Conference to context is surprising. Such discussion as there was of the general rule of interpretation at the 1964 session of the Commission centred primarily on the need to incorporate the object and purpose of a treaty as part of that rule.[74] However, there was nothing to suggest that this change was envisaged as resulting in any significant broadening of the evidence that could be taken into account by an interpreter.[75]

B. *The analogy of domestic law*

Apart from ignoring the significance of the *Convention concerning the Employment of Women at Night* case[76] for the reception of evidence of surrounding circumstances more extensive than that suggested by the Commission's own draft of what became Article 31 of the Vienna Convention, this aspect of the Commission's work can be criticised for other reasons. Even if members of the Commission could have pleaded the excuse that the scope of the context/surrounding circumstances justification for examining a range of evidence that would otherwise have been excluded had not been canvassed extensively at the international level, it was certainly a matter of controversy in some municipal legal systems. As to why any notice should be taken of lessons learned from domestic law, it has to be acknowledged that the rules of treaty interpretation originated in, and were assimilated from, municipal law. Admittedly, the rules in question were, during the seventeenth and eighteenth centuries, ascribed to

[74] See the comments of Bartos (Yugoslavia), Yb ILC 1964, vol I, 279, para 64; ibid, 281, para 91; de Luna (Spain), ibid, 281, para 85; Chairman (Ago, Italy), 281, para 86; accepted by Waldock, ibid, 281, para 88. The only person to raise doubts about the subordinate nature of surrounding circumstances as a result of its inclusion in what became Article 32 was Rosenne who was reported as saying (ibid, 284, para 24): 'The article which would follow [the general rule of interpretation] and which would deal with subsidiary sources would cover preparatory work. He was not absolutely certain that the circumstances surrounding the conclusion of the treaty should be included under that same heading.'

[75] Indeed Waldock regarded his existing draft, with its reference to 'the context of the treaty as a whole', as already encompassing the objects and purposes of a treaty, see ibid, 281, para 87. This same thinking appeared in the Commission's final report on the law of treaties. The paragraph dealing with draft Article 27(1), which was the basis of Article 31(1) of the Convention, concentrated principally on the importance of context, but concluded with its only justification for the reference in draft Article 27(1) to 'in the light of its object and purpose': 'The Court has more than once had recourse to the statement of the object and purpose of the treaty in the preamble in order to interpret a particular provision' (Yb ILC 1966, vol II, 221, para (12)).

[76] (1932) PCIJ Ser A/B, No 50.

the dictates of natural law.[77] But by the nineteenth century there was a striking division of opinion amongst those who, in the absence of any general means of judicial settlement of disputes, regarded interpretation as largely unregulated by rules;[78] those who still relied upon the writings of, *inter alios*, Grotius and Vattel;[79] those prepared to rely upon examples of State practice to fashion a limited number of rules;[80] and those promoting instead a much more flexible approach to interpretation than that employed by municipal courts when dealing with contracts and other instruments.[81] There were also examples of a parallel being drawn between the interpretation of treaties at the international level and the interpretation of written instruments in domestic law,[82] and this phenomenon has continued into recent times.[83]

[77] Hence Grotius H, at the start of his chapter 'On Interpretation' in *De Jure Belli ac Pacis* (1646) Book III, Eng. trans., Carnegie (1925), 409, posited that 'natural reason demands that one to whom the promise has been made should have the right to compel the promisor to do what the correct interpretation suggests'. Similarly, in his chapter on 'The Interpretation of Treaties', Vattel E de, *The Law of Nations or The Principles of Natural Law* (1758), Eng. trans., Carnegie (1916), 199, having observed that in 'concessions, agreements, treaties, in all contracts, just as in laws, it is impossible to foresee and point out all the specific cases that might arise under them', went on to say that it was 'therefore necessary to lay down rules founded upon reason and authorised by the natural law and adapted to throw light upon what is obscure, decide what is uncertain, and frustrate the designs of one who enters into the contract in bad faith.'

[78] Hyde CC, *International Law Chiefly as Interpreted and Applied by the United States*, vol II (1922), 70; Lawrence TJ, *The Principles of International Law*, 7th edn. (1923), 302; Wheaton H, *Elements of International Law*, 6th Eng. edn (1929), 522; Westlake J, *International Law*, vol I (1910), 293, acknowledging, however, that some form of interpretation was nevertheless necessary.

[79] Halleck HW, *International Law*, 4th edn, vol I (1908), 317-320; see also Oppenheim L, *International Law*, vol I (1905), 559: 'Grotius and the later authorities applied the rules of Roman Law respecting interpretation in general to interpretation of treaties. On the whole, such application is correct in so far as those rules of Roman Law are full of common sense. But it must be emphasised that interpretation of treaties is in the first instance a matter of consent between the contracting parties. If they choose a certain interpretation, no other has any basis. It is only when they disagree that an interpretation based on scientific grounds can ask a meaning.'

[80] Phillimore R, *Commentaries upon International Law*, 3rd edn, vol II (1882), 97–132; Hall WE, *A Treatise on International Law*, 8th edn (1924), 390 ff.

[81] Westlake, loc cit, n 78; Hyde, op cit, 63 advocating the employment of whatever extrinsic evidence 'sheds light on the question involved'.

[82] *Van Bokkelen* case (1888) Moore, Int.Arb., vol II, 1807 at 1848; *Geofroy v Riggs*, 133 US 258 at 270 (1890); Lu JTC, *The Interpretation of Treaties* (1927), 38; Wright, 'The Interpretation of Multilateral Treaties' (1929) 23 AJIL 94.

[83] See Lauterpacht, 'Restrictive Interpretation and the Principles of Effectiveness in the Interpretation of Treaties' (1949) 26 BYIL 48 at 56, suggesting that most 'of the current rules of interpretation ... are no more than the elaboration of the fundamental theme that contracts must be interpreted in good faith ... That overriding rule must indeed be regarded as one of the general principles of law recognised by civilised states in the matter of interpretation'; *Re Italian Special Capital Levy Duties* (1949) 18 ILR 406 at 407: 'By reason of its

Despite the references in the case law and the literature to the close parallel between the rules of international law concerning treaty interpretation and their municipal counterparts for dealing with the interpretation of contracts or statutes, there has been little detailed examination of whether the latter throw much light upon the former. Nevertheless, the proposals ultimately drafted by the International Law Commission, and largely incorporated into the Vienna Convention, do have a familiar ring about them from the perspective of a municipal lawyer, reflecting a similarity which is close enough to suggest that a consideration of the latter might be helpful in an analysis of the former.

The hierarchy implicit in the relationship between Article 31 (the general rule) and Article 32 (the supplementary means of interpretation and particularly the limited role for preparatory work) is reminiscent of the common law position where extrinsic evidence of the latter type was barred from consideration by a court. In the domestic setting, this rule was at one time strictly applied not least because it enabled a judge to control the proceedings by limiting or excluding a jury's access to such information, and ultimately enabling him to interpret the written contract as a matter of law.[84] Many were the tactical battles fought over the admissibility of such evidence, because it was accepted that extrinsic evidence was 'admissible in respect to the subject matter, the situation and relations of the parties and all the circumstances, to explain any ambiguity apparent on the face of the instrument.'[85]

With the decline in the use of a jury in civil cases that has occurred in England and Australia, it was left to the judge alone to determine issues of fact as well as of law. From the point of view of limiting the role of the jury, there was no longer a need for an exclusionary rule. It was retained, however, at least to an extent, as a means of curtailing the length of trials through the judges' power to exclude what they might regard as unnecessary

character as a contractual instrument, the Treaty must be interpreted according to the canons of good faith'; *Pertusola* claim (1951) 18 ILR 414 at 419: 'there is scope for the application to the interpretation of treaties of most of the general principles which hold good in municipal law for the interpretation of contracts'; also in this last case, it was said that extreme versions of the ordinary meaning rule represented by such aphorisms as '*in claris non fit interpretatio*' had been 'repudiated by the most authoritative modern teaching of every country' (at 415); and, to like effect, *Italian Republic v Federal Republic of Germany* (1959) 29 ILR 442; *Southern Pacific Properties (Middle East) Ltd. v Arab Republic of Egypt* (1992) 106 ILR 502 at 547: 'The starting point on statutory interpretation, as in the interpretation of treaties and unilateral declarations, is the ordinary or grammatical meaning of the terms used.'

84 See McCormick, 'The Parol Evidence Rule as a Procedural Device for Control of the Jury' (1932) 41 Yale LJ 365.

85 Browne I, *A Treatise on the Admissibility of Parol evidence in Respect to Written Instruments* (1893, reprint 1982), 116, dealing with English and American authorities.

evidence.[86] The consequence, as far as Anglo-Australian law is concerned, has been the emergence of two contrasting views on the admissibility of extrinsic evidence, with no clear cut means of assimilating them.

On the one hand, there are vestiges of the former exclusionary rule so that evidence of surrounding circumstances is only 'admissible to assist in the interpretation of the contract if the language is ambiguous or susceptible of more than one meaning.'[87] In contrast, there is support for the proposition that evidence of surrounding circumstances should always be available in order that the court should be placed as far as possible in the position of the parties when they entered into their contract.[88] As Lord Wilberforce explained the position:[89]

> No contracts are made in a vacuum: there is always a setting in which they have to be placed. The nature of what is legitimate to have regard to is usually described as 'the surrounding circumstances' but this phrase is imprecise: it can be illustrated but hardly defined. In a commercial contract it is certainly right that the court should know the commercial purpose of the contract and this in turn presupposes knowledge of the genesis of the transaction, the background, the context, the matter in which the parties are operating.

To some extent the scope of the admissibility of surrounding circumstances is linked to the purpose for which it is sought to employ such evidence. The courts have always refused to indulge in an examination of the course of negotiations leading to the finalisation of a written contract

[86] As Lord Wilberforce observed in *Prenn v Simmonds* [1971] 1 WLR 1381 at 1384 of the prolonged negotiations that had taken place between the parties: 'The reason for not admitting evidence of these exchanges is not a technical one or even mainly one of convenience (though the attempt to admit it did greatly prolong the case and add to its expense). It is simply that such evidence is unhelpful. By the nature of things, where negotiations are difficult, the parties' positions with each passing letter are changing and until the final agreement, though converging, still divergent. It is only the final document which records a consensus.'

[87] *Codelfa Construction Pty Ltd v State Railway Authority of New South Wales* (1982) 149 CLR 337 at 352 per Mason J. However, as Mason J made clear (ibid), although susceptible of more than one meaning signified little more than the ability of the parties to suggest plausible alternative meanings, a contract could not satisfy this requirement 'if the words have a fixed meaning', when 'parol evidence is not admissible to show that the parties meant something different from what they have said' (*Bank of New Zealand v Simpson* [1900] AC 182 at 189). See also *Great Western Rly v Bristol Corp.* (1918) 87 LJ Ch 414.

[88] In the words of Lord Wright in *Inland Revenue Commissioners v Raphael* [1935] AC 96 at 143, the words used must 'be construed with reference to the facts known to the parties and in contemplation of which the parties must be deemed to have used them'; or of Lord Dunedin in *Charrington and Co. Ltd. v Wooder* [1914] AC 71 at 82: 'in order to construe a contract the court is always entitled to be so far instructed by evidence as to be able to place itself in thought in the same position as the parties to the contract were placed, in fact, when they made it—or, as it is sometimes phrased, to be informed as to surrounding circumstances.'

[89] *Reardon Smith Line Ltd. v Yngvar Hansen-Tangen* [1976] 1 WLR 989 at 995–996.

on the basis that the construction of that document is dependent upon the meaning attributable to its text and not upon any evidence of what the parties claimed they intended it to mean. As Mason J outlined the law in giving the principal judgment of the High Court of Australia in *Secured Income Real Estate (Australia) Ltd. v St. Martins Investments Pty Ltd.*:[90]

> The respondent also sought to rely on the oral testimony given by officers of the appellant and the respondent as to what was said and done during the course of negotiations leading up to the making of the contract, with a view to demonstrating that the parties had 'commercial' leases in mind. This was said to be evidence of surrounding circumstances to which recourse could be had in interpreting the contract. In truth the evidence is not evidence of surrounding circumstances; it is evidence of the antecedent oral negotiations and expectations of the parties and as such it cannot be used for the purpose of construing the words of a written contract intended by the parties to comprehensively record the terms of the agreement which they have made.

Despite a degree of uncertainty in the case law, the preferable view is that there is an embargo on the use of evidence of negotiations leading to the conclusion of a written contract, but only in so far as their attempted use is to establish the subjective intentions of the parties. Provided this aspect of the negotiations is avoided, they may be resorted to in order to place the court in the position of the parties at the time the contract was made. Once this has been achieved it is for the court to make an objective assessment of the meaning of the document, or that part of it, which is in dispute. To refer again to the judgment of Lord Wilberforce in *Reardon Smith Line Ltd. v Yngvar Hansen-Tangen*,[91] when 'one speaks of the intention of the parties, one is speaking objectively—the parties cannot themselves give direct evidence of what their intention was—and what must be ascertained is what is to be taken as the intention which reasonable people would have had if placed in the situation of the parties', as revealed to the court by the surrounding circumstances already established by the evidence.

C. *Comparisons between international law and municipal law*

There are obviously similarities and differences between the two legal orders. They are similar in that the primary source of meaning is the text of the written document. Hence, evidence of the negotiations which led to the adoption of that text is given a subordinate role. It is excluded altogether under Anglo-Australian law in so far as the attempt is made to introduce the court to the subjective intentions of the parties. It is only available in ascertaining the meaning of a treaty if, by application of the general rule of interpretation in Article 31 of the Vienna Convention, the

[90] (1979) 144 CLR 596 at 606. [91] [1976] 1 WLR 989 at 996.

treaty is ambiguous or if the result of applying Article 31 is absurd or unreasonable (Article 32). They are also similar in that a range of evidence may be presented to the court which the judge or judges will subsequently assert has been excluded from consideration. Accordingly the rules represent something of a fiction because the evidence has already been presented to the court though its influence on the judge(s) is disguised by the invocation of the rules in question.[92]

A finding that as a text has an ordinary meaning, which 'is sufficiently clear in itself', the preparatory work does not have to be considered,[93] is only made after that evidence has been brought before the court. Not that the preparatory work is necessarily ignored. In order to bolster its conclusions and make them appear more convincing to the parties to a case, international tribunals will attempt, as far as possible, to employ the evidence gleaned from that source 'to confirm the meaning resulting from the application of Article 31' (to use the words of Article 32 of the Vienna Convention). This is, of course, what the majority of the Permanent Court claimed to be doing in the *Convention concerning the Employment of Women at Night* case.[94]

The difficulty with the hierarchy established by Articles 31 and 32 is that it leaves open the answer to the question 'what happens when the *travaux préparatoires* turn out not to confirm but contradict the meaning arrived at by application of the general rule of interpretation?'[95] Judge Schwebel, who posed this question, admitted that, in the work of the Commission and elsewhere, '[s]urprisingly little attention was directed to

[92] In the words of a former attorney in the Office of the Legal Adviser of the US State Department, Vandevelde, 'Treaty Interpretation from a Negotiator's Perspective' (1988) 21 Vanderbilt JIL 281 at 296–297: 'The Vienna Convention does allow a court to refer to the negotiating history, however, even when the treaty text is clear, in order to confirm its interpretation—a rule that borders on the absurd. If the meaning is clear, a court need not confirm it, and examining the negotiating history serves no point. If a court examines the negotiating history anyway but in fact disconfirms the plain meaning, the court has no basis for following the interpretation that the history reveals. This absurdity is not manifest in practice because courts probably scrutinize the negotiating history whether the text seems clear or not. If the negotiating history supports a court's first impression, then the court labels the text as clear and can cite the negotiating history as confirming that meaning in accordance with article 32. If the negotiating history disconfirms the court's first impression, it can disregard it and cite its first impression as the clear meaning of the text or, alternatively, declare the text ambiguous and refer to the negotiating history in accordance with article 32. Of course, this procedure is contrary to the law as codified in articles 31 and 32, under which the negotiating history cannot vary the meaning of a clear textual provision.'

[93] *Admission of a State to the United Nations* case, ICJ Rep 1948, 57 at 63. The passage from which the words quoted were taken was employed by the Commission to support its draft of what became Article 32 of the Convention, Yb ILC 1966, vol II, 223, para (18).

[94] (1932) PCIJ Ser A/B, No 50 at 380, above p 23 and below at n. 98.

[95] *Maritime Delimitation and Territorial Questions* case, ICJ Rep 1995, 6 at 31.

this critical question'.[96] The answer lies in the very realities of such a situation.

Where there is an apparent conflict between an ordinary meaning and the preparatory work, the existence of the latter evidence may lead the tribunal to the conclusion that the meaning suggested by the application of Article 31 is nevertheless ambiguous. This was the basis of Judge Anzilotti's dissenting opinion in the *Convention concerning the Employment of Women at Night* case, though he was careful to avoid suggesting that he was departing from the primary ordinary meaning rule:[97]

> If Article 3, according to the natural meaning of its terms, were really perfectly clear, it would be hardly admissible to endeavour to find an interpretation other than that which flows from the natural meaning of its terms.
>
> But I do not see how it is possible to say that an article of a convention is clear until the subject and aim of the convention have been ascertained . . . Only when it is known what the Contracting Parties intended to do and the aim they had in view is it possible to say . . . that the natural meaning of terms used in a particular article corresponds with the real intention of the Parties.

The issue of the justification for relying upon material extrinsic to the text will be returned to shortly. However, the *Employment of Women at Night* case does illustrate a second possibility for dealing with an apparent dissonance between text and *travaux*, and that is to interpret the latter to conform with, and therefore confirm, the former, which was the approach adopted by the majority of the Court.[98]

Because of the reluctance to give the appearance of ignoring altogether the preparatory work (though justifiable on the wording of Articles 31 and 32 of the Vienna Convention), international tribunals can select, as an alternative approach, the downplaying of its significance, particularly if the tribunal is able to rely upon other sources of information pointing in a different direction. In the *Competence of the General Assembly* case,[99] the question was asked of the International Court whether the Assembly could admit an applicant State to membership in the United Nations under Article 4(2) of the Charter 'when the Security Council has made no recommendation for admission by reason of the candidate failing to obtain the requisite majority or of the negative vote of a permanent Member upon a resolution so to recommend?' The principal argument favouring such a power being vested in the Assembly stemmed from a letter from the Advisory Committee of Jurists to Committee II/1 of the San Francisco Conference in which it was stated that the use of the word decision in their proposed text of the provision signified that the Assembly might accept or reject a recommendation of the Council, whether it was favourable or

[96] Ibid. [97] (1932) PCIJ Ser A/B, No 50 at 383.
[98] Ibid, at 378–80. [99] ICJ Rep 1950, 4.

unfavourable.[100] If the Assembly was entitled to admit a State to membership following an adverse recommendation by the Security Council, it could also do so in the absence of a recommendation which could be regarded as equivalent to an unfavourable recommendation. This attempt to build upon the *travaux* was largely disregarded by the Court in a very brief reference to the issue.[101] The Court did so by giving a resounding endorsement of the primacy of the principle of interpretation that a provision should be given its natural and ordinary meaning in the context in which it occurs, as a consequence of which it was 'not permissible, in this case to resort to *travaux préparatoires*'.[102] Nevertheless, the Court did reinforce its conclusion that the power of the Assembly to admit was dependent on a prior favourable recommendation from the Council by reference to 'the structure of the Charter, and . . . by the relations established by it between the General Assembly and the Security Council'[103] in Articles 24, 4, 5 and 6 of the Charter, and by the way in which the two organs, particularly illustrated by the Assembly's Rules of Procedure, 'have consistently interpreted the text in the sense that the General Assembly can decide to admit only on the basis of a recommendation of the Security Council'.[104]

Despite some hesitation, there does seem to be an acceptance by the weight of judicial opinion in England and Australia that, even before issues of ambiguity are raised or considered, a court must have access to the circumstances surrounding the making of a contract before embarking upon its interpretation. Indeed, if intertemporality is to have any significance, it would seem to require an interpreter to be placed, so far as possible, in the position of the parties at that critical date. That principle would appear to be equally applicable to the interpretation of treaties at the international level. The question that now has to be addressed is whether, or to what extent, international law satisfies this requirement.

It has already been suggested that, on the face of it, the Vienna Convention does not meet this standard. In the Convention, the circumstances of the conclusion of a treaty can only be resorted to within the confines of Article 32, that is 'to confirm the meaning resulting from the application of article 31, or to determine the meaning when the interpretation according to article 31:

[100] *Pleadings*, 81 et seq. For a consideration of the *travaux* on this issue and on the related issue of whether the veto in Article 27(3) of the Charter was intended to apply to resolutions of the Security Council except for those relating to the maintenance of international peace and security, so that Article 27(3) should not have applied to Council resolutions on the admission of new members, see Klooz, 'The Role of the General Assembly of the United Nations in the Admission of Members' (1949) 43 AJIL 246.

[101] ICJ Rep 1950 at 9.

[102] Ibid at 8.

[103] Ibid.

[104] Ibid at 9.

(a) leaves the meaning ambiguous or obscure; or
(b) leads to a result which is manifestly absurd or unreasonable.'

However, this is not the entire picture because Article 32 is only a residual means of incorporating surrounding circumstances into the interpretative framework. It only covers those aspects of such circumstances not provided for in the general rule of interpretation in Article 31. The fact that there is a residual rule signifies that not all aspects of such circumstances are catered for in Article 31. Hence, neither the context of a treaty, referred to in Article 31(1) and defined in Article 31(2), nor the object and purpose of a treaty, also required to be taken into account by Article 31(1), nor the relevant rules of international law at that time under Article 31(3)(c), is sufficient of itself, nor would they be cumulatively, to satisfy the requirements of intertemporality. Whether international law achieves this standard, however, depends upon two possibilities: either the above three elements in Article 31 have been interpreted liberally enough to do so, or the limitations contained in Article 31 and 32 have been largely ignored. The next two sub-sections will deal with both those possibilities. The first will consider the elements specifically identified in Article 31(1); the second with the relevant rules of international law referred to in Article 31(3)(c). However, it will emerge from the cases discussed under both headings that evidence of surrounding circumstances is generally available and is not limited in the ways suggested by those headings.

1. *Context and object and purpose*

(a) *The Commission's apparent lack of regard for the jurisprudence of the Permanent Court*

It has already been pointed out[105] that the Permanent Court's opinion, and the dissenting declaration of four of the judges, in the *Convention on the Employment of Women at Night* case,[106] suggested that a broad view had been taken of context in that a range of material was taken into account and not regarded as excluded on the ground that it formed part of the preparatory work of the treaty. In his dissenting opinion in the same case, Judge Anzilotti excused his reference to such evidence, which he did regard as otherwise inadmissible, on the ground that it was needed to establish 'the subject and aim of the convention' because only when they were ascertained was it possible to say whether 'the natural meaning of terms used in a particular article corresponds with the real intention of the Parties'.[107] The absence of reference in the work of the International Law

[105] Above pp 23–24. [106] (1932) PCIJ Ser A/B, No 50.

[107] Ibid at 383. Judge Anzilotti's emphasis upon the object and purpose of a treaty seems to have had a significant effect upon the later jurisprudence of the Permanent Court. In the *Minority Schools* case (1935) PCIJ Ser A/B, No 64, the majority of the Court employed

Commission to the substance of the Court's opinion does indicate that it did not find favour with the Commission. Certainly Article 31(2) seems to be totally out of harmony with the Court's approach. The Commission and ultimately Article 31 of the Convention eschewed all mention of the intention of the parties, preferring instead the object and purpose of the treaty as a means of throwing light upon the ordinary meaning of a treaty text, though the Commission gave little indication that it regarded this factor as giving the interpreter the freedom to consult the background to the text which the Permanent Court had asserted in its later years under Anzilotti's influence.

(b) *The broad reception of evidence of surrounding circumstances by the present Court partly obscured by its regard for subjective intent in relation to compromissory clauses*

Whether the Permanent Court's approach retains any relevance for a wider application of context and object and purpose consistent with the acceptance of surrounding circumstances as a necessary foundation and starting point of the interpretative process is dependent upon how treaty interpretation has been approached in the years since the Vienna Convention was adopted. An example of a very broad view of the circumstances which a tribunal could take into account in interpreting the conventional bases of its jurisdiction is provided by the *Aegean Sea* case.[108] In particular, the decision would seem to demonstrate an endorsement of the importance of intertemporality to such an exercise.

In that case, brought by Greece against Turkey with regard to their competing continental shelf claims in the Sea, the International Court had

evidence of the circumstances surrounding the making of Albania's Declaration before the Council of the League of Nations of 2 October 1921 to establish the aim of the instrument as a basis for overriding the apparently clear meaning of its text. This led the minority to accuse the majority of departing from the principles of interpretation previously formulated by the Court. As Hyde commented ('The World Court Interprets Another International Agreement' (1935) 29 AJIL 479 at 482): 'the Court appears to be increasingly aware of the danger of concluding that textual or linguistic clarity is necessarily indicative of clearness of design of the parties to an international instrument, and perhaps under the salutory influence of Judge Anziolotti's dissenting opinion in the case concerning the Interpretation of the Convention of 1919 concerning the Employment of Women during the Night, is reluctant to acknowledge that a text is verbally clear even when there is room for such a conclusion.' Certainly, in the *Lighthouses* case (1934) PCIJ Ser A/B, No 62, the Court accepted Judge Anzilotti's view, expressed also in his dissenting opinion in the case (at 33), that preparatory work could be consulted to ascertain the intention of the parties, which presumably at this early stage in the treaty's existence was equivalent to the aim or purpose of the instrument, when it said (at 13): 'Where the context does not suffice to show the precise sense in which the Parties . . . have employed these words in their Special Agreement the Court, in accordance with its practice, has to consult the documents preparatory to the Special Agreement, in order to satisfy itself as to the true intention of the Parties.'

[108] ICJ Rep 1978, 3.

to consider two agreements upon which Greece relied to found the Court's jurisdiction. With regard to the first, the General Act for the Pacific Settlement of International Disputes 1928,[109] Greece had excluded from its acceptance *inter alia* 'disputes concerning questions which by international law are solely within the domestic jurisdiction of States, and in particular disputes relating to the territorial status of Greece, including disputes relating to its rights of sovereignty over its ports and lines of communication'. The initial issue of intertemporality concerned the scope of this reservation at the time it was made. After considering a letter to the Greek Foreign Minister of 9 September 1928, referred to by counsel as the '*travaux préparatoires*' of that reservation,[110] and a number of internal documents, submitted by Greece in response to a question asked by the Court, relating to Greece's instrument of accession to the General Act,[111] the Court decided that the above reservation in fact contained separate reservations, the one excluding matters relating to territorial status being independent of, and not limited by, the reservation as to questions of domestic jurisdiction.[112]

It is possible to explain the broad scope of the evidence which the Court was prepared to consider as justifiable, as a matter of treaty law. However, given the Court's apparent lack of concern about the relevance of Articles 31 and 32 of the Vienna Convention, it may be that the Court regarded itself as dealing with a compromissory clause to which the rules of treaty interpretation were only of indirect significance. The *Aegean Sea* case could, therefore, be treated as an example of the extent to which international tribunals are prepared to take account of the subjective intention of a party in assessing that party's purported acceptance of a tribunal's jurisdiction.

In the *Anglo-Iranian Oil Co.* case,[113] the Court's jurisdiction depended upon how it interpreted Iran's acceptance of the jurisdiction of the Permanent Court under Article 36 of that Court's Statute.[114] The International Court rejected the British contention that, interpreted as suggested by Iran, some of the words in the declaration would be superfluous; in the Court's view the principle that 'a legal text should be interpreted

[109] Article 17 of the General Act provided for the submission of disputes between parties to it to the Permanent Court. Article 37 of the Statute of the present Court reads: 'Whenever a treaty or convention in force provides for reference of a matter to . . . the Permanent Court of International Justice, the matter shall, as between parties to the present Statute, be referred to the International Court of Justice.'

[110] ICJ Rep 1978 at 26.

[111] Ibid at 27.

[112] Ibid at 27–28.

[113] ICJ Rep 1952, 93.

[114] The second (unnumbered) paragraph corresponds in substance to Article 36(2) of the present Statute. According to Article 36(5) of the present Statute: 'Declarations made under Article 36 of the Statute of the Permanent Court of International Justice and which are still in force shall be deemed, as between the parties to the present Statute, to be acceptance of the compulsory jurisdiction of the International Court of Justice for the period which they still have to run and in accordance with their terms.'

in such a way that a reason and a meaning can be attributed to every word in a text' applied to the interpretation of a treaty but not of a unilateral act which did not result from negotiations between two or more States.[115] The Court concluded, in favour of Iran, that the Iranian intention, adequately expressed in the text of the declaration, was 'manifest . . . to exclude from the jurisdiction of the Court disputes relating to all treaties or conventions accepted by it before the ratification of the Declaration'.[116] The Court reinforced this conclusion by invoking the Iranian law of 1931 whereby the Declaration had been approved by the Majlis (the Iranian parliament), in a form which made that intention clear. In relying upon this evidence, the Court refused to accept the British argument that it was 'a private document written only in the Persian language which was not communicated to the League or to any of the other States which had made declarations' accepting the Court's jurisdiction, justifying its use on the basis that it had been 'filed for the sole purpose of throwing light on a disputed question of fact, namely, the intention of the Government of Iran at the time when it signed the Declaration'.[117]

The Court's stance over the reception of this evidence is open to criticism, as indeed it was by members of the Court.[118] In the first place, on a number of occasions the Court has regarded declarations of acceptance of its jurisdiction as establishing a series of consensual or treaty like relationships between the States concerned.[119] Although such instruments are drafted unilaterally, their interpretation should be undertaken objectively as part of an international regime of dispute settlement.[120] Unfortunately, the Court's attitude in the *Anglo-Iranian* case has spilled over into other cases dealing with reservations in a purely treaty context.[121]

115 ICJ Rep 1952 at 105.

116 Ibid at 106.

117 Ibid at 107.

118 Judge McNair, ibid at 121; Judge Hackworth, ibid at 136–137.

119 *Right of Passage* case, ICJ Rep 1957, 125 at 146; *Nicaragua* case, ICJ Rep 1984, 392 at 418.

120 As Judge Read said in the *Anglo-Iranian Oil Co.* case, ICJ Rep 1952 at 142: 'I am unable to accept the contention that the principles of international law which govern the interpretation of treaties cannot be applied to the Persian Declaration, because it is unilateral. Admittedly it was drafted unilaterally. On the other hand, it was related, in express terms, to Article 36 of the Statute, and to the declarations of other States which had already deposited, or which might in the future deposit, reciprocal declarations. It was intended to establish legal relationships with such States, consensual in their character, within the regime established by the provisions of Article 36.' The similarity between the relationship established by such declarations and treaties was also recognised in the early work of the International Law Commission on the law of treaties, see draft Article 1(3) in Yb ILC 1959, vol II, 92. Although references to those declarations were deleted from the draft Articles and the commentaries thereon, nevertheless there was support for the proposition that 'the rules relating to such matters as the interpretation and termination of treaties applied to declarations under Article 36(2) of the Statute' (Yb ILC 1962, vol I, 56).

121 The *Aegean Sea* case, ICJ Rep 1978, 3, provides one example, though it is an example

(c) *Evidence of surrounding circumstances generally available or limited to cases of ambiguity?*

In both the *Anglo-Iranian Oil Co.* case[122] and the *Aegean Sea* case,[123] a good deal of attention was paid to the surrounding circumstances, even leaving to one side the more contentious evidence of subjective intention. In the former, the Court referred to the fact that Iran had 'denounced all treaties with other States relating to the regime of capitulations' and had entered into negotiations with those States 'with a view to replacing the denounced treaties by new treaties based upon the principle of equality'. The Court deduced from this that 'when the Government of Iran was about to accept the compulsory jurisdiction of the Court, it desired to exclude from that jurisdiction all disputes which might relate to the application of the capitulatory treaties, and the Declaration was drafted on the basis of this desire.'[124] Judge McNair, who had cast doubt on the admissibility of the evidence of the Iranian legislation,[125] also made reference to the 'historical considerations',[126] though he expressed the view, an issue not mentioned by the Court, that it was because of 'the real ambiguity in the text' of the Iranian declaration that it was 'both justifiable and necessary to go outside the text and see whether any light is shed by the surrounding circumstances.'[127] It was this information which made it easier for the judge 'to understand why the Iranian Government should desire to start with a clean slate in regard to the compulsory jurisdiction of

which should be treated with some caution. Turkey was not represented in the proceedings, so that it was for the Court to examine whether it had jurisdiction without any substantial submission from the respondent State. The evidence of Greece's 'subjective' intent was therefore employed to determine whether Greece's reservations to its acceptance of the General Act were wide enough to protect Turkey from the exercise of jurisdiction. Even if one accepts as preferable the contention advanced here that evidence of subjective intention is inadmissible, the evidence could nevertheless have been relied upon for a totally different reason. It constituted a declaration against interest in line with the Court's opinion in the *Status of South-West Africa* case, ICJ Rep 1950, 128 at 135–136, the interest in this case being that of Greece to limit the scope of its reservations so that they would not enable Turkey to rely upon them to protect itself from the proceedings instituted by the former. A more striking example is the *Belilos* case (1988) ECHR Ser A, No 132. On ratification of the European Convention for the Protection of Human Rights and Fundamental Freedoms 1950, Switzerland made what its acceptance called two 'interpretative declarations' and two 'reservations'. In acknowledging that one of the declarations could be treated as a reservation, the European Court of Human Rights was prepared 'to ascertain the original intention of those who drafted' the acceptance of the Convention (ibid, 23) by reference to documents which had passed between the Swiss Federal Council and Federal Assembly and which demonstrated Switzerland's intention to qualify its consent to be bound by the Convention in certain respects. For criticism of this decision, see Greig, 'Reservations: Equity as a Balancing Factor?' (1995) 16 Aust YBIL 21 at 32–34.

[122] ICJ Rep 1952, 93.
[123] ICJ Rep 1978, 3.
[124] ICJ Rep 1952 at 105.
[125] See above n. 112.
[126] ICJ Rep 1952 at 120.
[127] Ibid at 117–118.

the Court and to limit its obligations in that regard to treaties and conventions accepted by it after 19 September, 1932.'[128]

The Court gave no justification for its use of surrounding circumstances, presumably because it regarded the reason as self-evident. It is not altogether clear whether this was because of the existence of the ambiguity in the text as suggested by Judge McNair,[129] or because such evidence was automatically available to place a tribunal in the position of the parties when the treaty was made. This latter view of the case is supported by the explanation, given by the Court for its conclusion that 'it was the manifest intention of the Government of Iran to exclude from the jurisdiction of the Court disputes relating to the application of all treaties or conventions accepted by it before the ratification of the Declaration', that this intention had 'found an adequate expression in the text of the Declaration as interpreted above by the Court.'[130] However, that interpretation had not been based exclusively on the text, but had taken into account the historical record surrounding the making of the Declaration.

The same would be true of the *Aegean Sea* case. The record of background circumstances was admitted on that basis in dealing with Greece's claimed acceptance of the Court's jurisdiction under the General Act of 1929. Any ambiguity would have provided a ready excuse for an examination of the preparatory work, yet, apart from the reference to the letter of 1928 to the Greek Foreign Minister as 'the *travaux préparatoires* of the reservation',[131] there was no mention of the issue. That intertemporality and the fixing of the time of making of a treaty or of accession to it as a critical date dictate that the circumstances surrounding the event or events in question should be available to the interpreter is reinforced by two further factors. First, as a practical matter, the need for evidence of the circumstances surrounding the making of or accession to a treaty increases the further removed the time of interpretation is from the earlier event(s). Secondly, and more importantly, is the fact that, where the parties are themselves the interpreters of the treaty, the evidence is available to them as a matter of course. Where, by accident or design, a tribunal has jurisdiction over a dispute which involves the task of interpreting the treaty, the tribunal should not be so divorced from the position of the parties as the limitations explicit in Articles 31 and 32 of the Vienna Convention might suggest. In particular, the surrounding circumstances, whether allowable

128 ICJ Rep 1952 at 120.

129 Ibid at 117–118.

130 Ibid at 106. The Court's use of the background circumstances in reaching its conclusion differs from its more tentative use of the law by which the Majlis had approved the Declaration. Initially, the Court referred to it because it 'confirmed' that such was 'the intention of the Government of Iran' (ibid), but later accepted it on the basis that it had been 'filed for the sole purpose of throwing light on a disputed question of fact, namely, the intention of the Government of Iran at the time when it signed the Declaration' (ibid at 107).

131 ICJ Rep 1978, 3 at 26.

by reference to the three exceptions (context, object and purpose, and relevant rules of international law) contained in Article 31, or to the practice of the International Court, must constitute the essential basis for any process of interpretation.

To return to the *Aegean Sea* case,[132] it certainly exhibited the preparedness of the Court to consider a significant amount of 'historical evidence'[133] as an aid to interpreting the Greek reservations to the General Act of 1928. The Court did not seem to think, any more than it had in the *Anglo-Iranian Oil Co.* case, that the use of such evidence needed justification. However, when, in the former case, it went on to consider the other basis of jurisdiction relied upon by Greece, the Court seemed to think that it needed to provide some explanation of the evidence it employed.

Greece claimed to be entitled to rely upon a Joint Communiqué, issued on 31 May 1975 at the end of a meeting in Brussels between the Prime Ministers of Greece and Turkey, which recorded that they had 'decided' that the problems in the relations between the parties 'should be resolved peacefully by means of negotiations and as regards the continental shelf of the Aegean Sea by the International Court at The Hague'.[134] In considering whether this document constituted a binding undertaking to accept the jurisdiction of the Court in a case instituted unilaterally by one of the parties, the Court first pointed out that it had to determine 'the nature of the act or transaction embodied' in the Communiqué by having 'regard above all to its actual terms and to the particular circumstances in which it was drawn up'.[135] It then explained that the 'divergence of views' between the parties 'as to the interpretation of the Brussels Communiqué makes it necessary for the Court to consider what light is thrown on its meaning by the context in which the meeting of 31 May 1975 took place and the Communiqué was drawn up'.[136]

It could be argued that deciding whether the parties had intended to enter into a binding commitment by an instrument would allow a tribunal to rely upon a wider range of evidence than in relation to a simple question of deciding upon the meaning of a particular text.[137] However, it does

132 ICJ Rep 1978, 3. 133 Ibid at 30, 31. 134 Ibid at 39–40.
135 Ibid at 39. 136 Ibid at 41.
137 This would certainly be the situation under Anglo-Australian law: see *Pym v Campbell* (1856) 119 Eng Rep 903, in which what appeared to be a final record of a binding contract between the parties was not enforced because the defendant was allowed to introduce evidence to show that the parties had agreed that no contract was to come into existence until a second engineer (the first had already approved the invention before the written document was executed) approved the invention that was the subject matter of the contract and that the second engineer had in fact disapproved of it; and the words of McHugh JA in *Air Great Lakes Pty Ltd v KS Easter (Holdings) Ltd* (1985) 2 NSWLR 309 at 337: 'The intention to create a legally binding contract although a matter to be proved objectively, may, nevertheless . . . be proved by what the parties said and did as well as by what they wrote. The intention may be proved in that way even in a case where the document is intended to comprise all the

not seem that the Court, in the *Aegean Sea* case, believed that it was dealing with two separate issues,[138] but had used different phraseology to describe the one issue. After its comments about the nature of the Communiqué, all the Court did was to set out the 'relevant paragraphs' of that document[139] and then the arguments of the two sides on the matter.[140] The Court then explained that it was in light of these divergent views of the parties as to the meaning of the Communiqué that it was necessary for the Court to consider the context of the meeting and of the drawing up of the Communiqué.[141] However, the Court made no attempt to distinguish between the evidence that it employed as far as these two apparent questions were concerned. The circumstances or context which it examined comprised the details of the negotiations between the parties both before and after the Brussels meeting.[142]

(d) *Lack of explanation of the use of evidence of surrounding circumstances suggests that it is regarded as generally available as a necessary basis for the interpretative process and not dependent upon the specific requirements of Articles 31 or 32 of the Vienna Convention*

It is difficult to avoid the conclusion that the Court regarded the use of such evidence as less dependent upon the requirements of Article 32 as upon its general availability as part of the context or surrounding circumstances in all cases where States disagree as to the status or meaning of an instrument to which they are parties. This deduction may be further supported by the fact that, whereas the Court has consistently felt the need to underline the restrictions in relation to preparatory work,[143] there was

terms of their bargain. This is because the situation to be bound is a jural act separate and distinct from the *terms* of their bargain.'

[138] The Court took a different view in the *Maritime Delimitation and Territorial Questions* case, ICJ Rep 1994, 112 at 121, where it applied the pronouncement from the *Aegean Sea* case, ICJ Rep 1978 at 39, that 'the Court must have regard above all to [the alleged agreement's] actual terms and to the particular circumstances in which it was drawn up', to determine that the so-called 'Minutes of Doha' recorded the terms of an agreement binding upon Qatar and Bahrain, and then went on 'to an analysis of the content' of the Minutes of 1990 and earlier exchanges of letters of 1987 between Saudi Arabia and the two parties to the case 'and of the rights and obligations to which they give rise' (at 123). In other words, in the later case the Court undoubtedly treated the issues of whether a treaty had been intended, and what meaning should be attributed to it if it was, as two distinct matters to be decided.

[139] ICJ Rep 1978 at 39–40.

[140] Ibid at 40–1. Although Turkey did not appear in the proceedings before the Court, it did submit certain observations to the Court in a communication to the Registrar dated 25 August 1976, see ibid at 15, 40–41.

[141] Ibid at 41.

[142] Ibid at 41–44.

[143] This occurred during the time of the Permanent Court: see, for example, the *Lotus* case (1927) PCIJ Ser A, No 10, 16, a statement it often repeated, as in the *Convention concerning the Employment of Women at Night* case (1932) PCIJ Ser A/B, No 50, 378. However, in his comments about the work of the Court, Hudson MO, *The Permanent Court of International*

no hesitation in the *Agean Sea* case in its use of such evidence as part of the context or circumstances surrounding the issues in dispute between the parties. The final point worth making is that the Court has always taken a rather strict view of what constitutes ambiguity. In particular, the mere fact that the two sides are arguing for different meanings of a disputed provision does not in itself render it ambiguous in order to qualify the operation of Article 31 by recourse to the preparatory work.[144] In contrast, in the *Aegean Sea* case, the fact that the parties were in disagreement about the application of the disputed jurisdictional basis seemed sufficient to allow such evidence to be used. As the ambiguity requirement was not necessarily satisfied to the standard normally applied under Article 32, there is every reason for supposing that the Court was basing its reception of the evidence as a gloss on Article 31.

A case which involved a detailed examination by the Court of the historical record of a treaty, including the processes by which it was negotiated, was that of the *Interpretation of the WHO and Egypt Agreement*.[145] It arose out of the wish by all WHO members (except Egypt) who participated in the work of the Regional Office for the Eastern Mediterranean to relocate the Regional Office from Egypt. The 'principal' question asked of the Court by the WHO Assembly was as follows:[146]

1. Are the negotiation and notice provisions of section 37 of the Agreement of 25 March 1951 between the World Health Organisation and Egypt applicable in the event that either party to the Agreement wishes to have the Regional Office transferred from the territory of Egypt?

Justice 1920–1942 (1943), 652–655, did not regard such a rule as constituting a total barrier to the use of such evidence. In particular, Hudson pointed out (ibid, 652) that 'the construction of a text cannot be arrived at without a consideration of its setting, and the development of the negotiations forms part of the history which constitutes that setting.' From its inception, the present Court emphasised the subordinate role of preparatory work: see the *Admissions* case, ICJ Rep 1948, 57 at 63; the *Competence of the General Assembly* case, ICJ Rep 1950, 4 at 8, though prepared to use it to confirm an interpretation flowing from the general rule: see the *IMCO* case, ICJ Rep 1960, 150 at 159–160, 161 et seq; *Fisheries Jurisdiction* case, ICJ Rep 1973, 3 at 9–10. For a rejection of this view as a fiction, see the words of Judge Jessup in the *South-West Africa* cases, ICJ Rep 1966, 6 at 352: 'In my opinion it is not necessary—as some utterances of the two international courts might suggest—to apologise for resorting to *travaux préparatoires* as an aid to interpretation. In many instances the historical record is valuable evidence to be taken into account in interpreting a treaty. It is tradition, rather than law or logic, which has at times led to judicial statements that this evidence is used merely to confirm an interpretation which is supposed to have been already derived from the bare words of the text or even of the text in its context.'

144 It is apparent from the number of occasions on which the preparatory work has not been consulted because the meaning of the text was clear, or employed only to confirm that meaning, that a disagreement between the parties as to the meaning of a particular provision does not render the provision ambiguous; the disagreement can still be resolved by reference to the ordinary meaning of the text.

145 ICJ Rep 1980, 73.

146 Ibid at 76.

It has been suggested[147] that the reason why the Court felt free to use such a wide range of material, without discussing the limitations on the access to preparatory work in Article 32 of the Vienna Convention, was that the Court avoided the issue of how to interpret Section 37 by converting the question posed to the quite different one of 'What are the legal principles and rules applicable to the question under what conditions and in accordance with what modalities a transfer of the Regional Office from Egypt may be effected?'[148]

The significance of the employment by the Court of such a wide range of material cannot be dismissed quite so readily. In the first place the question can be asked whether the task of interpreting the WHO Assembly resolution initiating the Court's advisory jurisdiction differed so fundamentally from interpreting the section in an international agreement. Admittedly, Articles 31 and 32 of the Vienna Convention could only be applicable by analogy to a text of the former kind, but those provisions have been regarded as at least relevant to other consensual texts. Moreover, it could be suggested that, in so far as they represent general principles of law applicable to written contracts and other instruments in municipal law, they would seem to have a relevance for the interpretation of other written instruments under international law. Secondly, it is by no means clear that the International Court was drawing such a sharp distinction between the question originally asked, involving a question of treaty interpretation, and the approach necessary to determine how the question itself should be interpreted. As the Court observed:[149]

> But a rule of international law, whether customary or conventional, does not operate in a vacuum; it operates in relation to facts and in the context of a wider framework of legal rules of which it forms only a part. Accordingly, if a question put in the hypothetical way in which it is posed in the request is to receive a pertinent and effectual reply, the Court must first ascertain the meaning and full implications of the question in the light of the actual framework of law and fact in which it falls for consideration . . . The Court will therefore begin by setting out the pertinent elements of fact and of law which, in its view, constitute the context in which the meaning and implications of the first question posed in the request have to be ascertained.

If the context, conceived of in the broad fashion employed by the Court in this case, was necessary to an understanding of the WHO Assembly's resolution submitting the matter to the Court, the same should hold true for interpreting the text of a treaty. It is an essential starting point for the process of interpretation, dictated by the principle of intertemporality which requires the instrument under consideration to be placed in the time frame to which it belongs.

147 Thirlway, 'The Law and Practice of the International Court of Justice 1960–1989, Part Three' (1991) 62 BYIL 1 at 34.

148 ICJ Rep 1980 at 88.

149 Ibid at 76.

It is not only the approach adopted by the Court which seems difficult to distinguish from the interpretative process applicable to treaties. The same could be said of the Individual Opinions of a number of the judges. Judge Lachs, in his consideration of the relationship between the WHO-Egypt Agreement and the setting up of the Regional Office, had this to say:[150]

> it is clear from the merely matter-of-fact mention of the Regional Office in the 1951 Agreement that the presence of the Office in Alexandria is regarded as an accomplished fact . . . It follows that the instrument had no bearing upon [its] establishment.
>
> This view is reinforced by the historical background . . .

A similar opinion was expressed by Judge Ruda, who added that this 'interpretation is in accordance with the facts as I see them, which I now propose to describe.'[151] It is possible to regard these two pronouncements as conforming to the process prescribed in Article 32 of the Vienna Convention where the preparatory work and circumstances surrounding the conclusion of a treaty may be employed to confirm the meaning determined in accordance with the general rule set out in Article 31. However, there was nothing in either opinion to suggest that the use of the material in question was in any way limited to that specific purpose.

Judge Mosler regarded other host agreements as relevant to the interpretation of the 1951 Agreement, thus confirming his belief that he was involved in the process of treaty interpretation. He deduced from a comparison of the various treaties that there was 'a close link between the establishment or the continued existence of the office or service on the territory of the State and the agreement which regulates its legal status with respect to and within the legal order of that State.'[152] The Judge then examined the 'historical background' of the Agreement,[153] acknowledging that the 'measures which culminated in the placing of the Bureau at the disposal of the WHO ran parallel with the preparation and negotiation of the Agreement'.[154] He went on to say:[155]

> My interpretation of the events in question and of the probable intentions of the parties leads me to the conclusion that the arrangement whereby the Bureau's entry into operation as the Regional Office of the WHO was brought about was a stage in more extensive negotiations for the establishment of the Bureau as a regional institution of the WHO, with all the factual and legal consequences that entailed. The establishment of the seat of the regional organisation in Egypt consequently cannot be dissociated from the agreement regulating its status.

150 Ibid at 108.

151 Ibid at 115. Judge Oda also considered at considerable length the negotiating history of the 1951 Agreement as well as the 1948 Agreement between WHO and Switzerland in deciding that the former was irrelevant to the question asked, see ibid at 131.

152 Ibid at 126. 153 Ibid. 154 Ibid at 127. 155 Ibid.

It follows from this that Section 37 of the Agreement could not be ignored in any assessment of whether the Office could be relocated from Egypt. A similar approach was adopted, and conclusion reached, by Judge El-Erian. In support of his view that the 1951 Agreement was 'intended to regulate the legal status and activities of the Regional Office in Alexandria', he prefaced the use of the evidence in question with the following comment:[156]

> A careful examination of the circumstances of its conclusion, the purposes sought to be achieved by such an instrument and an analysis of its provisions clearly reveal that the Agreement is a 'host agreement'.

Despite variations in the purposes for which the surrounding circumstances were employed by the Court and by its individual members in the *WHO-Egypt Agreement* case, there was little hesitation in doing so. It may be that the Opinions of Judges Mosler and El-Erian were more striking in that both were more directly related to the interpretation of the 1951 Agreement rather than with simply testing the relevance of that Agreement to the question asked. In this connection, it would be true to say that some judges are more prepared than others to employ evidence of surrounding circumstances much more extensively than Articles 31 and 32 of the Vienna Convention would seem to allow.

In the *Territorial Dispute between Libya and Chad* case,[157] the International Court outlined the 'customary international law, reflected in Article 31 of the 1969 Vienna Convention on the Law of Treaties', and then applied it to the interpretation of Article 3 of the Treaty of 1955 between Libya and France,[158] concluding that Article 3 and Annex I of the Treaty were 'intended to define frontiers by reference to legal instruments which would yield the course of such frontiers'.[159] However, reference was made to snippets of the historical record as being part of the *travaux préparatoires*, not 'to elucidate the content of the 1955 Treaty; but . . . to confirm [the Court's] reading of the text, namely that the Treaty constitutes an agreement between the parties which, *inter alia*, defines the frontiers.'[160] In contrast, in his Separate Opinion, Judge Ajibola considered at some length the background to the 1955 Treaty. This was undertaken in order, first of all, to establish the object and purpose of the Treaty as envisaged by Article 31 of the Vienna Convention.[161] He then proceeded to use this and other evidence, gleaned from the 'volumes of diplomatic documents, including correspondence, agreements, notes or *procès verbaux*, and maps' submitted by the parties to the Court, as part of what he termed the 'integration approach' to treaty interpretation.[162] While the starting point for this was the context of the Treaty as identified by reference to Article

[156] ICJ Rep 1980 at 172. [157] ICJ Rep 1994, 6. [158] Ibid at 21–22.
[159] Ibid at 25. [160] Ibid at 27. [161] Ibid at 62. [162] Ibid at 66.

31(2) of the Vienna Convention,[163] the evidence employed was far broader in nature. For example, the Judge felt it necessary to explain on the basis of various sources including debates in the French National Assembly that France had not been entirely happy about the contents of the Treaty and that the Treaty had in fact been a compromise for both sides.[164] It would seem that the only acceptable explanation for the use of such evidence was as surrounding circumstances, because Judge Ajibola went on to make clear that, in this case, there was no need 'at all to resort to the *travaux* [*inter alia*] because the primary means of interpretation do not leave any residue of ambiguity or absurdity.'[165]

The final point which the *Libya/Chad* case illustrates is that, whether one regards the evidence as admissible as part of Article 31 as constituting a means of identifying the object and purpose of the treaty or as a gloss upon Article 31(2) through the medium of surrounding circumstances, or whether its use is justified under one of the exceptions to Article 32, the evidence is presented to the Court. The requirements of intertemporality are satisfied: the Court is in fact, or by way of a fiction, placed in the position of the parties at the time their treaty was made.

2. *The law existing at the time the treaty was made*

(a) *The role of Article 31(3)(c) of the Vienna Convention and its relationship to Waldock's draft Article 56*

It has already been suggested[166] that the International Law Commission's treatment of intertemporality was too narrow in that draft Article 56 was limited exclusively to matters of law: that (1) a 'treaty is to be interpreted in the light of the law in force at the time the treaty was drawn up'; and (2) that, subject to (1), 'the application of a treaty shall be governed by the rules of international law in force at the time when the treaty is applied'.[167] Although a specific provision dealing with the intertemporal law was omitted from the text, some of its effects, as far as the law is concerned, have been preserved by what became Article 31(3)(c) of the Vienna Convention:

There shall also be taken into account, together with the context:

. . .

(c) any relevant rules of international law applicable in the relations between the parties.

While this does not require notice to be taken of any intertemporal element, it certainly does not prevent account being taken of the time factor. Whether or not that was relevant in a particular case depended, in the Commission's final observations on the matter, on the parties' intentions

[163] Ibid. [164] Ibid at 68–69. [165] Ibid at 74.
[166] Above pp 2–5. [167] Yb ILC 1964, vol II, 8–9.

which could be accommodated in this context by the requirement of Article 31 that a treaty should be interpreted in good faith.[168]

Despite the Commission's ultimate ambivalence about intertemporality, Article 31(3)(c) would seem to encompass that issue in two ways. First, the reference to 'together with the context' suggests that what follows should be equally applicable to the interpretative process at the time of that context. As Article 31(3)(a) and (b) concern future events,[169] sub-paragraph (c) is the only one that could have a contemporaneous application. However, the fact that (a) and (b) deal with future events would seem to suggest that (c) should also incorporate a future element, that is to bring in relevant rules later 'applicable in the relations between the parties',[170] the fact that (a) and (b) deal with future events would seem to suggest that (c) should also incorporate a future element, that is, to relevant rules later 'applicable in the relations between the parties'. In this sense, if the parties' intentions so indicate, Article 31(3)(c) has the scope to cover both of the areas originally intended for draft Article 56.[171]

If one reads Article 31(3)(c) without the intervening sub-paragraphs (a) and (b), it would strongly suggest that the primary field of reference of (c) would be the law in force at the time the treaty was made, and this is certainly the aspect of draft Article 56 about which Waldock seemed to feel most confidence. In his commentary, he adverted to what he described as '[w]ell known instances of the application of the inter-temporal law to treaties',[172] all of which concerned the meaning to be attributed to a treaty at the time it was made. It has to be said, however, that the Commission's proposals and their subsequent endorsement by the Vienna Conference have produced something of an anomaly, at least in theory. It seems strange that the concept of surrounding circumstances should have been translated into the Vienna Convention as comprising, on the one hand, the restricted version of context as defined in Article 31(2), together with whatever can be added on in order to ascertain the object and purpose of the treaty, plus, on the other hand, *any* rules of international law subject only to the limitation of relevancy, the gap with regard to such circumstances only being remediable in the limited circumstances indicated in Article 32.

(b) *The cases advanced in support of draft article 56(1) were more concerned with the facts surrounding the making of a treaty than with the law existing at that time*

This lack of balance may in part be attributable to a misreading of some of

168 Yb ILC 1966, vol II, 222, para(16).

169 Thus, there should: 'also be taken into account, together with the context: '(a) any subsequent agreement between the parties regarding the interpretation of the treaty or the application of its provisions; (b) any subsequent practice in the application of the treaty which establishes the agreement of the parties regarding its interpretation.'

170 See below pp 51–56.

171 Yb ILC 1964, vol II, 9, above. p 5

172 Yb ILC 1964, vol II, 9, para (2).

the cases. It has already been pointed out that both before and after the Vienna Convention was finalised, there were examples of context or surrounding circumstances being given a wider interpretation than that indicated in Article 31(2) or Article 32 of the Convention. It can certainly be argued that some of the cases employed by Waldock to support draft Article 56(1) were authority for a much broader view of intertemporality. Indeed, they can be seen as clear evidence of the tendency of international lawyers to disguise questions of fact as issues of law, thus limiting intertemporality to matters of law rather than accepting it as of general application.

The *Grisbadarna* case[173] appears to be something of an exception. To understand what the parties meant by a boundary treaty of 1661 as it applied to their maritime territory, it was necessary to place the arbitrators, as far as possible, in the same position that the parties would have been in at the time the treaty was made. This could only be achieved by arming the arbitrators with evidence of the surrounding circumstances, including whatever rules of international law that may then have been relevant to an understanding of the treaty to be interpreted. The decision was explained by Waldock as follows:[174]

> The Tribunal declined to use either the median-line or thalweg principles for delimiting the maritime boundary under the treaty, on the ground that neither of these principles had been recognised in the international law of the seventeenth century. Instead it adopted the principle of a line perpendicular to the general direction of the land as being more in accord with the 'notions of law prevalent at that epoch'.

This description is, however, an over-simplification. The *compromis* drew a distinction between a determination by the arbitrators under the treaty, and a determination outside the treaty 'taking into account the circumstances of fact and the principles of international law'.[175] In light of the *compromis*, there would seem to be two alternative possibilities. If the arbitrators were simply interpreting and applying the 1661 treaty as suggested by Waldock, then the principle of intertemporality was directing them not just to the rules of international law contemporaneous with the treaty, but also to 'the circumstances of fact which existed at the time of

173 (1909) 11 UNRIAA 147; Eng. version Scott JB (ed.), *The Hague Court Reports* (1916), 121.

174 Yb ILC 1964, vol II, 9, para(2): the relevant parts of the award are in 11 UNRIAA at 160; and Scott, op cit n 173, at 129.

175 See Article 3 of the Agreement for Arbitration, Scott, op cit n 173, 133 at 134, 11 UNRIAA at 153–4: 'The tribunal of arbitration shall have power to determine how far the boundary-line shall be considered to be, either wholly or in part, determined by the boundary treaty of 1661, together with the chart appertaining to the same, and how each boundary-line is to be traced, and also, in so far as the boundary-line can not be considered as established by the treaty and chart in question, shall have power to determine the same, taking into account the circumstances of fact and the principles of international law.'

the treaty'.[176] If the arbitrators decided the case outside the 1661 treaty, then the intertemporality stemmed from the *compromis* in that the arbitrators regarded that instrument as directing them to the facts and law existing in 1661. There appears to be little doubt that the arbitrators believed that they were adopting the latter approach.[177]

One of the questions submitted to the tribunal established to hear the *North Atlantic Coast Fisheries* case[178] was the extent of the renunciation by the United States in a treaty of 1818 of the right of its inhabitants to take fish from within 'three marine Miles of any of the Coasts, Bays, Creeks or Harbours' of the King's Dominions in America. In making its determination, the tribunal undoubtedly relied upon the notion of intertemporality when it said that it could not 'take cognisance . . . of other principles concerning the territorial sovereignty over bays such as ten mile or twelve mile limits of exclusion based on international acts subsequent to the treaty of 1818'.[179] However, it is clear that the tribunal did not limit itself to a consideration of the then current state of international law, which, in any case, included evidence of State practice to which that ruling referred. In order to consider how the notion of 'bays' (which it took as being based on a geographical meaning) should be applied, the tribunal did take other evidence into account. As the tribunal explained:[180]

> The negotiators of the Treaty of 1818 did probably not trouble themselves with subtle theories concerning the notion of 'bays'; they most probably thought that everybody would know what was a bay. In this popular sense the term must be interpreted in the Treaty. The interpretation must take into account all the individual circumstances which for any one of the different bays are to be appreciated, the relation of its width to the length of penetration inland, the possibility and the necessity of its being defended by the State in whose territory it is indented; the special value which it has for the industry of the inhabitants of its shores; the distance which it is secluded from the highways of nations on the open sea and other circumstances not possible to enumerate.

There can be little doubt that the tribunal did not regard the definition of 'bay' in the treaty as being one prescribed by international law. International law was relevant to exclude a possible interpretation (a 10 or 12 miles rule), but not to attach a specific meaning to the term. The interpretation adopted by the tribunal was to emphasise the general geographical use of the word subject to account being taken in a particular case of a

176 See the text of the award, Scott, op cit n 173 at 127; 11 UNRIAA at 158.

177 See the text of the award, Scott, op cit n 173 at 126; 11 UNRIAA at 158. 'Whereas, as regards the question, "whether the boundary-line should be considered, either wholly or in part, as being fixed by the boundary treaty of 1661 and the map annexed thereto", the answer to this question should be negative, at least as regards the boundary-line beyond point A on the aforementioned map.'

178 (1910) 11 UNRIAA 167.

179 Ibid at 196.

180 Ibid at 198–199.

variety of factual matters. Those surrounding circumstances were therefore essential to the interpretation of the treaty.

Waldock also made reference to the *Rights of US Nationals in Morocco* case,[181] in which the International Court was asked to determine the scope of consular jurisdiction granted to the United States by Morocco by their treaty of 1836, replacing an earlier treaty of 1787, in 'substantially identical terms',[182] by the use of the words 'any dispute'. Waldock quoted the Court's assertion that, in deciding this issue, it was 'necessary to take into account the meaning of the word "dispute" at the times when the two treaties were concluded'.[183] However, if this was an instance of the application of the intertemporal law as suggested by Waldock,[184] it was only so in the broader sense of requiring the application of circumstances existing at the times the treaties were made to determine their meaning. The circumstances in question comprised a range of similar treaties between Morocco and other countries,[185] from which the Court concluded:[186]

> For this purpose it is possible to look at the way in which the word 'dispute' or its French counterpart was used in the different treaties concluded by Morocco: e.g., with France in 1631 and 1682, with Great Britain in 1721, 1750, 1751, 1760 and 1801. It is clear that in these instances the word was used to cover both civil and criminal disputes. . .
>
> Accordingly, it is necessary to construe the word 'dispute', as used in Article 20 [of the 1836 treaty], as referring to both civil disputes and to criminal disputes . . .

Without wishing to belabour the point further, this group of cases undoubtedly supports the view here advanced that intertemporality is a more extensive concept than Waldock was suggesting. It requires that the first and at times critical setting in which to place a treaty is that surrounding its inception and that this setting is not limited to the law in force at that time. Indeed, in the last of the cases dealt with, although the Court referred, in support of its conclusion to the fact that, under Moroccan law, 'the clear-cut distinction between civil and criminal matters had not yet been developed',[187] the evidence provided by the various treaties was more a matter of fact than it was of law in terms of the setting of the treaties of 1787 and 1836. Moreover, in none of the cases considered was any doubt raised as to the admissibility of such evidence of the circumstances surrounding, and forming the background to, the making of the treaties in question.

[181] ICJ Rep 1952, 176. [182] Ibid at 189.
[183] Ibid, cited in Yb ILC 1964, vol II, 9, para (2). [184] Ibid.
[185] See the US Counter-Memorial, *ICJ Pleadings*, vol I, 257 at 363–371.
[186] ICJ Rep 1952 at 189. [187] Ibid.

IV. CRITICAL DATE II: THE TIME OF INTERPRETATION AND THE MANAGEMENT OF CHANGE OVER THE LIFE OF A TREATY

A. Introduction: ascribing the effects of change to the acts or intentions of the parties

It has already been pointed out that draft Article 56(2) prescribed that 'the application of a treaty shall be governed by the rules of international law in force at the time when the treaty is applied.'[188] The principal objection to this formulation was that, as it was said to be subject to draft Article 56(1), there was no explanation of when it would not be excluded by the totally inconsistent requirement that a treaty was 'to be interpreted in the light of the law in force at the time when the treaty was drawn up.'[189] In addition, of course, the effects of intertemporality were defined exclusively in terms of the law.

In a sense, the time of interpretation will always be a significant date because it is then that attention is focused on the treaty and its interpretation. Whoever is the interpreter will be placed in the situation presented by the circumstances of the moment, and even his or her perception of past events surrounding the making of the treaty will be coloured by present experience, including some familiarity with the incidents of the intervening years and their effects.[190] There will always be an incentive therefore to give to the present an emphasis which logic might not always dictate. Nevertheless, the question to be examined here is the extent to which that emphasis has any legal foundation.

The rules of treaty law, as expressed in the Vienna Convention, do have some regard for changing circumstances. As already mentioned, as far as treaty interpretation is concerned, Article 31(3)(a) and (b) deal with the effect of subsequent agreements, whether express or to be implied from the practice of the parties, as matters to be 'taken into account'.[191] The amendment or modification of treaties by acts subsequent to their making

[188] Above p 3.

[189] See above n. 7.

[190] It is a failure to appreciate this factor which is the weakness in Jessup's criticism of Huber's view of the intertemporal law in the *Island of Palmas* case (1928) 2 UNRIAA 829 at 839 (above p 1) in 'The Palmas Island Arbitration' (1928) 22 AJIL 735 at 739–741. While it is true that, if Spanish title had been established at some date prior to the treaty of cession with the United States of 1898, that title should only have been regarded as relinquished by abandonment (ie as requiring a loss of the intention to retain sovereignty as well as a loss of possession), the existence of that earlier title can only be assessed in the light of later events and current perceptions of them. In the absence of an allocation of the island to Spain or acceptance of Spain's title, the subsequent history does not represent an abandonment of sovereignty but will inevitably be seen as evidence that such sovereignty had not been established. There is a similarity between this and the approach of the International Court in the *Kasikili/Sedudu Island* case, Judgment of 13 December 1999; text in (2000) 39 ILM 310, below pp 115, 122.

[191] Above p 46.

is covered in Articles 39, 40 or 41. Moreover, matters of termination or suspension clearly give rise to intertemporal issues, whether this occurs by the conclusion of a later treaty,[192] by a material breach of the original treaty,[193] or as a result of supervening impossibility of performance,[194] or of a fundamental change of circumstances to those existing at the time of the conclusion of a treaty,[195] or of the emergence of a new norm of the *jus cogens*.[196]

On the face of it, the only ways of keeping a treaty up to date over a period of time are by the parties agreeing to the necessary action either as a matter of interpretation under Article 31(3)(a) and (b), or as a matter of amendment or modification in accordance with Articles 40 or 41. In the case of a multilateral treaty with a large number of parties, such agreement may not be easy to achieve. One means of circumventing this problem is by way of interpretation, the justification for taking account of the changes brought about by subsequent events, or to subsequent perceptions, being ascribed to the original intentions of the parties. It is those intentions which enable the time of application of a treaty to become a critical date in the process of interpretation and to replace or supplement the time of making of the treaty for that purpose.

The existence of such an intention is of course very much a matter of inference from the circumstances. In other words, in the same way that the interpretation of a treaty depends upon an assessment of the circumstances surrounding its making, so the selection of the appropriate critical date(s) is also dependent upon such an assessment. However, as already pointed out, [197] it is also true to say that, in making such an assessment, the interpreter will inevitably be influenced by his/her own perception of the treaty as it stands at present, in light of its history over the intervening years. Two cases may be mentioned to illustrate the significance of intention in light of the circumstances to the choice between alternative possible critical dates.

In *Petroleum Development Ltd. v Sheikh of Abu Dhabi*,[198] the two arbitrators disagreed, so the unresolved issues were submitted to Lord Asquith as Umpire. The case concerned the extent of the area covered by a concession contract of January 1939, whereby the Sheikh granted to the company the sole right for 75 years to search for and exploit all mineral oils from an area described as 'the whole of the lands which belong to the ruler of Abu Dhabi and its dependencies and all the islands and the sea waters which belong to that area'.[199] The dispute arose when, in 1949, the Sheikh purported to grant similar rights to an American company over the

[192] See Articles 59 and 30.
[193] See Article 60, below pp 103–108.
[194] See Article 61.
[195] See Article 62.
[196] See Article 64, above p 21.
[197] Above p 50.
[198] (1951) 18 ILR 144.
[199] The translation of the Arabic contract provided by the Sheikh, which Lord Asquith interpreted for the reason given in the text as no wider than that of the claimant's translation (see ibid at 146–147).

continental shelf, rights which Petroleum Development Ltd claimed belonged to it by virtue of the 1939 agreement. Lord Asquith had no doubt that the original contract did not extend to the continental shelf of Abu Dhabi:[200]

> At that time neither contracting party had ever heard of the doctrine of the Continental Shelf, which as a legal doctrine did not then exist. No thought of it entered their heads . . . [I]t seems to me that it would be a most artificial refinement to read back into the contract the implications of a doctrine not mooted until seven years later, and, if the view which I am about to express is sound, not even today admitted to the canon of International Law.

Although, of course, not dealing with a treaty, the Umpire did give the impression that he was aware of, and was taking into account, the international nature of the transaction. Thus, as far as its interpretation was concerned, he explained his approach as follows:[201]

> while in this case evidence has been admitted as to the nature of the negotiations leading up to, and of the correspondence both preceding and following the conclusion of the Agreement, which evidence as material for construing the contract might, according to domestic English Law, be largely inadmissible, and to this extent the rigid English rules have been disregarded; yet on the other hand the English rule which attributes paramount importance to the actual language of the written instrument in which the negotiations result seems to me no mere idiosyncrasy of our system, but a principle of ecumenical validity. Chaos may obviously result if that rule is widely departed from: and if, instead of asking what the words used mean, the inquiry extends at large to what each of the parties meant them to mean, and how and why each phrase came to be inserted.

In other words, the Umpire placed the contract almost exclusively in the setting in which it was made, including both the relevant rules of international law relating to maritime territory and the surrounding circumstances reflected in the negotiations leading up to the conclusion of the agreement,[202] except in so far as they might constitute evidence of a party's subjective intentions. This setting was an appropriate application of the intertemporality principle to the agreement. Appraised in that setting, there was nothing to suggest that the Sheikh was intending to transfer, or the company expecting to receive, rights of exploitation which he might subsequently acquire by virtue of developing rules of international law.[203]

200 (1951) 18 ILR 144 at 152.

201 Ibid at 149.

202 Considered by the Umpire, ibid at 158–160.

203 As the agreement did cover certain possible subsequent changes brought about by a delimitation arrangement with other governments or by the establishment of a neutral area (Article 2(a) and (b), ibid at 146–147), there was an apparent absence of an intention to transfer rights to any other areas that might accrue to Abu Dhabi. Hence the agreement, these specific possibilities apart, was essentially based upon the *nemo dat quod non habet* principle

This decision may be contrasted with the *Aegean Sea* case.[204] One of the grounds upon which, Greece claimed, the International Court could exercise jurisdiction was that both Greece and Turkey were parties to the General Act for the Pacific Settlement of International Disputes 1928, which established the jurisdiction of the Permanent Court, a link preserved to bestow jurisdiction on the present Court by Article 37 of its Statute.[205] Whether this argument was correct depended on how the Court interpreted the reservation which Greece had made at the time it acceded to the General Act, excluding from its acceptance 'disputes concerning questions relating to the territorial status of Greece'.[206] Greece contended for a restrictive interpretation of 'territorial status' because the historical record showed that the great concern of States which had made similar reservations to various instruments of the time had been 'to protect themselves against possible attempts to modify territorial settlements established by the peace treaties' after the First World War.[207] However, the Court did not accept Greece's contention. While concern about attempts to undermine the peace settlements might have been 'the *motive* which led States to include in treaties provisions regarding "territorial status" ', it did

> not follow that they intended those provisions to be confined to questions connected with the revision of such settlements. Any modification of a territorial 'status' or 'situation' or 'frontier' is unpalatable to a State; and the strong probability is that a State which had recourse to a reservation of disputes relating to territorial status, or the like, intended it to be quite general.[208]

Having failed to limit the interpretation placed upon the reservation by reference to the historical circumstances with which Greece and other States were faced at the time Greece accepted the General Act, Greece sought to rely upon the *Abu Dhabi* case to establish that, as the continental shelf did not exist in legal doctrine at that time, the reservation should be limited only to matters of territorial status to which it would then have applied. This contention the Court also rejected:[209]

> While there may well be a presumption that a person transferring valuable property rights to another intends only to transfer the rights which he possesses at that time, the case appears to the Court to be quite otherwise when a State, in agreeing to subject itself to compulsory procedures of pacific settlement, excepts from that agreement a category of disputes which, though covering clearly specified subject-matters, is of a generic kind. Once it is established that the expression 'the territorial

at the time the agreement was made, a principle which worked in favour of the Netherlands in the *Island of Palmas* case (1928) 2 UNRIAA 829, in which, in response to the United States' contention that sovereignty over the island had been transferred to it by Spain by the Treaty of Paris 1898, the arbitrator pointed out (ibid at 842) that it was 'evident that Spain could not transfer more rights than she herself possessed.'

204 ICJ Rep 1978, 3.
205 See above p 35.
206 ICJ Rep 1978 at 20–21.
207 Ibid at 30.
208 Ibid.
209 Ibid at 32.

status of Greece' was used in Greece's instrument of accession as a generic term denoting any matters comprised within the concept of territorial status under general international law, the presumption necessarily arises that its meaning was intended to follow the evolution of the law and to correspond with the meaning attached to the expression by the law in force at any given time. This presumption, in the view of the Court, is even more compelling when it is recalled that the 1928 Act was a convention for the pacific settlement of disputes designed to be of the most general kind and of continuing duration, for it hardly seems conceivable that in such a convention terms like 'domestic jurisdiction' and 'territorial status' were intended to have a fixed content regardless of the subsequent evolution of international law.

This pronouncement was not based upon a consideration of Greece's reservation alone. As has already been noted, the interpretation of an acceptance of a jurisdictional clause has involved international tribunals in attempting to ascertain and to rely upon the subjective intention of the State involved.[210] In this case, the evidence, relevant to another but related issue, namely whether, as the Court concluded, the territorial status reservation was independent of, and not limited by the domestic jurisdiction exception in the same sub-paragraph of the reservation, did not assist the Greek case. Hence there was no alternative but to look at the scope of territorial status from a purely objective point of view. Indeed, that approach would seem to be dictated by the terms of the General Act, Article 39(2) of which allowed only the following reservations:[211]

(a) Disputes arising out of facts prior to the accession either of the Party making the reservation or of any other Party with whom the said Party may have a dispute;
(b) Disputes concerning questions which by international law are solely within the domestic jurisdiction of States;
(c) Disputes concerning particular cases or clearly specified subject-matters, such as territorial status, or disputes falling within clearly defined categories.

As already indicated above, it might have been the intention of the parties to the General Act that a State was entitled to demonstrate by evidence that its intention was to make a reservation narrower than the maximum allowed under Article 39. This Greece had been permitted to do (though unsuccessfully) with regard to the claimed link whereby its reference to domestic jurisdiction in the same part of the reservation had limited the scope of territorial status. That having failed, the territorial status part was left as an independent reservation in its own right. It would seem reasonable to suppose, therefore, that, by adopting the very words of a reservation permitted by Article 39(2), it was the intention of the parties, including Greece, that both should be objectively interpreted, independently of the subjective, but not publicised, intentions of the reserving

210 See above p 36.   211 ICJ Rep 1978 at 23.

State. It was on this basis that the Court went on to hold that the interpretation of such a reservation was not limited by the circumstances existing at the time of, and in the period immediately following, the conclusion of the General Act (when the continental shelf was unknown as a legal concept), but should take account of the subsequent development of territorial rights under international law (including those accruing as part of the continental shelf).[212]

While the time of interpretation is important as a purely practical matter, because changes of circumstances, be they of law or fact, are by then apparent to the interpreter, it is still doubtful whether that time can exist as a critical date in its own right. If it is to have legal, rather than simply practical, significance, the lesson of the *Aegean Sea* case is that its status is dependent upon the perceived intention of the parties existing at the time of the making of the treaty. It would seem to follow that that earlier date must always be critical. This view of the law is borne out by the International Court's advisory opinion in the *Namibia* case.[213]

At the time when the Mandate system was established by and under Article 22 of the Covenant of the League of Nations, a number of newly designated mandatory powers believed that Class C mandated territories could in time be annexed by them. Not only had this not occurred, but the objective of the sacred trust of civilisation in Article 22 under which the territories had been held had come to be recognised as 'the self-determination and independence of the people concerned'.[214] As to how this shift in attitude towards the future of dependant territories could be applied as part of the interpretative process, the Court explained as follows:[215]

> Mindful as it is of the primary necessity of interpreting an instrument in accordance with the intentions of the parties at the time of its conclusion, the Court is bound to take into account the fact that the concepts embodied in Article 22 of the Covenant . . . were not static, but were by definition evolutionary . . . The parties to the Covenant must consequently be deemed to have accepted them as such. That is why, viewing the institutions of 1919, the Court must take into consideration the changes which have occurred in the supervening half-century, and its interpretation cannot remain unaffected by the subsequent development of law, through the

[212] Judge De Castro dissented, holding that contractual obligations must be assessed, according to Articles 31 and 32 of the Vienna Convention, in their context and in light of the circumstances in which the treaty was concluded. It was only 'the interpretation of laws', like the UN Charter, which 'must be interpreted and applied in the context of the legal system in force at the time when the interpretation takes place (ICJ Rep 1978 at 68). In his view (ibid): 'It . . . seems permissible to conclude that the task of interpretation is to verify what was or could have been the will of Greece in 1931 when it used the expression "territorial status" in reservation (b) to its accession to the General Act. The function of intertemporal law is different; it is by the operation of the rules of intertemporal law that new sovereign or exclusive rights over the continental shelf have been attributed to Greece or Turkey.'

[213] ICJ Rep 1971, 16.

[214] Ibid at 31.

[215] Ibid.

Charter of the United Nations and by way of customary law. Moreover, an international instrument has to be interpreted and applied within the framework of the entire legal system prevailing at the time of the interpretation.

The use made of the apparent intention of the parties complies with the requirement of intertemporality in relation to the conclusion of a treaty. That intention can only be deduced from the circumstances surrounding the act of conclusion, in assessing how the text of the treaty is to be interpreted. This approach is broader than that allowed for by Article 31 of the Vienna Convention which is limited to the object and purpose of the treaty, and does not seem to cater for the emergent purpose to become a relevant factor on the basis of the evolutionary nature of the instrument as envisaged by the parties at the time of its making. Yet it was this later explanation of the position which coincides most closely with that given by the Court in the *Namibia* case, when it concluded that, 'viewing the institutions of 1919, the Court must take into consideration the changes which have occurred . . . and . . . the subsequent development of the law'. It is less clear what the Court was signifying by its final comment that 'an international instrument has to be interpreted and applied within the framework of the entire legal system prevailing at the time of the interpretation'. Does this mean more than that, as a practical matter, the entire circumstances, of fact as well as the law, existing at the time of interpretation are bound to shape the vision of the treaty in the mind's eye of the interpreter?

A similar doubt as to whether current values can be applied directly to a treaty, or whether their application needs to be based upon the original intentions of the parties, can be seen in the *Gabčikovo–Nagymaros Project* case.[216] The Treaty between Hungary and Czechoslovakia of 1977 concerning the construction and operation of the Gabčikovo–Nagymaros System of Locks on the River Danube included undertakings to ensure that the quality of water was not impaired[217] and 'compliance with the obligations for the protection of nature arising in connection with the construction and operation of the System of Locks'.[218] The Court certainly expressed the view that the application of contemporary environmental standards stemmed from the nature of the obligations themselves:[219]

These articles do not contain specific obligations of performance but require the parties . . . to take new environmental norms into consideration when agreeing upon the means to be specified in the Joint Contractual Plan.

By inserting these evolving provisions in the Treaty, the parties recognised the potential necessity to adapt the Project. Consequently, the Treaty is not static, and is open to adapt to emerging norms of international law.

216 ICJ Rep 1997, 7. 217 Article 15, ibid, at 22.
218 Article 19, ibid, at 23. 219 Ibid, at 67–88.

This factor was reiterated later in the Judgment:[220]

In order to evaluate the environmental risks, current standards must be taken into consideration. This is not only allowed by the wording of Articles 15 and 19, but even prescribed, to the extent that these articles impose a continuing—and thus necessarily evolving—obligation on the parties to maintain the quality of water of the Danube and to protect nature.

However, the Court concluded its consideration of this aspect of the case with a much broader basis for its application of contemporary environmental values, whether in the form of new norms or standards:[221]

Throughout the ages, mankind has, for economic and other reasons, constantly interfered with nature. In the past, this was often done without consideration of the effects on the environment. Owing to new scientific insights and to a growing awareness of the risks for mankind—for present and future generations—of pursuit of such interventions at an unconsidered and unabated pace, new norms and standards have been developed, set forth in a great number of instruments during the last two decades. Such new norms have to be taken into consideration, and such new standards given proper weight, not only when States contemplate new activities but also when continuing with activities begun in the past.

Does this statement amount to an assertion that all treaties containing a reference to environmental standards are by nature evolutionary, or that they are so presumptively, in the absence of a clear expression of a contrary intent by the parties? Or was it simply a warning that whatever the effects of a treaty amongst the parties, it could not absolve them from responsibility in their dealings with other States? This last mentioned possibility seems unlikely because it is a statement of the obvious. Hence it could be taken as signifying that, though the provisions of the 1977 Treaty were evolutionary, it may well be that all environmental treaties are from their nature subject to the requirements of the developing standards of international environmental law.

It may not be possible to provide a definitive answer as to the Court's meaning, the above passages having all the signs of being a compromise between two alternative views. On the one hand, there was support for a broad view of the role of community values in the interpretation of environmental treaties. Thus, Judge Weeramantry had this to say of the 'intertemporal aspect of the present case' in relation to Article 31 of the Vienna Convention:[222]

220 Ibid, at 77–78.

221 Ibid, at 78. The Court prefaced this pronouncement with the following observation (ibid): 'The Court is mindful that, in the field of environmental protection, vigilance and prevention are required on account of the often irreversible character of damage to the environment and of the limitations inherent in the very mechanism of reparation of this type of damage.'

222 Ibid, at 114, going on to say: 'Environmental rights are human rights. Treaties that

Environmental concerns are live and continuing concerns whenever the project under which they arise may have been inaugurated. It matters little that an undertaking has been commenced under a treaty of 1950, if in fact that undertaking continues in operation in the year 2000. The relevant environmental standards that will be applicable will be those of the year 2000.

On the other hand, Judge Bedjaoui was adamant that the primary point of reference for the interpretation of any treaty was 'the intentions of the parties at the time of its conclusion',[223] intentions which 'are presumed to have been influenced by the law in force at the time the Treaty was concluded, the law which they were supposed to know, and not by future law, as yet unknown'.[224] In his view, therefore, 'the essential basis for the interpretation of a treaty remains the "*fixed reference*" to contemporary international law at the time of its conclusion. The "*mobile reference*" to the law which will subsequently have developed can be recommended only in exceptional cases'.[225] In the *Namibia* case,[226] 'the situation was special . . . the definition of the "*sacred trust*" [was] evolutionary',[227] but the 1977 Treaty was quite different and was, therefore, subject to the normal rules of interpretation:[228]

In general, it is noteworthy that the classical rules of interpretation do not require a treaty to be interpreted *in all circumstances* in the context of the entire legal system prevailing at the time of the interpretation, in other words, in the present case, that the 1977 Treaty should be interpreted 'in the context' and in the light of the new contemporary law of the environment or of international watercourses. Indeed, it is quite the opposite that these rules of interpretation prescribe, seeking as they do to recommend an interpretation consonant with the intentions of the parties at the time the Treaty was concluded.

Accordingly, it was only in 'very special situations' that the subsequent law could be taken into account 'as an element of interpretation or modification of the obligations of a treaty'.[229]

affect human rights cannot be applied in such a manner as to constitute a denial of human rights at the time of their application. A Court cannot endorse actions which are a violation of human rights by the standards of their time merely because they are taken under a treaty which dates back to a period when such action was not a violation of human rights.' See also the same Judge's endorsement of the intertemporal principle applying to how facts are appreciated, as well as to changes in the law, in the *Request for an Examination of the Situation in the Nuclear Tests* case, ICJ Rep 1995, 288 at 340. Support for this broader view is to be found in Judge Herczegh's Dissenting Opinion, in the *Gabčikovo–Nagymaros* case, ICJ Rep 1997 at 178.

223 Words taken from the *Namibia* Advisory Opinion, ICJ Rep 1971, 16 at 31.

224 ICJ Rep 1997 at 121.

225 Ibid, at 122.

226 ICJ Rep 1971, 16.

227 ICJ Rep 1997 at 122.

228 Ibid, at 123. As Judge Bedjaoui added (ibid): 'In general, in a treaty, a State incurs specific obligations contained in a body of law as it existed at the conclusion of the treaty and *in no wise incurs evolutionary and indeterminate duties.*'

229 Ibid, at 124 (heading D).

It is difficult to accept the broader interpretation of the Court's judgment in the *Gabčikovo–Nagymaros Project* case that, at least in certain areas of the law, in this context the environment or, according to Judge Weeramantry, human rights in general, the date of interpretation will inevitably constitute, not just a significant stage, but a critical date, in the process of interpretation. The Court's ascription of the need to take account of developments in the law to the intentions of the parties as expressed in Articles 15 and 19 in particular of the 1977 Treaty,[230] while at the same time apparently endorsing a much wider role for 'new norms . . . to be taken into consideration' and for 'new standards [to be] given proper weight',[231] is symptomatic of the interpreter's dilemma. His or her perception of the treaty is inevitably that of the present, even though the text upon which the interpretation is based represents the thoughts of the parties at the time the treaty was made. If the former is, as a matter of law, to qualify as a critical date then the present realities must, by some means, create a legal justification for that step to be taken. The lesson from the *Namibia* and *Gabčikovo–Nagymaros* cases would seem to be that the Court is prepared to accept that present realities can establish such a qualification, but prefers to consider treaties individually (that is, in accordance with its assessment of the parties' intentions), rather than to lay down any general rule (for example, in respect of all treaties, or perhaps only in respect of those of a particular type, such as those dealing with the environment or human rights) whereby the time of interpretation would, at least presumptively, represent a critical date in the life of a treaty.

B. *Extension of the powers of international organisations ascribed to the intentions of the parties to their constitutional treaty*

How this might be achieved can best be examined in relation to the field of international constitutional law. It is in that field that the inference will most readily, if not inevitably, be drawn that the parties to the original treaty must have intended that the process of interpretation could make up for a lack of express powers to deal with a particular problem by filling gaps in the instrument in question. As Judge Spender said of the UN Charter in his Separate Opinion in the *Expenses* case:[232]

> It was intended to apply to varying conditions in a changing and evolving world community and to a multiplicity of unpredictable situations and events. Its provisions were intended to adjust themselves to the ever changing pattern of international existence.

[230] N. 220 above.
[231] N. 221 above.
[232] ICJ Rep 1962, 151 at 185.
[232] ICJ Rep 1962, 151 at 185.

In interpreting such a treaty, therefore, the time of interpretation must be regarded as critical, because that flows from the parties' original intentions.

There is a further question to be addressed as to how far the apparent intentions of the parties will mould the outcome in the light of the circumstances existing at the time of the interpretation. In the *Reparations* case,[233] the International Court was asked to consider whether, in 'the event of an agent of the United Nations in the performance of his duties suffering injury in circumstances involving the responsibility of a State, has the United Nations, as an Organisation, the capacity to bring a claim . . . with a view to obtaining reparation due in respect of the damage caused (a) to the United Nations, (b) to the victim or to persons entitled through him?'.[234] With regard to (a), the affirmative answer was traceable to the role entrusted to the United Nations by States parties to the Charter. From the Charter, it could be deduced that 'the Organisation was intended [by those parties] to exercise and enjoy, and is in fact exercising and enjoying, functions and rights which can only be explained on the basis of a large measure of international personality', which meant that 'it is a subject of international law and capable of possessing international rights and duties and that it has capacity to maintain its rights by bringing international claims'.[235] There was no reason to doubt that 'the Organisation has the capacity to bring an international claim against one of its Members which has caused injury to it by a breach of its international obligations towards it'.[236] It could not be 'supposed that in such an event all the Members of the Organisation, save the defendant State, must combine to bring a claim against the defendant for the damage suffered by the Organisation'.[237]

The curious aspect of this part of the Court's Opinion is that it avoids any mention of the need to imply such a power, despite the fact that no such power is mentioned in the Charter. It is as if the Court was identifying two types of non-express authority; the first flowing as a matter of course from the express powers and functions of the United Nations, and the second dependent upon a further act of implication. With regard to (a), the Court regarded the competence in question to bring a claim on its own behalf as a situation in the first category. This can be deduced from a number of passages in the Opinion, most notably where the Court asserted that the Members of the Organisation, 'by entrusting certain functions to it, with the attendant duties and responsibilities, have clothed it with the competence required to enable those functions to be effectively discharged',[238] and where it stated that:[239]

233 ICJ Rep 1949, 174.
234 Ibid at 176–177.
235 Ibid at 179.
236 Ibid at 180.
237 Ibid at 180–181.
238 Ibid at 179.
239 Ibid at 180.

The functions of the Organisation are of such a character that they could not be effectively discharged if they involved the concurrent action, or the international plane, of fifty-eight or more Foreign Offices, and the Court concludes that the Members have endowed the Organisation with capacity to bring international claims when necessitated by the discharge of its functions.

It is only when the Court proceeded to (b), the right of the United Nations to claim on behalf of the agent, or those entitled through him, that the Court relied upon the doctrine that, under international law, 'the Organisation must be deemed to have those powers which, though not expressly provided in the Charter, are conferred upon it by necessary implication as being essential to the performance of its duties'.[240] As to how a necessity existed in such circumstances, the Court found it in the fact that 'the Organisation may find it necessary, and has in fact found it necessary, to entrust its agents with important missions to be performed in disturbed parts of the world'. In order 'to ensure the efficient and independent performance of these missions and to afford effective support to its agents, the Organisation must provide them with adequate protection'. Member States owed obligations to the Organisation in undertakings made in the Charter and in complementary agreements. The 'effective working of the Organisation . . . and the independence and effectiveness of the work of its agents require that those undertakings be strictly observed', so that it was 'necessary that, when an infringement occurs, the Organisation should be able to call upon the responsible State to remedy its default, and, in particular, to obtain from the State reparation for the damage that the default may have caused to [the] agent'.[241]

As the justification for its conclusion provided under (a) was obscure, and the justification for (b) open to doubt, the approach (though not necessarily the conclusions reached) adopted by Judge Hackworth would seem to be preferable. In his view, an affirmative answer to (a) or (b) both depended upon the doctrine of implied powers, which rightfully applied to (a),[242] but not to (b). As he explained his view of the position:[243]

Powers not expressed cannot truly be implied. Implied powers flow from a grant of expressed powers, and are limited to those that are 'necessary' to the exercise of powers expressly granted. No necessity for the exercise of the power in question has been shown to exist. There is no impelling reason, if any at all, why the Organisation should become the sponsor of claims on behalf of its employees, even though limited to those arising while the employee is in line of duty. These employees are still nationals of their respective countries, and the customary methods of handling such claims are still available in full vigour. The prestige and efficiency of the Organisation will be safeguarded by an exercise of its undoubted right under . . . (a) *supra*. Even here it is necessary to imply power, but . . . the

[240] Ibid at 182. [241] Ibid at 183. [242] Ibid at 196–197.
[243] Ibid at 198. See also Judge Badawi, ibid at 216; Judge Krylov, ibid at 217.

necessity is self-evident. The exercise of an additional extraordinary power in the field of private claims has not been shown to be necessary to the efficient performance of duty of either the Organisation or its agents.

It can certainly be said, in favour of the Hackworth view, that it is difficult to accept that there was an absolute necessity that the United Nations could make such a claim. It was at most reasonably necessary, not on the basis of any intention on the part of Member States that the Charter should be specifically interpreted in such a way (it was after all acknowledged by the Court that it was 'faced with a new situation'),[244] but because of the possible fallibility of diplomatic protection. As the Court pointed out:[245]

It is essential that—whether the agent belongs to a powerful or to a weak State; to one more affected or less affected by the complications of international life; to one in sympathy or not in sympathy with the mission of the agent—he should know that in the performance of his duties he is under the protection of the Organisation. The assurance is even more necessary when the agent is stateless.

The implication of authority founded upon the express powers or functions of the organisation may be based upon some inferred intention on the part of the creators of the constitutional treaty in question, but the necessity for the implication is judged by the needs of the time of interpretation. As to the degree of necessity required, the fact that it is, as suggested above, qualified rather than absolute is reflected in a number of later pronouncements by the International Court.

In the *Expenses* case,[246] the Court encouraged an expansion of the powers of the United Nations, or at least of the powers of the General Assembly and of the Security Council in ways not envisaged by Chapter IV, and Chapters VI and VII, of the Charter respectively. It did so by relying upon the purposes of the Organisation set out in broad terms in Article 1 of the Charter in the following well-known pronouncement:[247]

[244] Ibid at 182. [245] Ibid at 183–184. [246] ICJ Rep 1962, 151.

[247] Ibid at 168. The Court's differing approaches to questions (a) and (b) in the *Reparations* case or the difference between absolute necessity on the one hand and qualified necessity or appropriate action on the other as in the *Expenses* case are reflected in Seyersted's distinction between implied powers and inherent powers. As he explained (Seyersted F, *United Nations Forces* (1966), 155): 'While a minority of the members will always have the right to challenge the legality, from an internal point of view, of acts performed to attain aims other than those defined in the constitution, the minority cannot challenge acts performed in order to attain aims covered in the constitution merely on the basis that such acts were not "essential" or "necessary" to attain these aims. Thus, it is not necessary to look for specific provisions in the constitution, or to resort to strained interpretations of text and intentions, or to look for precedents or constructions to justify legally the performance by an intergovernmental organisation of a sovereign or international act not specifically authorised in its constitution. As an intergovernmental organisation it has an *inherent* power to perform such acts.' In Seyersted's view this explanation is supported by the presumptive legality accorded 'appropriate' action by the Court in the *Expenses* case, see op cit, 404. As the present text suggests it is difficult to

When the Organisation takes action which warrants the assertion that it was appropriate for the fulfilment of one of the stated purposes of the United Nations, the presumption is that such action is not *ultra vires* the organisation.

The structure of the Charter as originally envisaged was for the purposes to be pursued through the use of the specific powers granted to the various organs of the United Nations, augmented, presumably, by such powers that might be implied from the grant of those express powers. Here the Court seemed to be suggesting that powers might equally well flow from the purposes of the United Nations. As the actions of the General Assembly in relation to UNEF, and of the Assembly and the Security Council concerning ONUC, fell within the Organisation's responsibility for the maintenance of international peace and security, there could be no doubting their presumptive validity. Instead of saying that only necessary action was not *ultra vires* (or even omitting any limitation at all so that an 'action which warrants the assertion that it was . . . for the fulfilment of one of the stated purposes' would not be *ultra vires*), the Court limited the presumption of legality to 'appropriate' action. But what was meant of 'appropriate' in this context?

The first point to notice is that the 'appropriate' links the action with the purposes of the Organisation: it does not refer directly to the appropriateness of the organ which took the action. If one considers only the former aspect, that is the appropriateness of the action, then it would be as well to regard that test as signifying only that the action must be reasonably necessary for achieving the purpose in question. This would have the virtue of maintaining consistency with the *Reparations* case,[248] where the requirement adopted by the Court for the United Nations to be able to present a claim on behalf of one of its agents who had been the victim of conduct by a State, entailing the responsibility of that State, was one of qualified (that is of reasonable) necessity, rather than one of absolute necessity. However, the Court's pronouncement is defective with regard to the latter aspect, in that it suggests that any UN organ has the capacity to take action for any of the purposes of the Organisation and that such action will have presumptive validity. As Judge Winiarski warned in his Dissenting Opinion:[249]

> The Charter has set forth the purposes of the United Nations in very wide . . . terms. But . . . it does not follow, far from it, that the Organisation is entitled to seek to achieve those purposes by no matter what means. The fact that an organ of the United Nations is seeking to achieve one of those purposes does not suffice to render its action lawful. The Charter . . . carefully created organs and determined their competence . . .

accept the validity of the act of an organ within an institution which has no competence with regard to the kind of action it is undertaking, even if the institution does.

248 ICJ Rep 1949, 174 above p 60.

249 Ibid at 230.

The Court's approach may have been acceptable in relation to the General Assembly and the Security Council in the field of international peace and security, where they had overlapping competences. However, the presumption advanced by the Court was far too broad as it could not possibly apply to an action by an organ outside its competence, but justified on the ground that the action was designed to further one of the purposes of the Organisation. To prevent this potentially excessive application of the Court's pronouncement, it would seem to be necessary to take the 'appropriate' as signifying that the action must both have that quality from the perspective of the organ taking action and also be reasonably necessary for fulfilling (one of) the purposes of the United Nations.

However one regards the reference to appropriate in the Court's Opinion, it has to be said that the reliance on the purposes of the Organisation as justifying the valid taking of action by the Organisation, or by one of its organs on its behalf, has great potential for extending the powers of the Organisation, certainly beyond those that could be implied from existing express powers. The purposes of the United Nations are, of course, much more broadly stated than the purposes of, for example, the various specialised agencies, set up to deal with particular areas of international activity, such as health, civil aviation, food and agriculture, or maritime matters, but all share the similarity that their purposes are, for the most part, expressed in 'indefinite' terms.[250] Accordingly, it is open to an organ to rely upon an expansive interpretation of those purposes in taking action which it regards as appropriate/reasonably necessary for achieving those purposes. However, in terms of intertemporality, it is an appropriateness or reasonable necessity that is assessed by reference to the needs of the time of interpretation, whether actual, or even to a degree prospective, and is not to be judged by the standards and aspirations of the time when the constitution was adopted.

In the *Effect of Awards by the UN Administrative Tribunal* case,[251] the International Court was asked whether the General Assembly had 'the right on any grounds to refuse to give effect to the award of compensation made by that Tribunal in favour of a staff member of the United Nations whose contract of service has been terminated without his consent?'.[252] The Court had no doubt that the power to establish a tribunal to adjudicate in disputes between the Organisation and its staff members arose 'by necessary intendment out of the Charter'.[253] It did not justify this conclusion by reference to the express powers of the General Assembly to establish a subsidiary organ, because the issue was not the validity of the existence of the Tribunal, but the scope of the authority granted to it. The Court relied partly upon the steps which the Assembly and the Secretary-

[250] Judge Winiarski, referring to Article 1 of the UN Charter, ibid.
[251] ICJ Rep 1954, 47. [252] Ibid at 48. [253] Ibid at 57.

General had already taken in furtherance of Article 101 of the Charter,[254] and partly upon what it regarded as one of the purposes (aims) of the United Nations:[255]

When the Secretariat was organised, a situation arose in which the relations between the staff members and the Organisation were governed by a complex code of law. This code consisted of the Staff Regulations established by the General Assembly, defining the fundamental rights and obligations of the staff, and the Staff Rules, made by the Secretary-General in order to implement the Staff Regulations. It was inevitable that there would be disputes between the Organisation and staff members as to their rights and duties. The Charter contains no provision which authorises any of the principal organs of the United Nations to adjudicate upon these disputes, and Article 105 secures for the United Nations jurisdictional immunities in national courts. It would, in the opinion of the Court, hardly be consistent with the expressed aim of the Charter to promote freedom and justice for individuals and with the constant preoccupation of the United Nations . . . to promote this aim that it should afford no judicial or arbitral remedy to its own staff for the settlement of any disputes which may arise between it and them.

While a purpose/aim of the Charter might be ascribable to the content of that document at the time of its making, implicit, if not explicit, in the above passage is the significance of events up to the time of interpretation. The complexity of the regulations and rules governing appointments, and the nature of the various types of appointment resulting therefrom, rendered an appropriate dispute settlement process necessary, even necessary in an absolute sense. Moreover, the aim/purpose identified by the Court as the promoting of 'freedom and justice for individuals' was not one specifically stated in the Charter, but only to be inferred from Article 1(3) of that instrument[256] in the light of the Organisation's 'constant preoccupation' with such matters.

[254] According to Article 101:

'1. The staff shall be appointed by the Secretary-General under regulations established by the General Assembly.

. . .

3. The paramount consideration in the employment of the staff and in the determination of the conditions of service shall be the necessity of securing the highest standards of efficiency, competence, and integrity. Due regard shall be paid to the importance of recruiting the staff on as wide a geographical basis as possible.'

[255] ICJ Rep 1954 at 57.

[256] According to Article 1(3), the purposes of the United Nations include: 'To achieve international co-operation . . . in promoting and encouraging respect for human rights and for fundamental freedoms for all . . .' For a case where an international tribunal preferred to rely upon the narrower ground of an extensive reading of the express powers of the organ which established it, rather than upon the proposition that its creation was in furtherance of the purposes of the United Nations in the maintenance of international peace and security, see *Prosecutor v Tadic* (1995) 105 ILR 419. The International Criminal Tribunal for the Former Yugoslavia was confronted with an objection to the validity of its creation by the Security Council. An Appeals Chamber held that it had been properly established under the UN

The existence of a need for an adjudicatory system did not necessarily entail one with the authority to reach decisions binding upon the parties and more particularly on the United Nations. The Court acknowledged that the Assembly had a discretion as to how it should provide a satisfactory system. In fact, when it established UNAT, the Assembly chose to adopt just such a system, Article 10(2) of the Tribunal's Statute prescribing that its judgments 'shall be final and without appeal'. This discretion existed by virtue of the implied power which the Assembly had to establish an adjudicatory process in a form it regarded as suitable.[257]

C. *Community values in treaty interpretation*

The emphasis given to the circumstances existing at the time of interpretation enables account to be taken of what might be termed relevant community values and of the changes that may have occurred to them over the lifespan of the treaty. These values may be of a moral or of a practical kind. Moral values are openly recognised through the *jus cogens* provisions contained in Articles 53 and 64 of the Vienna Convention.[258] There is an obvious practical community value in acceptance of the need to arm the United Nations (or other international organisations) with powers to deal with new situations within its (or their) field of competence.[259] It is true that the introduction of something as amorphous as community values into treaty interpretation is open to the criticism that it will inevitably threaten the sanctity of the text and encourage departures from the intentions which that text reveals. Nevertheless, there is a degree of support for it in some of the literature and, to a limited extent, in the jurisprudence of the International Court, and certainly in the opinions given by a number of members of the Court.

Charter. Even if, as the Chamber was prepared to accept, the Council's discretion to take action under Article 39 of the Charter to deal with a threat to international peace and security was limited to measures provided for in Articles 41 and 42 (ibid at 467), the scope of Article 41 was wide enough to encompass the creation of an international criminal court as a measure 'not involving the use of armed force . . . employed to give effect to [the Council's] decisions' (ibid at 469–470).

257 As the Court expressed it (ICJ Rep 1954 at 58): 'it is contended that . . . an implied power can only be exercised to the extent that the particular measure under consideration can be regarded as absolutely essential. There can be no doubt that the General Assembly in the exercise of its power could have set up a tribunal without giving finality to its judgments. In fact, however, it decided, after long deliberation, to invest the Tribunal with power to render judgments which would be "final and without appeal", and which would be binding on the United Nations. The precise nature and scope of the measures by which the power of creating a tribunal was to be exercised, was a matter for determination by the General Assembly alone.'

258 Above pp 20–21.

259 See above p 59 and further below pp 74–75.

The reference to community values has echoes of the views of the Yale School. McDougal and his associates[260] incorporated into their principles of treaty interpretation an idea which they variously described as the 'basic constitutive policies of the larger community' or 'the requirements of fundamental community policy',[261] or, in keeping with the trademark of the Yale School, 'the goals of (the system of) public order'.[262] If it came to a conflict between fundamental community policy and 'the genuine shared expectations of the parties' to the treaty, as expressed in the treaty or gleaned from the contextual evidence of its making, however, it was the former which should prevail.[263]

While this hypothesis may be justifiable in the limited area of *jus cogens*, its wider application would seem to be doubtful. Indeed, the weakness of the McDougal construct lay not just in its deliberate imprecision,[264] but also in its supporting evidence. The examples related to the more limited propositions that treaties should be interpreted in harmony with and not in derogation from the *jus cogens*,[265] or from rights established by general international law.[266] More fundamentally, the most that community values, the rules of the *jus cogens* apart, can or might offer is a guide as to how a treaty should be interpreted. An individual treaty might not raise any particular issue of community values, other than that of preserving the integrity of the treaty. This would be the case with many bilateral agreements, or those involving a limited number of parties. In such circumstances, the primary requirements would be to apply the treaty in accordance with the parties' wishes (or expectations) as expressed in that instrument. Accordingly, the involvement of community values as an aspect of interpretation is likely to be greater in the case of a multilateral treaty of a constitutional or legislative nature or, though in fact bilateral, where it forms part of a multilateral regime.

With these limitations in mind, it is nevertheless possible to demonstrate the significance of community values from a number of strands. In the first place the invalidity provisions of the Vienna Convention, and not just

260 McDougal MS, Lasswell HD and Miller JC, *The Interpretation of International Agreements and World Public Order* (1967).

261 Ibid, 41. 262 Ibid, 44. 263 Ibid.

264 See Fitzmaurice, '*Vae Victis* or Woe to the Negotiators! Your Treaty or Our "Interpretation" of It' (1971) 65 AJIL 358 at 370–372.

265 Hall WE, *A Treatise on International Law* (7th edn 1917), 344: 'a sense cannot be adopted which leads to . . . incompatibility with an accepted fundamental principle of law'; Oppenheim L, *International Law* (7th edn 1948): 'It is a unanimously recognised customary rule of International Law that obligations which are at variance with universally recognised principles of International Law cannot be the object of a treaty.'

266 Hudson MO, *The Permanent Court of International Justice, 1920–1942* (1943), 655: 'Any international instrument must be interpreted in the light of prevailing international laws by which the parties must be taken to have charted their course'; *Kronprinz Gustaf Adolf* (1932) 2 UNRIAA 1239 at 1246–1247.

Article 53,[267] based for the most part on general principles of law, are undoubtedly reflections of the values of the international community, as well as of the municipal systems from which they were drawn. Secondly, the development of the rules of international law cannot be divorced from the changes in international society, because its legitimacy is 'rooted in the will of the international community characterised by common interests and shared values'.[268] It is not to be supposed that the interpretation of rules contained in treaties can be segregated from such values.

International jurisprudence is not without support for the proposition that community needs and values are relevant to treaty interpretation, though, as in the *UN Administrative Tribunal* case,[269] the intimation of their significance may be *sotto voce*. Alternatively, as in the *Namibia* case,[270] the reference may be clearer, though ascribed to the original intention of the parties to the Covenant of the League upon Article 22 of which the Mandates regime was based. Some individual members of the Court have not been so reticent, however, often linking the development of international law, as well as the rules of treaty interpretation, to their own formulations of what may be taken to represent the values of the international community.

Perhaps the earliest exponent of such an approach was Judge Alvarez who opted for what he called 'the law of social interdependence'[271] by means of which international law required of States altruism and co-operation instead of the self-interested concerns of the past.[272]

It was the Court's volte-face in the *South West Africa* cases[273] which produced various invocations of community values in criticism of the Court's denial of jurisdiction. Judge Tanaka asserted a degree of judicial creativity, but one circumscribed by 'what can be logically inferred from the *raison d'être* of the legal system, legal institution or norm'.[274] Nevertheless, the continuation of the supervision of the mandate could be deduced not 'from mere necessity or desirability but from the *raison d'être*

[267] Above pp 20–21, 660.

[268] Binder G, *Treaty Conflict and Political Contradiction* (1988), 63.

[269] ICJ Rep 1954, 47, above p 65.

[270] ICJ Rep 1971, 16, above pp 55–56; and in the *Gabčikovo–Nagymaros Project* case ICJ Rep 1997, 7, above at nn. 218–20.

[271] *Admissions* case, ICJ Rep 1948, 57 at 69–70.

[272] Judge Alvarez lost no opportunity of emphasising his message: see inter alia *Corfu Channel* case, ICJ Rep 1949, 4 at 40 ff; *Competence* case, ICJ Rep 1950, 4 at 14–19; *Status of South West Africa* case, ICJ Rep 1950, 128 at 175–176; *Anglo-Norwegian Fisheries* case, ICJ Rep 1951, 116 at 148–150; also Judge Azevedo in the *Competence* case, ICJ Rep 1950 at 23–24; Judge Bustamante in the *South West Africa* cases, ICJ Rep 1962, 319 at 351; Judge Bedjaoui in the *Threat or Use of Nuclear Weapons* case, ICJ Rep 1996, 226 at 270–1; Judge Weeramantry, ibid at 490.

[273] ICJ Rep 1966, 6; in contrast to ICJ Rep 1962, 319.

[274] ICJ Rep 1966 at 277.

and the theoretical construction of the mandates system as a whole'. In his view, 'social and individual necessity constitutes one of the guiding factors for the development of the law by way of interpretation as well as legislation'.[275]

Judge Jessup was more explicit. Both the development of the law and the interpretation of treaties were influenced by society's changing values:[276]

> The law can never be oblivious to the changes in life, circumstance and community standards in which it functions. Treaties—especially multipartite treaties of a constitutional or legislative character—cannot have an absolutely immutable character.

Hence, in interpreting the mandate agreement, 'the judicial task of the Court . . . is to be performed by applying appropriate objective standards', the relevant standard in this case being 'one which takes account of the views and attitudes of the contemporary international community',[277] or, as Judge Padilla Nervo expressed it:[278]

> The interpretation of the Mandate and the obligations of the Respondent is to be made, taking into account, besides the text and spirit of the relevant instruments, the circumstances existing now in 1966, not only those which prevailed in 1920. The aims, the convictions, the needs of the peoples and States for the maintenance of peace in the closely interdependent world of our day is, and should be a fundamental consideration in the mind of the Court.

It has only been in more recent times, when humanitarian and environmental issues have been raised in litigation, that, as a consequence, community values have emerged as a major factor in the context of the relevant legal issues.

[275] Ibid. It is less clear whether Judge Tanaka was claiming societal need as the basis for the continuation of international supervision of the mandate, for he went on to specify that such continuation could be attributed to 'the reasonably assumed intention of the parties', an approach which represented 'a compromise with voluntarism . . . derived from the concept of sovereignty' (ibid at 277–278). It was this approach which the Court later employed in the *Namibia* case, ICJ Rep 1971, 16 at 31 to declare that 'the concepts embodied in Article 22 of the Covenant . . . were not static, but were by definition evolutionary' so that the 'parties to the Covenant must consequently be deemed to have accepted them as such'.

[276] ICJ Rep 1966 at 439.

[277] Ibid at 441.

[278] Ibid at 463. In the Judge's view these principles were applicable directly as a normal aspect of treaty interpretation, and because of the dynamic nature of the treaties. As he explained (at 464): 'The Court is well aware of [the] realities [of today] and shall consider, in its interpretation of the relevant international instruments and obligations, the prevailing ideas and circumstances of today regarding human rights and fundamental freedoms, as well as regarding the actual meaning and universal recognition embodied now in the concepts "material and moral well-being and social progress", which is a dynamic concept.'

In the *WHO Nuclear Weapons* case,[279] there was less reason for taking them into account as the Court did not proceed beyond the preliminary issue of whether the WHO had a competence, under its Constitution, to ask the question it had submitted to the Court. The Court answered in the negative. It reinforced this response by redefining the question presented to it as involving the legality of the use of nuclear weapons, a matter which it regarded as more properly falling within the aegis of the UN General Assembly or Security Council. Hence, it was not for the WHO, an institution of limited competence, to usurp their roles by submitting such a question to the Court.

It is possible to counter the Court's approach by taking the line (1) that the redefinition of the question was to distort it, as the question had specifically asked whether, in 'view of the health and environmental effects, . . . the use of nuclear weapons by a State in war or other armed conflict [would] be in breach of its obligations under *international law including* the WHO Constitution'; and (2) if the words in italics were excised, the question would seem to fall squarely within the Organisation's sphere of competence as determined by the criteria previously adopted by the Court to assess the powers of international institutions. The question then arises as to why this approach should be preferred to the one adopted by the Court. It is in this context that two of the principal dissenters, Judges Weeramantry and Koroma, called in aid their perception of relevant community values to support their preference. In their view, the international community's overriding concern with the health and welfare of mankind constituted justification enough for regarding the question submitted to the Court as falling within the competence of the WHO.[280]

The contemporaneous advisory opinion given by the Court in the *Legality of the Threat or Use of Nuclear Weapons* case,[281] in answer to the General Assembly's question whether 'the threat or use of nuclear weapons [was] in any circumstance permitted under international law?',

[279] ICJ Rep 1996, 66, see below p 75.

[280] Both Judges referred to the WHO's Committee of Experts' Report, Effects of Nuclear War on Health and Health Services (1984). Judge Weeramantry quoted from the Report, ibid, 6, ICJ Rep 1996 at 137, the passage beginning 'As doctors and scientists, the members of the committee feel that they have both the right and the duty to draw attention in the strongest possible terms to the catastrophic results that would follow from any use of nuclear weapons.' As Judge Koroma observed (ibid at 173): 'Such a catastrophe, it was argued, would be in violation of the health and environmental obligations undertaken by States under international law, particularly international humanitarian law, as well as under the Constitution of the WHO. Whether or not such obligations exist for States and whether they would be violated in the course of war or other armed conflict involving the use of nuclear weapons is, in my view, an eminently suitable matter for the Court to determine . . .' Indeed, as he went on to say (ibid at 174), in 'the face of such a catastrophe, the WHO has reached the conclusion that to cure the victims of nuclear attack would hardly be feasible, hence preventing the consequences is a more viable and realistic alternative.'

[281] ICJ Rep 1996, 226.

resulted in a more widespread invocation of community values as a reason for favouring a negative response to that question. Thus, Judge Bedjaoui, explaining his casting vote as President of the Court, commenced by pointing to the fact that, with nuclear weapons, 'humanity is living on a kind of suspended sentence'.[282] As to the compatibility of such weapons with international humanitarian law, he had this to say:

> By *its very nature the nuclear weapon, a blind weapon, therefore has a destabilising effect on humanitarian law, the law of discrimination which regulates discernment in the use of weapons. Nuclear weapons, the ultimate evil, destabilise humanitarian law*, which is the law of the lesser evil. The existence of nuclear weapons is therefore a major challenge to the very existence of humanitarian law, not to mention their long-term harmful effects on the human environment, in respecting which *the right to life* may be exercised.

It followed, in his view, that '*[a]tomic warfare and humanitarian law . . . appear to be mutually exclusive, the existence of the one automatically implying the non-existence of the other*'.[283] Nor did it follow that the right of self-defence could over-ride, even in extreme circumstances, a prohibition on the use of nuclear weapons:[284]

> The fact remains that the use of nuclear weapons by a State in circumstances in which its survival is at stake risks in its turn endangering the survival of all mankind, precisely because of the inextricable link between terror and escalation in the use of such weapons. It would thus be quite foolhardy unhesitatingly to set the survival of a State above all other considerations, in particular above the survival of mankind itself.

There are a range of other references to community values to be found in the dissenting opinions of Judges Shahabudeen,[285] Weeramantry[286] and

282 Ibid, at 268. 283 Ibid, at 273. 284 Ibid.

285 Ibid, at 386: 'once it is shown that the use of a weapon could annihilate mankind, its repugnance to the conscience of the international community is not materially diminished by showing that it need not have that result in every case; it is not reasonable to expect that the conscience of the international community will, both strangely and impossibly, wait on the event to see if the result is the destruction of the human species. The operative consideration is the risk of annihilation . . .'

286 Ibid, at 451: 'It would be a paradox if international law, a system intended to promote world peace and order, should have a place within it for an entity that can cause total destruction of the world system, the millennia of civilisation which have produced it, and humanity itself. A factor which powerfully conceals that contradiction, even to the extent of keeping humanitarian law at bay, is the use of euphemistic language—the disembodied language of military operations and the polite language of diplomacy. They conceal the horror of nuclear war, diverting attention to intellectual concepts such as self-defence, reprisals, and proportionate damage which can have little relevance to a situation of total destruction.' See also the Judge's use of a concern for the environment in traditional cultures and the European tradition on the basis that the 'ingrained values of any civilisation are the source from which its legal concepts derive, and the ultimate yardstick and touchstone of their validity' in the *Gabčikovo–Nagymaros Project* case, ICJ Rep 1997, 7 at 108.

Koroma.[287] In addition, in his separate opinion, Judge Ranjeva gave the following explanation of his reasons for reading the Court's Opinion as amounting to an assertion of the illegality of nuclear weapons:[288]

There can be no doubt that, in a matter of such importance for the peace and the future of mankind, the treaty solution remains the best means of achieving general disarmament and nuclear disarmament in particular. But the consensualism characteristic of international law cannot be limited either to a technique of contractual or conventional engineering or to the formalisation by majority vote of rules of international law. The law of nuclear weapons is one of the branches of international law which is inconceivable without a minimum of ethical requirements expressing the values to which the members of the international community as a whole subscribe. The survival of mankind and of civilisation is one of these values. It is not a question of substituting a moral order for the legal order of positive law in the name of some higher or revealed order. The moral requirements are not direct and positive sources of prescription or obligations but they do represent a framework for the scrutiny and questioning of the techniques and rules of conventional and consensual engineering. On the great issues of mankind the requirements of positive law and of ethics make common cause, and nuclear weapons, because of their destructive effects, are one such issue. In these circumstances, is illegality a matter of *opinio juris*? To this question the Court gives an answer which some would consider dubitative, whereas an answer in the affirmative . . . cannot be questioned and prevails.

It should not be thought that the invocation of community values was the sole preserve of those arguing for the total illegality of the threat, use or even possession of nuclear weapons. The policy of deterrence, based upon the right of self-defence and Article 51 of the UN Charter, had been effective in preventing the use of nuclear weapons since 1945,[289] and indeed the threat to use them had been instrumental in deterring Iraq from employing chemical or biological agents against the troops of Desert Storm.[290] As Judge Higgins pertinently observed at the conclusion of her dissenting opinion, it is not clear that 'either a pronouncement of illegality in all circumstances of the use of nuclear weapons or the answers formulated by the

[287] ICJ Rep 1997, 7, at 570: 'the Court, as well as taking cognisance of the unique characteristics of nuclear weapons when used, reached the following conclusions; that nuclear weapons have a destructive capacity unmatched by any conventional weapon; that a single nuclear weapon has the capacity to kill thousands if not millions of human beings; that such weapons cause unnecessary suffering and superfluous injury to combatants and non-combatants alike; and that they are unable to distinguish between civilians and combatants. When recourse is had to such weapons, it can cause damage to generations unborn and produce widespread and long-term effects on the environment, particularly in respect of resources necessary for human survival . . . The above findings by the Court should have led it inexorably to conclude that any use of nuclear weapons is unlawful under international law.'

[288] Ibid, at 296.

[289] See Judge Fleischhauer, ibid, at 309.

[290] See Judge Schwebel, ibid, at 323–329.

Court . . . best serve to protect mankind against the unimaginable suffering that we all fear.'[291]

D. *Community values and the Court's role in the UN System*

In most of the examples considered so far, community values have been invoked by individual judges of the International Court to support their views as to the inadequacies of the majority Judgment or Opinion. It should not be thought that such values do not influence the majority, as the *Namibia* case [292] clearly demonstrates. For the most part, when they are of significance, the Court may be less disposed to employ such strident language as that which appears in some of the dissenting opinions. This *sotto voce* approach to the issue of community values can be seen in the context of two aspects of the Court's work as it relates to the law of international organisations, the first concerning the Court's own advisory jurisdiction, and the second relating to its perception of the powers of such organisations.

With regard to the former, the Court has consistently taken the view that, as one of the principal organs of the United Nations, it should involve itself in community affairs so that its giving of a reply to a question asked by the General Assembly or Security Council 'represents its participation in the activities of the Organisation, and, in principle, should not be refused'.[293] In fact, the Court has gone so far as to assert that only 'compelling reasons' would justify its declining to give an advisory opinion.[294] Of particular significance has been its consistent refusal to regard the political elements involved in the asking of, or the answer to, a question as a relevant factor in deciding whether or not to exercise its advisory function.[295]

The Court's approach could be questioned on the ground that, in some cases, the opinion it provides, because of the political factors involved, is

291 Ibid, at 593.

292 ICJ Rep 1971, 16, above pp 55–56.

293 *Peace Treaties* case, ICJ Rep 1950, 65 at 71; *Reservations* case, ICJ Rep 1951, 15 at 19; *Privileges and Immunities* case, ICJ Rep 1989, 171 at 189.

294 *ILO Administrative Tribunal* case, ICJ Rep 1956, 77 at 86; *Expenses* case, ICJ Rep 1962, 151 at 155; *Privileges and Immunities* case, ICJ Rep 1989, 177 at 191; *Threat or Use of Nuclear Weapons* case, ICJ Rep 1996, 226 at 235.

295 As the Court said in the *Admissions* case, ICJ Rep 1948, 57 at 61: 'It has nevertheless been contended that the question put must be regarded as a political one and that, for this reason, it falls outside the jurisdiction of the Court. The Court cannot attribute a political character to a request which, framed in abstract terms, invites it to undertake an essentially judicial task, the interpretation of a treaty provision. It is not concerned with the motives which may have inspired this request, nor with the considerations which, in the concrete cases submitted for examination to the Security Council, formed the subject of the exchange of views which took place in that body.' See also *Expenses* case, ICJ Rep 1962, 151 at 155; *Threat or Use of Nuclear Weapons* case, ICJ Rep 1996, 226 at 234.

unlikely to contribute to the settlement of the dispute arising from the issue of interpretation.[296] Nevertheless, it is at least understandable that the Court should regard as overriding its community role in participating fully in the work of the United Nations. However, the Court has adopted an identical approach to requests for advisory opinions from the Specialised Agencies where the same community value does not seem to be operative, or at least not to an equivalent extent.

In the *Interpretation of the WHO and Egypt Agreement* case,[297] the International Court was asked by the World Health Assembly, *inter alia*, whether 'the negotiation and notice provisions of Section 37 of the Agreement between the WHO and Egypt [are] applicable in the event that either party to the Agreement wishes to have the Regional Office transferred from the territory of Egypt?'. The accusation had been made during the Assembly's consideration of the proposal to ask the question (but not repeated in submissions to the Court) that 'it was nothing but a political manoeuvre designed to postpone any decision concerning removal of the Regional Office from Egypt'.[298] Such a contention the Court regarded as 'counter to the settled jurisprudence of the Court' which 'establishes that if, as in the present case, a question submitted in a request is one that otherwise falls within the normal exercise of its judicial process, the Court has not to deal with the motives which may have inspired the request'.[299] The Court concluded by pointing out:[300]

> Indeed, in situations in which political considerations are prominent it may be particularly necessary for an international organisation to obtain an advisory opinion from the Court as to the legal principles applicable with respect to the matter under debate, especially when these may include the interpretation of its constitution.

The second aspect of the Court's advisory jurisprudence deserving attention concerns its promotion of an extension of the powers of the United Nations. The *Expenses* case[301] has already been mentioned in this connection.[302] The Court's reliance upon the purposes of the United Nations set

[296] For example, see the *Admissions* case, ICJ Rep 1948, 57, after which the impasse over the admission of new members to the UN was only resolved by an arrangement of the type regarded by the Court (at 65) as impermissible; *Expenses* case, ICJ Rep 1962, 151, following which a number of States still failed to pay contributions to the peace-keeping operations the costs of which the Court held could be apportioned between members by the General Assembly as expenses of the Organisation within Article 17 of the Charter.

[297] ICJ Rep 1980, 67.

[298] Ibid at 87.

[299] Ibid.

[300] Ibid.

[301] ICJ Rep 1962, 151.

[302] Above pp 62–64. It is not proposed to repeat here the earlier caveat that the Court's pronouncement in the *Expenses* case of presumptive legality with respect to action pursued in furtherance of the purposes of the organisation should not be regarded as justifying such action if taken by an organ lacking constitutional competence to perform the act in question.

out in Article 1 of the Charter as the foundation for action, that is presumptively legitimate, taken on the Organisation's behalf, provides a wide scope particularly to the Security Council and the General Assembly in the field of international peace and security. However, the Court's statement was not limited to those bodies nor to that purpose, but was of general application amongst UN organs and with regard to all of its purposes. Nor is there any reason to doubt that the same principle applies equally to any other intergovernmental organisation in relation to the purposes set out in its constituent treaty and to the powers expressly granted to it or to the various organs of which it is composed.[303] Moreover, the exercise of additional powers founded upon such sources is, as already explained, an essential element in providing such organisations with the means for dealing with novel problems and changing circumstances. This evolution is bound up with the dictates of intertemporality to enable them to face the challenges of an ever-developing present against which the purposes of each organisation and its competence must be constantly reassessed. It is this evolution which requires that the perspective of the time of interpretation must take into account not only the contemporary, but also the prospective, needs of the institution.

E. The discordant notes of the WHO Nuclear Weapons *case*

It was only with the *WHO Nuclear Weapons* case[304] that a potential dissonance emerged with regard to these various aspects of the Court's advisory competence and jurisprudence. The question asked by the WHO Assembly was as follows:[305]

> In view of the health and environmental effects, would the use of nuclear weapons by a State in war or other armed conflict be a breach of its obligations under international law including the WHO Constitution?

Given the controversy surrounding the WHO Assembly's decision to seek the Court's Opinion, and the fact that the *Threat or Use of Nuclear Weapons* case[306] was also before the Court at the behest of the UN General Assembly, it is not surprising that the Court declined to answer the question posed. As a matter of community policy this was an appropriate outcome. The only problem for the Court was to find a satisfactory justification for this result.

[303] Writers on the subject regard it as axiomatic that all such institutions are endowed with implied powers stemming from what is 'necessary to the fulfilment of the organisation's purposes or to the exercise of its functions and powers' (Skubiszewski, 'Implied Powers of International Organisations' in Dinstein Y (ed), *International Law at a Time of Perplexity* (1989), 855 at 858); Schermers HG and Blokker NM, *International Institutional Law*, 3rd rev edn (1995), 158, 162.

[304] ICJ Rep 1996, 66.

[305] Ibid at 68.

[306] ICJ Rep 1996, 226.

The Court's advisory jurisdiction is limited by Article 96 of the UN Charter and Article 65(1) of the Statute of the Court to legal questions. The fact that the question asked of the Court by the WHO Assembly concerned the legality of the use of nuclear weapons in light of a State's obligations under international law and the WHO Constitution meant that the question was legal, whatever the political ramifications involved.[307] The Court went on to decide that the question did not fall within the scope of WHO activities as required by Article 96(2) of the UN Charter,[308] nor within the competence of the WHO as required by Article X(2) of the Relationship Agreement between the WHO and the UN of 1948[309] and Article 76 of the WHO Constitution.[310] Accordingly, there was no need for it to consider whether, in the exercise of its discretion, the Court should have declined to give its Opinion. It is these last two issues which will now be examined in more detail.

1. *The competence of the Organisation*

With regard to the first issue, the competence of the WHO, the Court gave two reasons why the request for an advisory opinion was *ultra vires*. The Court also recognised, in dealing with the first issue, that the time of interpretation was the necessary date for assessing how the WHO Constitution should be interpreted. The Court pointed out that the relevant provisions of that document should be interpreted 'in accordance with their ordinary meaning, in their context and in the light of the object and purpose of the

[307] In the Court's own words (ibid at 73–74): 'The question put to the Court by the World Health Assembly does in fact constitute a legal question, as the Court is asked to rule on whether, "in view of the health and environmental effects, . . . the use of nuclear weapons by a State in war or other armed conflict [would] be a breach of its obligations under international law including the WHO Constitution". To do this, the Court must identify the obligations of States under the rules of law invoked, and assess whether the behaviour in question conforms to the obligations . . .

The fact that this question also has political aspects, as, in the nature of things, is the case with so many questions which arise in international life, does not suffice to deprive it of its character as a "legal question" . . . Whatever its political aspects, the Court cannot refuse to admit the legal character of a question which invites it to discharge an essentially judicial task, namely, an assessment of the legality of possible conduct of States with regard to the obligations imposed upon them by international law.'

[308] Above p 70.

[309] Article X(2) reads: 'The General Assembly authorises the World Health Organisation to request advisory opinions of the International Court of Justice on legal questions arising within the scope of its competence other than questions concerning the mutual relationships of the Organisation and the United Nations or other specialised agencies.'

[310] According to Article 76: 'Upon authorisation by the General Assembly of the United Nations or upon authorisation in accordance with any agreement between the Organisation and the United Nations, the Organisation may request the International Court of Justice for an advisory opinion on any legal question arising within the competence of the Organisation.'

WHO Constitution, as well as of the practice followed by the Organisation'.[311] Hence the date of interpretation will usually be critical because the practice of members of an organisation will more frequently be relevant to the interpretation of its constitution than will the practice of the parties to other multilateral instruments.

As to how the competence of the WHO was to be ascertained, the Court applied the general rule of interpretation it had thus expressed as a basis of concluding that the provisions of Article 2 of the WHO Constitution[312] 'may be read as authorising the Organisation to deal with the effects on health of the use of nuclear weapons, or of any other hazardous activity, and to take preventive measures aimed at protecting the health of populations in the event of such weapons being used or such activities engaged in'.[313] However, the preventive measures related to the aftermath of the use of the weapons, not to the prevention of their being used in the first place. As the Court explained:[314]

> The question put to the Court in the present case relates, however, *not to the effects* of the use of nuclear weapons on health, but to the *legality* of the use of such weapons *in view of their health and environmental effects*. Whatever these effects might be, the competence of the WHO to deal with them is not dependent on the legality of the acts that caused them. Accordingly, it does not seem to the Court that the provisions of Article 2 of the WHO Constitution . . . can be understood as conferring upon the Organisation a competence to address the legality of the use of nuclear weapons, and thus in turn a competence to ask the Court about that.

311 ICJ Rep 1996 at 76.

312 WHO Assembly resolution WHA 46.40 which requested the Advisory Opinion referred specifically to the following subparagraphs of Article 2 (ibid at 76–77): '(a) To act as the directing and co-ordinating authority on international health work; . . . (k) to propose conventions, agreements and regulations, and make recommendations with respect to international health matters and to perform such duties as may be assigned thereby to the Organisation and are consistent with its objective; . . . (p) to study and report on, in co-operation with other specialised agencies where necessary, administrative and social techniques affecting public health and medical care from preventive and curative points of view, including hospital services and social security; . . . (v) generally to take all necessary action to attain the objective of the Organisation.'

The objective of the WHO is 'the attainment by all peoples of the highest possible level of health', that being described as 'a state of complete physical, mental and social well-being and not merely the absence of disease or infirmity'. Some of the dissenting judges employed a larger number of the sub-paragraphs in considering the competence of the WHO in the context of nuclear weapons, see Judge Weeramanty, ICJ Rep 1996 at 129 and 132; Judge Koroma, ibid at 180–1.

313 Ibid at 76.

314 Ibid. Doubts over the WHO's competence in this respect were strongly pressed in the Health Assembly and by the Organisation's Legal Counsel at the time the proposal to seek an advisory opinion was under consideration, see Rostow, 'The World Health Organisation, The International Court of Justice, and Nuclear Weapons' (1995) 20 Yale JIL 151 at 157–61.

If the Court is suggesting that the competence of the WHO is limited entirely to considering the effects of other hazardous activities or of the use of other hazardous materials, its view is far from convincing. A number of examples can be given of hazardous materials or activities which one would reasonably regard as falling within the aegis of a body involved in world health to the extent of the WHO with a view to the regulation or even proscription of the use of the material or of the conduct in question: the use of narcotics or tobacco;[315] or the use of unsafe sexual practices as a contributing factor in the spread of AIDS. In particular the scope of the Court's Opinion created doubts about whether the WHO could involve itself in attempts to regulate the tobacco industry.[316] In terms of intertemporality, it is regrettable that the Court did not take more account of the prospective needs of the Organisation in this regard.

It is difficult, therefore, to accept this aspect of the Court's Opinion. It did attempt to reinforce its conclusion by reference to what it termed 'the principle of speciality' by which international organisations 'are invested by the States which create them with powers, the limits of which are a function of the common interests whose promotion those States entrust to them'.[317] The Court then explained the effects of this principle in the form of the express and implied powers attaching to an organisation. Despite the relatively broad formulation of the basis for the implication of powers which it employed,[318] the Court applied a narrow interpretation of the

315 See Akande, 'The Competence of International Organisations and the Advisory Jurisdiction of the International Court of Justice' (1998) 9 European JIL 437 at 447. For the WHO's past reluctance to involve itself in health regulation but the assumption that it can and should concern itself in controlling the tobacco industry, see Taylor, 'An International Regulatory Strategy for Global Tobacco Control' (1996) 21 Yale JIL 257 esp at 278–283.

316 The WHO is attempting to circumvent the problem by working towards a framework convention on tobacco control. Given that the Assembly unanimously supported resolution WHA52.18, in which it decided *inter alia*:

> '1(1) . . . to establish an intergovernmental negotiating body open to all Member States to draft and negotiate the proposed WHO framework convention on tobacco control and possible related protocols;
> (2) in order to prepare the work of the body referred to above, to establish a working group on the WHO framework convention on tobacco control open to all Member States which will prepare proposed draft elements of the . . . convention, report on progress to the Executive Board at its 105th session, and complete its work and submit a report to the Fifty-third World Health Assembly.'

this would seem to satisfy the requirements of the parties' agreement that the matter fell within the competence of the Organisation. In response to the report, resolution WHA53.16 recognised that it established 'a sound basis for initiating the negotiations by the Intergovernmental Negotiating Body' and requested the Director-General 'to convene the first session of the Negotiating Body in October 2000'.

317 ICJ Rep 1996 at 78.

318 As the Court said (ibid at 79): 'The powers conferred on international organisations are normally the subject of an express statement in their constituent instruments. Nevertheless, the necessities of international life may point to the need for organisations, in order to achieve their objectives, to possess subsidiary powers which are not expressly provided for in

'necessary implication as being essential to the performance' of an organisation's duties requirement[319] to the position of the WHO, concluding that:[320]

> In the opinion of the Court, to ascribe to WHO the competence to address the legality of the use of nuclear weapons—even in view of their health and environmental effects—would be tantamount to disregarding the principle of speciality; for such competence could not be deemed a necessary implication of the Constitution of the Organisation in the light of the purposes assigned to it by its member States.

This view of the necessary implication test is hardly compatible with the way in which that test was applied in the *Reparations* case.[321] In that case, the Court regarded the United Nations as endowed with the capacity to bring an international claim on behalf of an agent injured in the service of the Organisation. Such a power could only be regarded as necessary or essential in a less than absolute sense. It was only on a strict application of what was necessary or essential that the WHO did not have the competence to consider the legality of the use of nuclear weapons or other hazardous materials.

If one separates the nuclear weapons issue from the suggestion that the WHO is not competent to consider the legality of the use of other hazardous substances or activities, it may be possible to rely upon the Court's alternative justification for its Opinion. This it regarded as stemming from the nature of the UN system which was 'designed to organise international co-operation in a coherent fashion by bringing the United Nations, invested with powers of general scope, into relationship with various autonomous and complementary organisations, invested with sectoral powers'.[322] It followed from 'the logic of the overall system contemplated by the Charter' that, though the WHO has '"wide international responsibilities", those responsibilities are necessarily restricted to the sphere of public "health" and cannot encroach on the responsibilities of other parts of the UN system. And there is no doubt that questions concerning the use of force, the regulation of armaments and disarmament are within the competence of the United Nations and lie outside that of the specialised agencies'.[323]

This aspect of the Court's determination has been criticised on two principal grounds. In the first place, it has been suggested that the Court misread the substance of the question posed so that it was less easily reconcilable with the objectives of the WHO.[324] Secondly, it has been

the basic instruments which govern their activities. It is generally accepted that international organisations can exercise such powers, known as "implied" powers.'

319 Taken from the *Reparations* case, ICJ Rep 1949, 174 at 182, quoted above p 61.

320 ICJ Rep 1996 at 79.

321 ICJ Rep 1949, 174, above p 62.

322 ICJ Rep 1996 at 80.

323 Ibid.

324 As Judge Weeramantry said in his Dissenting Opinion, ibid at 111: 'Moreover, the

argued that the Court's decision was based upon the proposition that the various specialised agencies have independent areas of competence, whereas in many circumstances they will have overlapping responsibilities.

It is certainly true that the Court redefined the question posed by the World Health Assembly but, given the motives behind the request,[325] the Court's redefinition does not seem to have missed the point of what the Assembly was really seeking from the International Court. Once that reinterpretation was adopted, the issue of overlap did not arise. When a certain matter falls so substantially within the competence of one organisation (in this case the United Nations and in particular the General Assembly or the Security Council), it is reasonable to accept that another organisation with only an indirect or insignificant responsibility in the area can only exercise that limited responsibility in conjunction with or at the invitation of the former institution having primary responsibility for the matter. The advantage of this approach is that it avoids the unparalleled restrictiveness of the Court's application of the doctrine of implied powers to the WHO Constitution, to the detriment of the Organisation's future role in relation to the possible regulation of hazardous activities and of the use of hazardous materials. Leaving a constitution, whether that of the United Nations or of a Specialised Agency, room to 'expand' to cope with new challenges is an essential aspect of intertemporality in relation to international organisations.

2. *The limits of the Court's advisory jurisdiction*

The second aspect[326] of the *WHO* case to be considered concerns the Court's avoidance of the issue that it should have declined to exercise its advisory function on the ground of judicial propriety. It will be recalled that, having decided that the question posed fell outside the competence of the WHO, the Court thought it unnecessary to deal with the aforementioned issue. However, given that the political manoeuvring which accompanied the adoption of the resolution requesting the Court's opinion led to the redefinition of that question by the Court, it is at least worth asking

Court does not focus its attention precisely on the terms of WHO's question, but addresses, rather, the question of general legality or illegality of the use of nuclear weapons. This takes the discussion further away from the immediate concerns of WHO, as reflected in its carefully worded question, and nearly equates it to the question of general illegality asked by the General Assembly. Had the Court proceeded on the basis of an examination of State obligations regarding health and the environment under international law and under the WHO Constitution, it would have been more apparent how closely these were related to the work of WHO.' See also Judge Shahabuddeen, ibid at 97–98; and Judge Koroma, ibid at 190, referring to his view that the Court's conclusion was arrived at partly 'as a result of a fundamental misconstruction of the question posed'.

325 Some of the background is given by Judge Oda in his Separate Opinion, ibid at 90–96.

326 See above p 76.

whether those political factors would not have provided a justification for the Court to decline to give an opinion in the exercise of its discretion. If the Court had adopted this course as a basis for so declining, it would have avoided the need to impose such a restrictive interpretation on the competence of the WHO.

The Court's avoidance of the issue in the *WHO* case at least suggests that such a possibility is still open. However, it is doubtful whether the political ramifications of a question asked are regarded by the Court as sufficient justification for it to decline to exercise its jurisdiction. The existence of political factors allegedly militating against the acceptance of the judicial settlement of disputed issues has for the most part been subsumed in a consideration of whether or not a question posed was a legal one, and thus subject to the Court's jurisdiction under Article 96 of the Charter and Article 64 of its Statute.[327] In the *Threat or Use of Nuclear Weapons* case,[328] dealing with the question submitted to the Court by the UN General Assembly,[329] the Court did distinguish between the issue of its jurisdiction and that of its discretion. With regard to the former, it followed its established jurisprudence that the existence of political aspects to a question did 'not suffice to deprive it of its character as a "legal question" '.[330] As far as the latter issue was concerned, the Court relied upon 'its responsibilities as "the principal judicial organ of the United Nations" ' under Article 92 of the Charter. Hence, when considering a request, the Court 'should not, in principle, refuse to give an advisory opinion'; in accordance with its consistent jurisprudence, 'only "compelling reasons" could lead it to such refusal'.[331]

As already mentioned,[332] the status of the Court as one of the principal organs of the United Nations justifies its view that only compelling reasons should lead it to decline to exercise its jurisdiction with regard to questions submitted to it by the Security Council or the General Assembly. There seems to be no obvious reason why the Court should adopt the same approach to questions submitted by a Specialised Agency. It is true that the terminology of 'compelling reasons' came from the Court's Opinion in a case involving the ILO Administrative Tribunal in its handling of appeals by UNESCO officials.[333] However, that case concerned the totally different matter of the Court's role under Article XII of the Tribunal's Statute and had nothing to do with the question of whether political factors would

[327] See above pp 73–74.

[328] ICJ Rep 1996, 226.

[329] By General Assembly Resolution 49/75K of 15 December 1994 (ibid at 228) the Assembly: 'Decides . . . to request the International Court of Justice urgently to render its advisory opinion on the following question: "Is the threat or use of nuclear weapons in any circumstance permitted under international law?".'

[330] ICJ Rep 1996 at 234.

[331] Ibid.

[332] Above pp 73–74.

[333] *Administrative Tribunal of the ILO* case, ICJ Rep 1956, 77.

justify the Court in declining to fulfil that role. According to Article XII:[334]

1. In any case in which the Executive Board of an international organisation which has made the declaration specified in Article II, paragraph 5, of the Statute of the Tribunal challenges a decision of the Tribunal confirming its jurisdiction, or considers that a decision of the Tribunal is vitiated by a fundamental fault of the procedure followed, the question of the validity of the decision given by the Tribunal shall be submitted by the Executive Board concerned, for an advisory opinion, to the International Court of Justice.
2. The opinion given by the Court shall be binding.

The only legal impediment to the Court fulfilling its function as an appellate body concerned an alleged lack of equality between the parties. This stemmed from two sources: the fact that the procedure outlined in Article XII enabled only UNESCO to challenge decisions of the Tribunal, and Article 66 of the Statute of the International Court which allowed only States and international organisations to appear before the Court or to make written or oral submissions to the Court. With regard to the latter, the defect was cured, 'on the one hand, by the procedure under which the observations of officials were made available to the Court through the intermediary of UNESCO and, on the other hand, by dispensing with oral proceedings.'[335] As far as the former aspect was concerned, the Court regarded the inequality issue as irrelevant,[336] or at least only nominal.[337] Certainly the inequality suggested was not sufficiently compelling to prevent the Court answering the question posed:[338]

Notwithstanding the permissive character of Article 65 of the Statute in the matter of advisory opinions, only compelling reasons could cause the Court to adopt in this matter a negative attitude which would imperil the working of the régime established by the Statute of the Administrative Tribunal for the judicial protection of officials. Any seeming or nominal absence of equality ought not to be allowed to obscure or to defeat that primary object.

[334] Text ibid at 78. UNESCO had made a declaration in accordance with Article II(5), ibid at 81.
[335] Ibid at 86.
[336] As the Court said (ibid at 85): 'However, the inequality thus stated does not in fact constitute an inequality before the Court. It is antecedent to the examination of the question by the Court. It does not affect the manner in which the Court undertakes that examination.'
[337] The Court continued as follows (ibid): 'Also, in the present case, that absence of equality between the parties to the Judgments is somewhat nominal since the officials were successful in the proceedings before the Administrative Tribunal and there was accordingly no question of any complaint on their part. That being so, it is not necessary for the Court to express an opinion upon the legal merits of Article XII of the Statute of the Administrative Tribunal.'
[338] Ibid at 86.

Despite the transposition of the 'compelling reasons' test from its original context to the situation where the Court was asked for an advisory opinion by the UN General Assembly, there was no justification for applying the principle in a case where the request emanated from a Specialised Agency and a question was raised as to whether the alleged political factors were sufficiently troublesome for the Court, in its discretion, to decline to exercise jurisdiction. The existence of such factors was considered briefly by the International Court in the *Interpretation of the Agreement between WHO and Egypt* case.[339] The first of the propositions relied upon by the Court, to the effect that its 'jurisprudence establishes that if, as in the present case, a question submitted in a request is one that otherwise falls within the normal exercise of its judicial process, the Court has not to deal with the motives which may have inspired the request',[340] would seem to be equally applicable both to the issue of jurisdiction,[341] and to that of its discretion.[342] And the same is true of its subsequent comment that 'in situations in which political considerations are prominent it may be particularly necessary for an international organisation to obtain an advisory opinion from the Court as to the legal principles applicable with respect to the matter under debate, especially when these may include the interpretation of its constitution'.[343]

Apart from the fact that the Court is the principal judicial organ of the United Nations, and not of the Specialised Agencies, so that participation in the work of the Organisation is not a relevant justification for exercising its advisory jurisdiction at the behest of the latter, there is a secondary issue and that concerns the matter of whether there may not be political considerations of differing types or significance involved in the operation of the Court's discretion. This is a possibility which has not been adverted to by the Court. Even with respect to requests by the General Assembly or the Security Council, it may not be enough, even if it is now firmly established in the Court's jurisprudence, for the Court to be guided solely by its role as a principal organ of the United Nations and to regard its participation in the work of the Organisation as an overriding criterion. There is no such justification for ignoring political factors in cases where it is one of the Specialised Agencies which is seeking to invoke the Court's advisory jurisdiction.

In the *Interpretation of the Agreement between WHO and Egypt* case,[344] two political aspects of the background circumstances of the case

339 ICJ Rep 1980, 73.

340 Ibid at 87.

341 Two of the cases cited concerned primarily the Court's jurisdiction to interpret a treaty provision as being a legal question: *Admissions* case, ICJ Rep 1948, 57 at 61–162; *Competence* case, ICJ Rep 1950, 4 at 6–7.

342 The third of the cases cited, the *Expenses* case, ICJ Rep 1962, 151 at 155, was more concerned with the discretion issue.

343 ICJ Rep 1980 at 87.

344 ICJ Rep 1980, 73.

were raised. First, the reason why the attempt was being made to move the Regional Office from Egypt was that the Arab States of the area were using it as a means of expressing their disapproval of Egypt for entering into the Camp David Peace Agreements with Israel in September 1978.[345] Secondly, when the request for an advisory opinion was debated in the World Health Assembly in May 1980, supporters of the proposal for the transfer of the Regional Office alleged that the request was 'nothing but a political manoeuvre designed to postpone any decision concerning removal of the Regional Office from Egypt'.[346] It was in the context of this latter issue (though it was not one which had been raised in any submission to the Court) that the Court made its comment about its jurisprudence establishing that 'if, as in the present case, a question submitted in a request is one that otherwise falls within the normal exercise of its judicial process, the Court has not to deal with the motives which may have inspired the request', backing it up with its observation that it was 'in situations in which political considerations are prominent [that] it may be particularly necessary for an international organisation to obtain an advisory opinion from the Court as to the legal principles applicable with respect to the matter under debate'.[347]

It has to be said of the Court's response that it would have made more sense in relation to the first aspect (using the removal of the Office as means of 'punishing' Egypt for its conduct towards Israel), than the second (requesting an Opinion from the Court as a delaying tactic). It is highly likely that there will be non-legal reasons for proposing or supporting the removal of the headquarters or of a regional office of an agency from the territory of a particular State. However, the question being asked related to the exclusively legal issue of the rules applicable to such a transfer, particularly those operating between the agency and the host State of the headquarters or office in question. Accordingly, in such circumstances, it could be said that the Court's jurisprudence demonstrated that the motives of the States supporting the transfer were irrelevant to the answering of the question presented to the Court. This reaction by the Court would seem to be entirely misplaced with regard to the other issue. No case was in fact

[345] The texts are given in (1978) 17 ILM 1466. Egypt raised the objection that the request for the transfer was 'politically motivated' at the 1979 (32nd) session of the World Health Assembly, see ICJ Rep 1980 at 85.

[346] Ibid at 87.

[347] Ibid. It has to be admitted that the Court's view of the sectoral division of competence between the UN and WHO with regard to the legality of nuclear weapons and their regulation, based upon its conception of an integrated UN 'system' stemming from the relationship agreements between the UN and the specialised agencies, is in harmony with its application of the presumption that it, as the principal judicial organ of the UN, should not in principle decline to answer questions submitted to it by the General Assembly, to requests for advisory opinions from the specialised agencies.

made to the Court to the effect that the real reason behind the request for an advisory opinion was to delay implementation of the proposal for the transfer of the Regional Office. But, if such an allegation could have been substantiated, would it not thus have been shown that the request constituted an abuse of process so that the proper course would have been for the Court to have declined to give an opinion? In such circumstances, the motives of the request's supporters would not have been irrelevant, but a crucial factor with regard to the contention that the Court should not entertain such a request.

An abuse of process argument would in theory be as determinative in a case where the request emanated from the General Assembly or the Security Council as in one where the requesting body was one of the Specialised Agencies. However, the possibility that political factors might be involved as a ground for the Court declining to give an opinion in the latter circumstance is arguably more open to it on the Court's existing case law. Indeed, as already suggested,[348] such an avenue would have had obvious advantages in the *WHO Nuclear Weapons* case.[349] The Court did take account of political factors in its redefinition of the question asked by the World Health Assembly.[350] However, the consequence of adopting this course was that, in order to avoid answering the question asked, the Court employed a very restrictive view of the WHO's competence as it related to the legality or otherwise of the use of hazardous materials or of the engagement of States in hazardous activities, to the detriment of possible future avenues of endeavour by the Organisation. Given that the case concerned the relationship, not of the Court and the United Nations, but of the Court and one of the Specialised Agencies, there was no need for the Court to have felt bound to exercise its discretion in favour of giving an opinion. It should only do so where the political realities suggest that the Court's answer can perform a useful function. Where those factors (in this case dressing up the real issue to be determined in the guise of a different question) suggest that there is something akin to an abuse of process involved in the submission of the case to the Court, the existence of those factors could justify the Court exercising its discretion in favour of declining to give its opinion.

This outcome would have had the practical benefit of protecting the principle of intertemporality from the Court's negative reaction to the powers of the WHO. It has to be admitted, however, that the Court might have regarded the adoption of such a course as unsatisfactory in that it would have left the Organisation free to pursue its incursion into the field

[348] Above pp 80–81.

[349] ICJ Rep 1996, 66.

[350] As it was alleged the Court did in the *Interpretation of the Agreement between WHO and Egypt* case, ICJ Rep 1980, 73 at 191 ff.

of nuclear weapons. If, to prevent this occurring, the Court was determined to provide some other ground for not giving an Opinion, it should have shown a greater awareness of the future intertemporal needs of the international community in the field of health. By insisting upon the priority of the United Nations in matters of international peace and security, the Court could have curtailed the involvement of the WHO in the politics of nuclear weapons, while leaving it open to that Organisation to consider the regulation of other hazardous materials or activities as falling within its competence as the guardian of international public health. It is at this stage that it is necessary to consider a further aspect of the powers of international organisations, which reinforces the role of intertemporality in the development of those powers, and that is the importance of the practice of a particular organisation and its members in relation thereto as a vehicle for extending those powers.

V. INTERTEMPORALITY AND THE PRACTICE OF AN ORGANISATION

A. The role of subsequent practice

In addition to inherent or implied powers, it is generally accepted that the powers of an organisation can be extended by practice. There is a debate over the means whereby such 'customary powers', as they are sometimes called,[351] can be created, especially with regard to whether such powers can be imposed upon a recalcitrant minority.[352] The answer to this question may be linked to the issue of whether a distinction can usefully be drawn between the practice of the parties and the practice of the organisation. If the matter is regarded exclusively from the point of view of the parties,[353] it would seem that the provisions of the Vienna Convention concerning the interpretation of treaties should be dominant. If it is wished to argue that constitutional treaties are not subject to the Convention's

[351] See, for example, Schermers HG and Blokker NM, *International Institutional Law*, 3rd rev edn (1995), 158.

[352] We are not here concerned with institutions which have bestowed upon them or one of their organs the authority to make determinative interpretations of their constitution such as is the case with financial organisations like the IMF and IBRD: see Amerasinghe, 'Interpretation of Texts in Open International Organisations' (1994) 65 BYIL 175 at 178–179; and see generally Kirgis 'Specialised Law-Making Processes' in Schachter O and Joyner CC (eds), *United Nations Legal Order* (1995), vol 1, 109.

[353] This was the view of Judge Spender, forcibly expressed in the *Expenses* case, ICJ Rep 1962, 151 at 187–190, and then in the following words at 192: 'My present view is that it is not possible to equate "subsequent conduct" with the practice of an organ of the United Nations. Not only is such an organ not a party to the Charter but the inescapable reality is that both the General Assembly and the Security Council are but the mechanisms through which the Members of the United Nations express their views and act. The fact that they act through such an organ, where a majority rule prevails and so determines the practice, cannot, it seems to me, give any greater probative value to the practice established within that organ than it would have as conduct of the Members that comprise the majority if pursued outside of that organ.'

rules in this respect,[354] the claim that such treaties are different is enhanced by reference to the international personality of these organisations. It follows from this that the practice of an organisation is distinct from the practice of the individual member States.[355] By this route it might more readily be possible to establish that the objections of a minority to a particular constitutional development can be overridden because that is the institutional will.[356] However, it has to be said that a form of contract or consensual theory has also been employed to justify the same conclusion.[357] This was certainly Lauterpacht's opinion. Having suggested that

[354] This seems to have been the view of the International Law Commission when it observed (Yb ILC 1964, vol II, 204, para (14)): 'The problem of the effect of the practice of organs of an international organisation upon the interpretation of its constituent instrument raises the question how far individual Member States are bound by the practice. Although the practice of the organ as such may be consistent, it may have been opposed by individual Members or by a group of Members which have been outvoted. This special problem appears to relate to the law of international organisations rather than to the general law of treaties and the Commission did not consider that it would be appropriate to deal with it in the present articles.' As Judge de Visscher said in the *Status of South West Africa* case, ICJ Rep 1950, 128 at 189: 'one must bear in mind that in the interpretation of a great international constitutional instrument, like the United Nations Charter, the individualistic concepts which are generally adequate in the interpretation of ordinary treaties do not suffice.' Quoted with approval by Judge Jessup in the *South West Africa* cases, ICJ Rep 1966, 6 at 353. See also to similar effect Judge de Castro in the *Namibia* case, ICJ Rep 1971, 16 at 184; and Judge Shahabuddeen in the *Threat or Use of Nuclear Weapons* case, ICJ Rep 1996, 226 at 395.

[355] See the comments of Díaz González, the International Law Commission's Special Rapporteur in introducing the Fourth Report on relations between States and international organisations (text in Yb ILC 1989, vol II Pt 1, 153), that (Yb ILC 1989, vol I, 282, para 3) it was by treaty that States 'established the permanent functional organs, independent of themselves', and (ibid, 283, para 11) that among the 'constituent elements of an international organisation' were 'the means, which consisted of the functions and powers of the organisation and reflected some degree of autonomy *vis-á-vis* its members. In legal terms, that autonomy was reflected in the existence of decision-making machinery which in turn reflected the organisation's own will—which was not necessarily the same as that of each of its members—thereby attesting to the reality of its legal personality.'

[356] See Amerasinghe, op cit, n. 352 at 200: 'While the organ is generally composed of representatives of member States, what is relevant is not the view of the members of the organ *per se* but the resulting conduct of the organ taken as an entity in itself. The size of the majority in favour of the practice should not be relevant provided the conduct constitutes an act of an organ as a body and is attributable to the organ.'

[357] In fact Amerasinghe went on to posit, as an alternative justification, the argument that (ibid): 'since the parties to the constitution, whether they are original parties or become parties subsequently, have agreed to the mechanisms of decision-making by the organisation, they have also agreed to accept the decisions of the organisation taken under the constitution, even though they have voted against or may disagree with such decisions, as reflecting proper conduct on the part of the organisation. Henc, that a member State is in an opposing minority and does not immediately agree to a decision involving practice is of no consequence, because ultimately the member concerned had agreed, by implication and directly at the time it became a party to the constitutive treaty, to accept the decision as reflecting the will of the organisation, even though it disagreed with it at the time it was made.'

the practice of an organisation could be constituted 'on the basis of majority voting and often against the dissenting views of a minority',[358] he subsequently explained[359] that it was

> probably necessary to recognise that recourse to the practice of international organisations now stands on an independent legal basis; that is to say, that there exists a specific rule of the law of international organisation to the effect that recourse to such practice is admissible and that States, on joining international organisations, impliedly accept the permissibility of constitutional development in this manner.

Whatever the logic of differentiating between institutional and other treaties from the point of view of the applicability of the Vienna Convention, the International Court has not gone that far. In the *WHO Nuclear Weapons* case,[360] for example, it adopted the formal position that 'the constituent instruments of international organisations are multilateral treaties, to which the well-established rules of treaty interpretation apply'.[361] Then, having quoted from the *Expenses* case relating to the UN Charter,[362] the Court addressed the issue of interpretation in the following way:[363]

> [T]he constituent instruments of international organisations . . . can raise specific problems of interpretation owing, *inter alia*, to their character which is conventional and at the same time institutional; the very nature of the organisation created, the objectives which have been assigned to it by its founders, the imperatives associated with the effective performance of its functions, as well as its own practice, are all elements which may deserve special attention when the time comes to interpret these constituent treaties.

At this point the Court quoted Article 31 of the Vienna Convention with its reference to subsequent practice 'which establishes the agreement of the parties' regarding the treaty's interpretation. It would seem from this presentation of the legal position that the Court was affirming the contractual nature of the WHO Constitution at least as far as the Vienna Convention was concerned. On the other hand, while the practice of the organisation was an aspect of its institutional nature, this did not take its evaluation away from the requirements of Article 31(3)(b) with its emphasis upon the need

358 'The Development of the Law of International Organisations by the Decisions of International Tribunals' (1976-IV) 152 Hag Rec 377 at 459.

359 Ibid at 460.

360 ICJ Rep 1996, 66.

361 Ibid at 74.

362 Ibid at 74–75, where the Court quoted the following words from its opinion in the *Expenses* case, ICJ Rep 1962, 151 at 157: 'On the previous occasions when the Court has had to interpret the Charter of the United Nations, it has followed the principles and rules applicable in general to the interpretation of treaties, since it has recognised that the Charter is a multilateral treaty, albeit a treaty having certain special characteristics.'

363 ICJ Rep 1996 at 75.

for 'agreement' rather than necessarily just a majority view. Finally, and of particular significance for the purposes of this volume, the Court regarded the time of interpretation ('when the time comes to interpret these ... treaties') as necessarily critical in a proper assessment of the significance of the various factors which it had just identified.

In dealing with subsequent conduct, the Court was ambivalent as to whether it was dealing with the practice of the organisation or that of the parties. On the one hand, it held that the rather meagre 'practice of the WHO' bore out its conclusion that the question did not fall within the Organisation's field of competence.[364] However, it justified this outcome by stating that:[365]

> Resolution WHA46.40 itself, adopted, not without opposition, as soon as the question of the legality of nuclear weapons was raised at the WHO, could not be taken to express or to amount on its own to a practice establishing an agreement between the members of the Organisation to interpret its Constitution as empowering it to address the question of the legality of the use of nuclear weapons.

The clear message would appear to be, therefore, that such practice, if it had existed, would have brought the question within the WHO's field of competence. It is certainly true that the member States of an organisation can, by express agreement amending the latter's constitution, extend the powers available to the organisation.[366] It would also seem to follow that the parties may, by tacit agreement implied from the practice under a treaty, modify the instrument, even to the extent of granting additional powers to the organisation concerned.

This possibility formed part of the draft articles adopted by the International Law Commission on the law of treaties,[367] though it was not

[364] Ibid at 81. [365] Ibid.

[366] The requirements for such an amendment depend upon the provisions of the treaty in question. According to Article 73 of the WHO Constitution: 'Texts of proposed amendments to this Constitution shall be communicated by the Director General to Members at least six months in advance of their consideration by the Health Assembly. Amendments shall come into force for all Members when adopted by a two-thirds vote of the Health Assembly and accepted by two thirds of the members in accordance with their respective constitutional processes.'

[367] According to draft Article 68 as adopted by the International Law Commission in 1964 (Yb ILC 1964, vol II, 198): 'The operation of a treaty may also be modified: ... '(b) By subsequent practice of the parties in the application of the treaty establishing their agreement to an alteration or extension of its provisions.' This particular aspect of the provision became Article 38 of the Commission's Final Draft (Yb ILC 1966, vol II, 236), but retaining the same Commentary. The Commission, having quoted the following passage from the *Air Transport Services Agreement* arbitration (1963) 38 ILR 182 at 249: 'This course of conduct may, in fact, be taken into account not merely as a means useful for interpreting the Agreement, but also as something more: that is as a possible source of a subsequent modification, arising out of certain actions or certain attitudes, having a bearing on the juridical situation of the parties and on the rights that each of them could properly claim', added the following comment:

included in the final text of the Vienna Convention. It has been contended that the rejection by the Vienna Conference of the Commission's draft Article 38 has had the consequence that 'a treaty may not be modified by subsequent practice in applying the treaty, even if the practice should establish the agreement of the parties to modify the provisions of the treaty'.[368] This view would seem to be untenable for a number of reasons. The Commission certainly regarded the draft provision as representing the then current legal position, and it is difficult to accept that its rejection by the Conference had the legislative effect of abolishing the principle. The meaning and application of a treaty are as much subject to the common will of the parties as was its initial formation. As international law does not place any restriction upon how obligations are assumed whether by agreement or otherwise,[369] nor are any imposed on the making of treaties or their modification by the Vienna Convention,[370] changes to a treaty may be achieved by the tacit consent of the parties. This possibility raises a number of problems which were influential in the Vienna Conference's rejection of draft Article 38. For example, the tacit amendment of a treaty to which they are parties will create difficulties for States the constitutions of which require the satisfaction of certain procedures for the undertaking of treaty obligations. Moreover, in the case of multilateral treaties which prescribe specific means for their amendment, there is the issue of how to reconcile the alleged tacit amendment with the means set out in the treaty. This will be a particular problem in relation to a treaty which comprises the constitution of an international organisation. Nevertheless, the general tenor of the Court's approach in the *WHO Nuclear Weapons* case has endorsed the possibility of the tacit modification of an international constitution through the practice of its members, notwithstanding the fact that the treaty in question makes provision for its own amendment.

'Although the line may sometimes be blurred between interpretation and amendment of a treaty through subsequent practice, legally the processes are distinct. Accordingly, the effect of subsequent practice in amending a treaty is dealt with in the present article as a case of modification of treaties.'

368 Zoller, 'The "Corporate Will" of the United Nations and the Rights of the Minority' (1987) 81 AJIL 610 at 616. Curiously, Zoller then went on to assert that, because the international personality of the United Nations 'would be obliterated if the UN legal order were equated with, and reduced to, the law of treaties between states . . . institutional law has been and must be supplemented with "established practices" or "rules" tailored to the needs of the system' (at 630). Even if one *were* prepared to accept Zoller's statement quoted in the text, the above pronouncement in this note would not necessarily be inconsistent with it as the 'institutional law' (which presumably is that contained in the organisation's constitution) is not being amended, but only 'supplemented', by the 'practices' of the organisation in question.

369 *Eastern Greenland* case (1933) PCIJ Ser A/B, No 53 at 70–71; *Temple* case, ICJ Rep 1961, 17 at 31–32; *Nuclear Test* cases, ICJ Rep 1974, 253 at 267–268; *Aegean Sea* case, ICJ Rep 1978, 3 at 39; *Frontier Dispute* case, ICJ rep 1986, 554 at 573–574; *Maritime Delimitation and Territorial Questions* case, ICJ Rep 1994, 112 at 120 et seq.

370 Articles 3, 11 and 39.

It is less clear what conduct might constitute the necessary agreement to such a change. When it rejected the idea that Resolution WHA46.40 amounted to practice establishing such an agreement, the Court's use of the words 'between the members of the Organisation'[371] suggested that what was required was the agreement of the parties as a whole. It would seem that this inference is supported by the Court's subsequent assertion that the fact that a resolution has been decided upon by the requisite majority is not conclusive as to its consequences when it said:[372]

> the question whether a resolution has been duly adopted from a procedural point of view and the question whether a resolution has been duly adopted *intra vires* are two separate issues. The mere fact that a majority of States, in voting on a resolution, have complied with all the relevant rules of form cannot in itself suffice to remedy very fundamental defects, such as acting *ultra vires*, with which the resolution might be afflicted.

The issue of the effectiveness of a resolution to constitute the will of the organisation and therefore to bind a dissenting minority would seem to be of a similar kind. Unless the organ in question has been granted the authority to determine disputes between members over the interpretation and application of the constitution, such conduct by a majority of the parties can hardly represent the practice of the organisation. It will at most be evidence of, but not conclusive as to, how the constitution should be interpreted.

B. *Amendment, interpretation and the weight of practice*

Apart from evaluating the alleged practice (to determine whether it represents just the views of the parties, or at least a majority of them, or can be considered as establishing the 'corporate' will of the organisation), it may also be necessary to distinguish between an amendment and a mere interpretation of the text in order to decide whether the conduct in question has the consequence contended for. Hence, at least in theory, where the practice departs from the ordinary meaning of the text in a way that does not seem to be justifiable on the ground that it is consistent with a plausible interpretation of the text in question,[373] the process would seem to be

[371] ICJ Rep 1996 at 81, above at n. 365.

[372] Ibid, at 82.

[373] As Waldock had said at the Vienna Conference on the Law of Treaties, 1st sess, 39th Mtg, 214, para 55: 'The Commission had taken account of the difference between the interpretation of a treaty on the basis of subsequent practice and the question whether a subsequent practice departed so far from any reasonable interpretation of the terms as to constitute a modification.' See also the comments by Lachs in the Commission that, 'occasionally, the subsequent practice of the parties transformed a treaty so profoundly that it was made to serve a purpose diametrically opposed to the one for which it had been concluded'. The example being given was that of the 1948 Treaty between Belgium, France, Luxembourg, the

classifiable as one of amendment and not interpretation. On the other hand, where the disputed issue is not covered by the terms of the treaty, there thus being a gap in the treaty's provisions, it is more readily regardable as being resolvable by interpretation and not amendment by the relevant conduct.

This is relevant to a consideration of the effect which practice might have had in the interpretation to be placed upon the WHO Constitution in the *Nuclear Weapons* case.[374] One of the reasons why the Court's view of the competence of the Organisation can be regarded as so narrow was that the power sought to be exercised was nowhere proscribed. There was nothing in the Constitution to suggest that the regulation or prohibition of hazardous conduct or of the use of hazardous materials was prohibited. Hence, in the absence of such a forbidden proscription, the issue for the Court should have been regarded as one of interpretation, not amendment, of the instrument, so that the Court's invocation of Article 31(3)(b) of the Vienna Convention would seem to have been appropriate for this purpose.

Related to the amendment/interpretation issue is that of the weight or extent of the practice necessary to support the amendment or interpretation being advanced. The International Law Commission's Commentary on draft Article 38 on amendment stated that 'the Commission intended to indicate that the subsequent practice, even if every party might not itself have actively participated in the practice, must be such as to establish the agreement of the parties as a whole to the modification in question',[375] and a similar explanation was provided with regard to what became Article 31(3)(b) of the Vienna Convention.[376] In other words, the weight and extent of the practice must be judged against the standard required to establish an agreement amongst the parties. As to the reaction that amendment in derogation of the text of a treaty should require more concrete evidence than an understanding as to the meaning of the provision, the

Netherlands and the United Kingdom for collaboration in economic, social and cultural matters and for collective self-defence (19 UNTS 51), designed in part, according to the preamble and Article VII, to enable the parties to take necessary steps in the event of a renewal by Germany of a policy of aggression, to which the Federal Republic later acceded (YB ILC 1964, vol I, 286, para 45); and that, 'in international organisations, changes could be brought about by way of practice and interpretation in such a manner as to give to certain provisions of the constituent instrument a meaning which was very remote from that envisaged by the parties at the time of signature' (ibid, para 46).

[374] ICJ Rep 1996, 66.

[375] Yb ILC 1966, vol II, 236, para (2).

[376] Yb ILC 1966, vol II, 222, para (15): 'The text provisionally adopted in 1964 spoke of a practice which "establishes the understanding of all the parties". By omitting the word "all" the Commission did not intend to change the rule. It considered that the phrase "the understanding of the parties" necessarily means "the parties as a whole". It omitted the word "all" merely to avoid any possible misconception that every party must individually have engaged in the practice where it suffices that it should have accepted the practice.'

explanation probably lies in the fact that subsequent practice of less than agreement quality or consistency may nevertheless be relevant to the interpretation of a treaty under Article 32 of the Vienna Convention. According to that provision, supplementary means of interpretation may be employed 'in order to confirm the meaning resulting from the application of article 31, or to determine the meaning when the interpretation according to article 31: (a) leaves the meaning ambiguous or obscure; or (b) leads to a result which is manifestly absurd or unreasonable'.

It is apparent from the jurisprudence of the Permanent Court that subsequent practice could be used for these purposes. With regard to the confirmation of the meaning established by the text, in the *Interpretation of the Treaty of Lausanne* case,[377] the Court was asked about the character of a decision taken by the Council of the League regarding the frontier between Turkey and Iraq, then under British Mandate. When the matter was under discussion by the Council, the statements made by the Rapporteur, 'which were confirmed by the unanimous vote of all members of the Council, including the British and Turkish representatives, show that there was no disagreement between the Parties as regards their obligation to accept as definitive and binding the decision or recommendation to be made by the Council, with a view to fixing the frontiers'. In the Court's opinion, the 'fact that they have accepted beforehand the Council's decision upon the question now before it may therefore be regarded as confirming the interpretation which . . . flows from the actual wording of the article'.[378] Similarly, in the *Competence of the ILO to Regulate Agricultural Labour* case,[379] the Court endorsed the proposition which later constituted Article 32(a) of the Vienna Convention, when it said:[380]

> As regards the inclusion of agriculture, the Court is unable to find in [the ILO Constitution] read as a whole any real ambiguity. The Court has no doubt that agricultural labour is included in it. If there were any ambiguity, the Court might, for the purpose of arriving at the true meaning, consider the action which has been taken under the Treaty. The Treaty was signed in June, 1919, and it was not until October, 1921, that any of the Contracting Parties raised the question whether agricultural labour fell within the competence of the International Labour Organisation. During the intervening period the subject of agriculture had repeatedly been discussed and had been dealt with in one form or another. All this might suffice to turn the scale in favour of the inclusion of agriculture, if there were any ambiguity.

When the practice is sufficiently clear to establish an agreement between the parties, it should not matter whether the agreement constitutes an amendment or an interpretation of the treaty provision in question. Indeed, in a particular case, it may be difficult to determine whether the

[377] (1925) PCIJ Ser B, No 12.
[378] Ibid at 25.
[379] (1922) PCIJ Ser B, No 2.
[380] Ibid at 39–40.

text is sufficiently clear to rule out a contrary agreement as an interpretation thereof. A good example of this is provided by the *Namibia* case.[381] The International Court had to consider the effect of Article 27(3) of the UN Charter, whereby decisions of the Security Council on non-procedural matters 'shall be made by an affirmative vote of nine members including the concurring votes of the permanent members', on Resolution 276 (1970) of the Council, which had been declared adopted notwithstanding the fact that two permanent members, France and the United Kingdom, had abstained. However, from the earliest days of the Council's proceedings, resolutions had been declared validly adopted, even where one of the permanent members had abstained from voting. The Court had no doubt that Resolution 276 (1970) constituted a valid decision of the Council:[382]

The proceedings of the Security Council extending over a long period supply abundant evidence that presidential rulings and the positions taken by members of the Council, in particular its permanent members, have consistently and uniformly interpreted the practice of voluntary abstention by a permanent member as not constituting a bar to the adoption of resolutions . . . This procedure followed by the Security Council . . . has been generally accepted by Members of the United Nations and evidences a general practice of that Organisation.

In this case, the practice of some of the parties to the Charter, that is to say, of the permanent members of the Security Council, and of those UN members which had, over the years, been elected as non-permanent members of the Council, had been augmented by the acceptance of the value of this practice by members of the United Nations as a whole. Hence, it was appropriate to regard the practice as that of the Organisation, rather than as that of a majority of the parties to the Charter. However, the Court's pronouncement did not go so far as to explain how the practice was given legal effect. On one view, it is tantamount to a modification or amendment of the Charter. Certainly the Court was at pains to emphasise evidence suggesting the universal acceptance of the practice, so that the 'consent' of the parties could be said to have existed. For those who regarded Article 27.3 as having a clear meaning which required the concurring votes of *all* permanent members, the practice of UN members must be taken to have constituted a *de facto* revision of the Charter the *de jure* effect of which the Court was now recognising.

The dividing line is a narrow one, and there is an alternative reading possible of Article 27.3. Put simply, it is that the provision cannot possibly signify 'all' the permanent members because the last part of the paragraph *requires* abstention in certain circumstances ('in decisions under Chapter VI, and under paragraph 3 of Article 52, a party to a dispute shall abstain

[381] ICJ Rep 1971, 16. [382] Ibid at 39–40.

from voting'). To make sense of the first part of Article 27.3 it cannot require the concurring votes of permanent members in all circumstances. Once that is recognised, the existence of the proviso requiring abstention in certain circumstances at least suggests that abstention may be possible in other circumstances at a member's discretion. Viewed in this light, the text contains an ambiguity, so that it would in any case be permissible to have resort to the practice of the parties to resolve the uncertainty. As Judge Dillard observed,[383] the South African

> contention is rested on an analysis of legislative history and on the theory that the language of Article 27(3) is so clear and unambiguous that no interpretative process, whether by subsequent conduct or otherwise, is permissible. The contention reveals the weakness of an indiscriminate application of the textual approach when coupled with the plain and ordinary meaning canon of interpretation. Had the critical clause read: '*all five* permanent members, *who must be present and voting* . . .', the contention might have been justified. In the absence of such a precise prescription the subsequent conduct of the parties is clearly a legitimate method of giving meaning to the Article in accordance with the expectations of the parties, including, in particular, the permanent members.

It would seem, therefore, that subsequent practice can be considered under both Article 31 and Article 32 of the Vienna Convention. The International Law Commission appeared to accept that this was so when, having cited various Opinions of the Permanent Court, it made the comment that the 'value of subsequent practice varies according [to the extent to which] it shows the common understanding of the parties as to the meaning of the terms'.[384] Indeed, in the *Competence of the ILO* case, the relatively short period before the practice was challenged might have cast doubt as to its conclusiveness as an example of conduct that was of the type envisaged by Article 31(3)(b) of the Vienna Convention. However, as already mentioned, the approach adopted by the present Court in the *WHO Nuclear Weapons* case[385] seems to have been that the Convention rules were equally applicable to situations when the practice being examined was that of an organisation rather than that of the parties to its constituent treaty.

C. *Summation*

The relationship between practice and competence with regard to international organisations may not be an easy one to assess. In the *Expenses* case,[386] the Court endorsed the authority of the General Assembly to

383 Ibid at 153–154.

384 Yb ILC 1966, vol II, 222, para (15), the cases in question being those referred to above p 93.

385 ICJ Rep 1996, 66, above p 89.

386 ICJ Rep 1962, 151.

undertake or to control peace-keeping operations and to make provision for the financing of such activities. While the reference to the limits of the Assembly's authority was ultimately directed towards budgetary matters, the discussion was linked to the specific authority granted to the Assembly in the field of international peace and security by Article 11(2) of the UN Charter and the restriction in that provision that, when 'action is necessary', the question 'shall be referred to the Security Council'. The Court held that the 'provisions of the Charter which distribute functions and powers to the Security Council and to the General Assembly give no support to the view that such distribution excludes from the powers of the General Assembly the power to provide for the financing of measures designed to maintain international peace and security'.[387] As to the exclusion of 'action' from the Assembly's competence by virtue of Article 11(2), the Court concluded that this limitation had 'no application where the necessary action is not enforcement action', an interpretation of the provision borne out by the 'practice of the Organisation throughout its long history'.[388]

It is difficult to identify from the Court's Opinion where the express powers ended and where it was necessary to rely upon implied powers available to the Organisation and exercised through its political organs, particularly in this context by the General Assembly. However, it does not appear that the Court regarded the practice cited to it as giving rise to any additional customary powers. While that practice may have justified the conclusion reached as to the meaning of the limitation in Article 11(2), the position with regard to the Assembly's budgetary authority was not so clear cut. Although a majority of member States of the Organisation had supported the Assembly's budgetary powers with respect to peace-keeping operations (for otherwise the budgets would not have been approved), a persistent minority, including France and the Soviet Union, had objected to the imposition of peace-keeping costs on members as part of the normal budget of the Organisation. A practice which has majority support may be of evidential value under Article 32 of the Vienna Convention, but certainly does not constitute 'the agreement of the parties' regarding the treaty's interpretation.[389] However, this issue was avoided by the Court first holding that the Assembly's powers extended to peace-keeping operations, as long as the latter were not coercive, and then regarding all expenses arising from activities within the Organisation's competence as subject to the Assembly's normal budgetary authority. In light of the first

[387] Ibid at 164.

[388] Ibid at 165.

[389] As Ress explained in the context of the *Expenses* case ('Interpretation' in Simma B (ed), *The Charter of the United Nations: A Commentary* (1994), 25 at 41): 'The interpreter must not completely disregard such practice on the part of the Organisation, even if it is not universally accepted and cannot, therefore, reach the significance of quasi-authentic appraisal, because this practice contains "a message" which the interpreter must at least take notice of and which must be considered as an important interpretational possibility.'

of these two conclusions, there was no real need for the Court to have made its comments about the presumption of legality in a case where 'the Organisation takes action which warrants the assertion that it was appropriate for the fulfilment of one of the stated purposes of the United Nations' and its assertion that, if 'the action was taken by the wrong organ, it was irregular as a matter of [the] internal structure [of the Organisation], but this would not necessarily mean that an expense incurred was not an expense of the Organisation'.[390]

There are some parallels between the position of the General Assembly in the *Expenses* case, and that of the WHO in the *Nuclear Weapons* case.[391] In the first place, both the purposes of United Nations under Article 1 of the charter are the functions of the WHO under Article 2 of the Constitution, to achieve its objective in Article 1 of 'the attainment of all peoples of the highest possible level health', were extensive. Secondly, in the case of the General Assembly under the Charter, it had broad powers to deal with matters relating to international peace and security, subject to the limitation of authority in the case of enforcement action, which was held not to apply to the two operations in question; in the case of the WHO, its Constitution contained no explicit exclusion of its competence to consider the regulation of nuclear weapons or of other hazardous materials or activities. A third similarity relates to the objections that were raised to the use of the General Assembly's budgetary authority to impose obligations upon member States to pay for peace-keeping operations[392] compared to the objections made by member States of WHO[393] to the requesting of the advisory opinion from the Court raising, in the Court's view, the issue of the legality of nuclear weapons.

There was, however, a striking difference on this issue in the Court's approach to the two cases. It has already been pointed out how the Court avoided giving any significance to the fact of dissent among UN members by treating the text of Article 17 as in itself justifying the conclusion adopted. In the WHO case, on the other hand, the existence of dissent formed a significant element in the Court's reasoning that the Organisation's competence did not extend to the regulation of the use of nuclear weapons or of hazardous materials or activities. As the Court explained:[394]

[390] Ibid at 168. The potential 'tyranny of the majority' is built into Article 17 of the Charter, but does it necessarily follow that the majority is also the sole arbiter of whether an expenditure is properly part of the expenses of the Organisation within that provision? See generally Zoller, op cit n. 368.

[391] ICJ Rep 1996, 66.

[392] The various objectors are referred to in the Dissenting Opinion of Judge Moreno Quintena, ICJ Rep 1962, 151 at 244.

[393] Details of the voting appear in the Dissenting Opinion of Judge Weeramantry, ICJ Rep 1996, 66 at 106.

[394] Ibid at 81.

Resolution WHA 46.40 itself, adopted, not without opposition, as soon as the question of the legality of nuclear weapons was raised at the WHO, could not be taken to express or amount on its own to a practice establishing an agreement between the members of the Organisation to interpret its Constitution as empowering it to address the question of the legality of the use of nuclear weapons.

This pronouncement would have been acceptable enough if recourse to the practice of the World Health Assembly had been necessary either to amend the constituent treaty of the Organisation, or at least to justify a not readily obvious interpretation of a provision of that treaty. However, this was not a situation where the power claimed was prohibited by the treaty, nor was an implied power to deal with the regulation of hazardous materials or activities so unusual that such a power could only be established by the tacit agreement of the parties acting to extend the competence of the WHO. It is true that the Court's statement related to a competence to consider the legality of nuclear weapons, but the objections relied upon should have been distinguished from the competence of the Organisation to deal in general with the regulation of hazardous activities and the use of hazardous materials. It was the Court's failure to distinguish between the two which led it to make a number of statements about the regulation of the latter which are unacceptable in law and could limit unduly the scope of the WHO's legitimate activities.

The practice of the Organisation was undoubtedly a relevant factor for the Court to take into account, but only in part as a matter of treaty interpretation. In that context, it should have been considered as permitted by virtue of Article 32 of the Vienna Convention, as in terms of consistency and extent it came nowhere near to satisfying the standard required by Article 31(3)(b). Properly understood, this evidence did show qualified support for the involvement of the WHO in matters of regulation and what should be done with regard to hazardous activities and the use of hazardous materials; but it also demonstrated the unease of a large minority of members of the Organisation at its involvement in such a politically sensitive issue as the outlawing of any use of nuclear weapons. Apart from the significance of this material for the question of whether the Court should have declined, in the exercise of its discretion, to answer the request, it was also relevant in two other ways. It had been taken into account by the Court in its reinterpretation of the question posed by the World Health Assembly, but it had also influenced the Court in its consideration of the issue of whether the WHO could involve itself in a matter which was more properly for the General Assembly or Security Council to address. Either of these alternatives would have been more satisfactory bases for the Court to have declined to have given an Opinion than the ground of a lack of competence to deal with the regulation of activities, or of the use of materials, hazardous to health.

While it is possible to identify practice that *may* be relevant to the interpretation of a constitutional text, it is a less easy task to determine what practice will affect the outcome of that process by an international tribunal.

As a starting point it can be said with confidence that, where there is substantial approval of, and acquiescence in (there being no real dissent from), a specific reading of a provision, that reading will constitute the agreement of the parties, whether one regards it as falling within Article 31(3)(b) of the Vienna Convention or as a modification of the provision as a matter of customary law.[395] At the other end of the scale is a situation where a group of member States is opposed to the application of a text in the manner represented by the conduct in question. In theory, a distinction should be drawn between an interpretation or a modification of the constitution, because only in the latter case should it be essential to demonstrate an agreement between the parties by participation or acquiescence in the change in issue. Where there is a dissenting minority, then the view favoured by the majority can only succeed on the basis that it constitutes a matter of interpretation of the relevant text. In such circumstances, as the practice cannot amount to the agreement of the parties under Article 31(3)(b), it should nevertheless be available to the interpreter under Article 32,[396] although account would also have to be taken of the views of the minority.

To fit the *WHO Nuclear Weapons* case,[397] in which the Court concentrated exclusively on the former provision, into this framework, it would be necessary to add the qualification that, where there is such a lack of agreement in the views of the members of an organisation, their inconsistent practice will only be relevant to the process of interpretation, even under Article 32 of the Vienna Convention, if those views are maintained over a sufficient length of time.[398] If one side does not maintain its position, it will provide some evidence that the opposing view was correct. If

[395] *Namibia* case, ICJ Rep 1971, 16.

[396] This seems to be in keeping with the view expressed by Judge Fitzmaurice in his Separate Opinion in the *Expenses* case (ICJ Rep 1962, 151 at 201–2): 'Nevertheless, while the existence of these considerations renders it impossible to regard the practice of the United Nations as conclusive in the matter . . . it cannot be less than very material; and even if a majority vote cannot in the formal sense bind the minority, it can, if consistently exercised in a particular way, suffice to establish a settled practice which a tribunal can usefully and properly take account of.'

Judge Spender took a contrary position (ibid at 191–192). '. . . it is not evident on what ground a practice consistently followed by a majority of Member States not in fact accepted by other Member States could provide any criterion of interpretation which the Court could properly take into consideration in the discharge of its judicial function.'

[397] ICJ Rep 1996, 66.

[398] See the words of Judge Fitzmaurice, above n. 396, referring to a practice as being 'settled' and based upon a vote 'consistently exercised'.

both sides back down, there will be little reason for the interpreter to refer to the earlier conduct in giving a meaning to the relevant text.

In the *Nuclear Weapons* case, it may be that the discordant practice had not existed for a sufficiently long period for the practice to have been regarded as admissible under Article 32. Otherwise, there is no reason why the Court could not have considered the opposing views as admissible under that provision as the issue appeared to be one of interpretation rather than of modification of the WHO Constitution. It fell into the former category because it was a health-related matter and there was no bar, actual or apparent, in the Constitution, to the regulation by WHO of hazardous activities or of the use of hazardous substances. The problem with the adoption of this classification in relation to the WHO Constitution is that it sits uncomfortably with the Court's refusal to employ the doctrine of implied powers to extend the competence of the Organisation. If the issue had been one of interpretation, there would have been no need to refer to the practice of the Organisation, as that doctrine would have been sufficient to extend WHO's competence. The rejection of implied powers for such a purpose, and the reference to the practice of the Organisation, suggest that the Court was dealing with the modification, and not just the interpretation, of the WHO Constitution.

As a matter of intertemporality, of setting an issue in the context of the time of interpretation, which is a necessary element in considering how a text and the original intentions of the parties should now be perceived, the views or practice of the members of an institution, though discordant, are obviously evidence relevant to resolving those questions. However, intertemporality also requires that a prospective evaluation should be made of the issue in relation to the powers which that institution might need to employ with regard to the future exercise of its functions. This requirement ties in with the relevance of community values. The political realities of the *WHO* case cast doubts upon whether the regulation of nuclear weapons was a necessary function of that Organisation. But this did not mean that the regulation of other hazardous activities or of the use of other hazardous materials fell outside the Organisation's competence. A prospective view of the likely future needs of the Organisation, and of what community values might require, strongly suggested that such a power should be available and should readily be implied. It should not have been left to the achievement of some ill-defined virtual majority agreement of the members in satisfaction of Article 31(3)(b) of the Vienna Convention.

VI. INTERTEMPORALITY IN RELATION TO TREATY TERMINATION OR SUSPENSION

A matter which would seem to be firmly attached to the time at which a later event occurs is the termination or suspension of a treaty. This is clearly the case with regard to most of the grounds of termination. Thus a treaty may be terminated or withdrawn from (Article 54(b) of the Vienna Convention) or suspended (Article 57(b)) 'at any time by consent of all of the parties', or where that intention may be implied by their entering into 'a later treaty relating to the same subject matter' or where 'the provisions of the later treaty are so far incompatible with those of the earlier one that the two treaties are not capable of being applied at the same time' (Article 59). The same is true with regard to provisions dealing specifically with later events, breach (Article 60), supervening impossibility of performance (Article 61), fundamental change of circumstances (Article 62), and emergence of a new peremptory norm of general international law (Article 64).

In a number of other cases, the ground for termination, withdrawal or suspension seems to be rooted in a treaty's origins. Thus, a party may take such a step 'in conformity with the provisions of the treaty' (Article 54(a), Article 57(a)). Denunciation or withdrawal may take place if:

(a) it is established that the parties intended to admit the possibility of denunciation or withdrawal; or
(b) a right of denunciation or withdrawal may be implied by the nature of the treaty (Article 56(1)).

Similarly, although '[t]wo or more parties to a multilateral treaty may conclude an agreement to suspend the operation of the provisions of the treaty, temporarily and as between themselves alone', this is only permitted if:

(a) the possibility of such a suspension is provided for by the treaty; or
(b) the suspension in question is not prohibited by the treaty and
    i does not affect the enjoyment by the other parties of their rights under the treaty or the performance of their obligations;
    ii is not compatible with the object and purpose of the treaty (Article 58(1)).

Such a division between the time of the making of a treaty and the time of termination is more a matter of emphasis than a strict selection of one in preference to the other as a critical date. Even where there appears to be a selection of one in preference to the other, for example, the references to the provisions of the treaty in Articles 54 and 57, or to the parties' intentions or the nature of the treaty in Article 56; or to the possibility being provided for by the treaty or to the rights and obligations of the parties under the treaty or the object and purpose of the treaty under Article 58; the circumstances surrounding the conclusion of the treaty cannot be isolated entirely from events subsequent to the treaty as a means of identifying what the treaty involves. Nor is it possible to consider the provisions of the Vienna Convention dealing specifically with later events without considering aspects of the treaty at the time it was concluded. In some instances, these are expressly referred to in the provisions themselves, as in the case of the definition of a material breach of a treaty in Article 60(3)(b) as *inter alia* 'the violation of a provision essential to the accomplishment of the object and purpose of the treaty'; or the various aspects of Article 62 whereby a fundamental change of circumstances must relate 'to those existing at the time of the conclusion' of the treaty, circumstances which must have 'constituted an essential basis of the consent of the parties to be bound by the treaty', but cannot be 'the result of a breach by the party invoking it . . . of an obligation under the treaty'.

In most cases, whichever aspect is given priority in the provisions of the Vienna Convention, the termination of, withdrawal from, or suspension of, a treaty will involve two elements: an investigation of the circumstances, including the rights and obligations expressed in the treaty, existing at the time the treaty was made; and an assessment of the act, and the events surrounding it, whereby it is alleged that the treaty has been, or can be, brought to an end.

An example of the significance of both these factors is provided by the *Namibia* case.[399] In 1966, following years of intransigence by South Africa with regard to its alleged non-compliance with the obligations of the Mandate agreement, under which it had administered South West Africa, the UN General Assembly had purported to terminate the agreement. As the International Court had already held that the United Nations was the successor of the League of Nations, as a party to the Mandate agreement, with the General Assembly as the appropriate supervisory organ of the due performance of the agreement,[400] one of the issues was whether the Assembly had been entitled to exercise, on behalf of the United Nations, a right to terminate the agreement on the ground of a material breach of that agreement by the other party, South Africa.

In adjudicating upon this issue, the International Court first of all considered the circumstances surrounding the making of the Mandate agreement. South Africa had argued that Class C Mandates, like that over South West Africa, were subject to the control of the Mandatory power to such an extent that the arrangement was but an interlude before annexation. This contention was rejected by the Court on the ground that such an interpretation was inconsistent with the provisions of Article 22 of the Covenant and of the Mandate agreement in relation to South West Africa. In the Court's view,[401] 'the final outcome of the negotiations [concerning that Article], however difficult of achievement, was a rejection of the notion of annexation. It cannot tenably be argued that the clear meaning of the mandate institution could be ignored by placing upon the explicit provisions embodying its principles a construction at variance with its object and purpose'.

[399] ICJ Rep 1971, 16.
[400] *Status of South West Africa* case, ICJ Rep 1950, 128.
[401] ICJ Rep 1971 at 30.

The Court also regarded as critical the situation existing at the time of the act of termination. It did so for two different reasons, the first of which has already been discussed.[402] In its view, Article 22 of the Covenant, and particularly 'the concept of the sacred trust' which it embodied, 'were not static, but were by definition evolutionary'. As the Court explained:[403]

> The parties to the Covenant must consequently be deemed to have accepted them as such. That is why, viewing the institutions of 1919, the Court must take into consideration the changes which have occurred in the supervening half-century, and its interpretation cannot remain unaffected by the subsequent development of law, through the Charter of the United Nations and by way of customary law. Moreover, an international instrument has to be interpreted and applied within the framework of the entire legal system prevailing at the time of the interpretation. In the domain to which the present proceedings relate, the last fifty years . . . have brought important developments. These developments leave little doubt that the ultimate objective of the sacred trust was the self-determination and independence of the peoples concerned.

The second reason did not relate to an assessment of the obligations arising out of Article 22 of the Covenant and the Mandate agreement. It was necessary for the Court to examine the act of termination and the circumstances surrounding that act. Resolution 2145(XXI) of the General Assembly which had purported to terminate the Mandate had sought to justify the taking of this step by declaring:[404]

> That South Africa has failed to fulfil its obligations in respect of the administration of the Mandated Territory and to ensure the moral and material well-being and security of the indigenous inhabitants of South West Africa and had, in fact, disavowed the Mandate.

The Court had no doubt that, 'even if the mandate [system] is viewed as having the character of an institution',[405] a particular mandate was 'in fact and in law . . . an international agreement having the character of a treaty or convention'.[406] Accordingly the position was governed by Article 60 of the Vienna Convention, 'concerning termination of a treaty relationship on account of breach' which 'may in many respects be considered as a codification of existing customary law on the subject'.[407] According to Article 60, only a material breach of a treaty justifies termination, but the Court had no doubt that this had occurred.[408]

402 Above pp 55–56. 403 Ibid at 31. 404 Quoted, ibid at 46.
405 Ibid.
406 *South-West Africa* cases, ICJ Rep 1962, 319 at 330, quoted ICJ Rep 1971 at 47.
407 Ibid.
408 See also the Court's reaction to the South African contention that the policy of apartheid as applied to Namibia was designed to promote the interests of the inhabitants of the Territory (ibid at 57): 'Under the Charter of the United Nations, the former Mandatory had pledged itself to observe and respect, in a territory having an international status, human

The Court provided no explanation of its use of Article 60 beyond the reference to the fact that the provision represented 'existing customary law on the subject'. Presumably the 'existing' refers to the time of termination rather than the time of adjudication. Although the Vienna Conference had not yet been held at the former time, the Commission's final set of draft Articles, which also date from 1966, was expressed in almost identical terms as far as a material breach was concerned.[409] The only other possibilities are that termination of a treaty can or should be effected in accordance with the law in force at the time the treaty was made, or that the evolutionary nature of the treaty system in question under Article 22 of the Covenant meant that its performance and termination, as well as the scope of its obligations, had to be judged in accordance with the intertemporal law, that is the law relevant to the changing requirements of the system.

These latter two possibilities are not so fanciful as it may at first appear. The application of the law contemporaneous with the creation of the Mandate would have produced a similar result. One of the cases cited in the Commission's final commentary on the law of treaties was the *Tacna-Arica* arbitration,[410] which dates from the same period as the Mandates system. The Commission explained the case's relevance as follows:[411]

> There Peru contended that by preventing the performance of article 3 of the Treaty of Ancon, which provided for the holding of a plebiscite under certain conditions in the disputed area, Chile had discharged Peru from her obligations under that article. The Arbitrator, after examining the evidence, rejected the Peruvian contention, saying:[412] 'It is manifest that if abuses of administration could have the effect of terminating such an agreement, it would be necessary to establish such serious conditions as the consequence of administrative wrongs as would operate to frustrate the purpose of the agreement, and, in the opinion of the Arbitrator, a situation of such gravity has not been shown.'
>
> This pronouncement seems to assume that only a 'fundamental' breach of article 3 by Chile could have justified Peru in claiming to be released from its provisions.

In other words, the conduct of Chile, judged against the requirements of a material breach in Article 60(3) of the Vienna Convention, would not have amounted to 'a repudiation of the treaty'.

As to the law of the time of termination, Article 60 was designed to replace the notion that an innocent State could employ an alleged material

rights and fundamental freedom for all without distinction as to race. To establish instead, and to enforce, distinctions, exclusions, restrictions and limitations exclusively based on grounds of race, colour, descent or national or ethnic origin which constitute a denial of fundamental human rights is a flagrant violation of the purposes and principles of the Charter.'

409 Draft Article 57, Yb ILC 1966, vol II, 253.
410 (1925) 2 UNRIAA 921.
411 Yb ILC 1966, vol II, 254, para (4).
412 2 UNRIAA at 943–944.

breach of a bilateral treaty as entitling that State, without more ado, to declare the treaty as at an end. The scheme of the Convention is that a State claiming that its acceptance of the treaty was vitiated by one of the grounds of invalidity, or that the treaty was terminated or suspended, or that it was entitled to withdraw from the treaty, can only invoke the particular ground as a basis of pursuing the procedural requirements laid down in Articles 65 and 66 of the Convention.[413] In relation to *Namibia (South West Africa)*, however, the UN General Assembly in Resolution 2145(XXI) simply decided that, because South Africa had 'failed to fulfil its obligations' under the Mandate, and had, 'in fact, disavowed the Mandate', the Mandate was 'therefore terminated'.[414] There would seem to be a number of possible justifications for the taking of such peremptory action without satisfying the procedural requirements indicated in Articles 65 and 66 of the Convention.

In the first place, it could be argued that the impasse over the irreconcilable views of the parties (the United Nations and South Africa) had persisted for such a lengthy period that any further notice of the alleged non-performance of its obligations by South Africa would have been superfluous. While this was certainly the Court's perception of the reality of the situation,[415] it is not a satisfactory view of the significance attached

[413] Article 65 reads in part:

1. A party which . . . invokes either a defect in its consent to be bound by a treaty or a ground for impeaching the validity of a treaty, terminating it, withdrawing from it or suspending its operation, must notify the other parties of its claim. The notification shall indicate the measure proposed to be taken with respect to the treaty and the reasons therefor.
2. If, after the expiry of a period which, except in cases of special urgency, shall not be less than three months after the receipt of the notification, no party has raised any objection, the party making the notification may carry out . . . the measure which it has proposed.
3. If, however, objection has been raised by any other party, the parties shall seek a solution through the means indicated in Article 33 of the Charter of the United Nations.

Article 66 deals with the situation that arises if, under Article 65(3), 'no solution has been reached within a period of 12 months following the date on which the objection was raised'. Article 66(a) allows any party 'to a dispute concerning the application or the interpretation of article 53 or 64' (the *jus cogens* provisions) to submit the matter to the International Court ('unless the parties by common consent agree to submit the dispute to arbitration'); but any other dispute arising out of the invalidity, termination or suspension of a treaty may only be submitted to the conciliation procedures, which contain no power for the award of a binding decision, contained in the Annex to the Convention, though of course the parties to the dispute may have other avenues for settlement available to them.

[414] The text of these parts of the Resolution appears in ICJ Rep 1971 at 46, see above p 103.

[415] As the Court explained the circumstances, ibid at 44–45: 'Further fruitless negotiations were held from 1952 to 1959. In total, negotiations extended over a period of thirteen years, from 1946 to 1959. In practice the actual length of negotiations is no test of whether the possibilities of agreement have been exhausted; it may be sufficient to show that an early deadlock was reached and that one side adamantly refused compromise. In the case of

by the Commission to what became Article 65. The Commission's proposals were designed to provide an orderly process to replace and prevent the possibility of arbitrary abrogation, and there was no sign that the process was intended to apply to short term, but not to long running, disputes over the operation of a particular aspect of a treaty.[416]

The second possibility is based on the fact that Mandate agreements formed part of a regime under the aegis of the Council of the League of Nations and of the General Assembly of the United Nations, as successor to the League. It was a *lex specialis* which empowered the General Assembly to terminate an agreement in the case of default by a mandatory of its obligations under the agreement. Support can be found for this approach in the Separate Opinions of Judge Dillard,[417] and of Judge De Castro.[418] The Court's position was more equivocal. As already explained,[419] the primary ground for its conclusion was that the Assembly had been exercising the right to terminate on behalf of the United Nations as a party to a bilateral agreement which had been broken by the other party. However, it also linked the power to take such a step to the Assembly's role as the 'supervisory institution, competent to pronounce, in that capacity, on the conduct of the mandatory with respect to its international obligations, and competent to act accordingly'.[420]

The third alternative is related to the Court's initial reference to Article 60 of the Vienna Convention as only 'in many respects' representing customary international law.[421] It would seem that one of the respects in which Article 60 could not have been considered as constituting customary

Namibia . . . this stage had patently been reached long before the United Nations finally abandoned its efforts to reach agreement. Even so, for so long as South Africa was the Mandatory Power the way was still open for it to seek an arrangement. But that chapter came to an end with the termination of the Mandate.'

416 In the words of the Commission's Commentary to what was then Draft Article 62 (YB ILC 1966, vol II, 262, para (1)): 'Many members of the Commission regarded the present article as a key article for the application of the provisions . . . dealing with the invalidity, termination or suspension of the operation of treaties. They thought that some of the grounds upon which treaties may be considered invalid or terminated or suspended . . ., if allowed to be arbitrarily asserted in face of objection by the other party, would involve real dangers for the security of treaties. These dangers were, they felt, particularly serious in regard to claims to denounce or withdraw from a treaty by reason of an alleged breach by the other party . . . Accordingly, the Commission considered it essential that the present articles should contain procedural safeguards against the possibility that the nullity, termination or suspension of the operation of a treaty may be arbitrarily asserted as a mere pretext for getting rid of an inconvenient obligation.' Similar provisions are contained in the Vienna Convention on the Law of Treaties between States and International Organisations or between International Organisations 1986, Text in (1986) 25 ILM 543, justified by the Commission along similar lines, Yb ILC 1982, vol II, Part 2, 63.

417 ICJ Rep 1971 at 163.

418 Ibid at 213–214.

419 Above, pp 103–104.

420 Ibid at 49–50.

421 Ibid at 47.

international law was that the procedural requirements had not become established in State practice.[422] Until that time aggrieved States had regarded it as their right to denounce, suspend or withdraw from a treaty in the case of any of the grounds specified in Part V of the Convention. Unless some limitation on the right existed in the treaty itself, the right was unhampered by external procedural requirements. The act would only be subject to examination by an international tribunal if there was some jurisdictional link between the parties. However, the link did not have to be by virtue of some other arrangement. The link could be provided in the denounced or suspended treaty as far as testing the validity of the act of denunciation or suspension was concerned.

This principle was affirmed by the International Court in the *Jurisdiction of the ICAO Council* case.[423] Pakistan argued that the Court lacked jurisdiction because India had purported to suspend the treaties, on which the Court's jurisdiction was claimed to be based, in its dealings with Pakistan. The Court rejected this contention:[424]

> If a mere allegation, as yet unestablished, that a treaty was no longer operative could be used to defeat its jurisdictional clauses, all such clauses would become potentially a dead letter, even in cases like the present, where one of the very questions at issue on the merits, and as yet undecided, is whether or not the treaty is operative—i.e. whether it has been validly terminated or suspended. The result would be that means of defeating jurisdictional clauses would never be wanting.

If a choice has to be made between the three possibilities outlined above, it would be preferable to select the second. As suggested already,[425] the first would provide an unsatisfactory precedent for general application, though justifiable on the basis of South Africa's continuing refusal to abide by what the vast majority of States regarded as its obligations under the Mandate. With regard to the third, it is probable that, at the time the *Namibia* Advisory Opinion was given, that possibility was also correct. The contemporaneous *ICAO* case strongly suggests that, at that time, the procedural requirements in Articles 65 and 66 of the Vienna Convention did not represent customary international law. Given that the procedural requirements of the Vienna Convention have been largely ignored by States, it is clear that those requirements could not as such have become part of customary international law.

As far as intertemporality is concerned, issues of termination and

[422] Venezuela was one of the States which sought to introduce a provision (for the subsequent adoption of Article 4, see below pp 108–109) limiting the application of the Vienna Convention by preventing its having retroactive effect, and specifically mentioning what became Article 60 as constituting a progressive development of the former law relating to the termination of a treaty on account of a breach of its terms: see Vienna Conference, Second Session, 317, 100th Mtg. Cttee of the Whole, para 64.

[423] ICJ Rep 1972, 46.

[424] Ibid at 53–54.

[425] Above pp 105–106.

suspension inevitably require a consideration of both the obligations and rights arising under the treaty and of the circumstances leading up to and surrounding the act of termination and suspension. The first is necessary as a matter of interpretation, which may require, on the basis of the parties' intentions, an examination of later events including changes in the law; the latter partly as a matter of interpretation and partly in order to determine whether the act of termination or suspension complies with the requirements of the treaty and of the law contemporaneous with that act. Nevertheless, the Court has achieved a substantial reconciliation between alternatives one and three in the course of its Judgment in the *Gabčikovo–Nagymaros Project* case when it said that Articles 65 to 67, 'If not codifying customary law, at least generally reflect customary international law and contain certain procedural principles which are based on the obligation to act in good faith'.[426]

VII. RETROACTIVITY OF THE VIENNA CONVENTION

A. *Application of the Convention to non-parties*

There is one final aspect of intertemporality which should be mentioned and that is the non-retroactivity principle. This is a basic part of treaty law, applicable to all treaties in the absence of an indication of a contrary intention.[427] However, the significance of the principle for the operation of the Vienna Convention was only raised at a late stage of the Vienna Conference.[428] It became a matter of concern because many of the provisions being adopted were regarded by States present at the Conference as constituting new rules, based on the progressive development of the law, rather than simply the codification of existing rules.[429] Article 4 as adopted attempted to strike a balance between the non-retroactivity of the former rules, and the effectiveness of the latter as pre-existing customary international law:

[426] ICJ Rep 1997, p 7 at 66.

[427] According to Article 28 of the Vienna Convention: 'Unless a different intention appears from the treaty or is otherwise established, its provisions do not bind a party in relation to any act or fact which took place or any situation which ceased to exist before the date of entry into force of the treaty with respect to that party'

[428] The proposals, one by Venezuela (A/CONF.39/C.1/L.399), and one by Brazil, Chile, Iran, Kenya, Sweden, Tunisia and Venezuela (the last named having withdrawn its own) (A.CONF.39/C.1/L.400), appear in the UN Conference on the Law of Treaties, Docs of the Conference, 252–25.

[429] See the comments of the Venezuelan representative, UN Conference on the Law of Treaties, 2nd Session, 316–317, 100th Mtg Cttee of the Whole, paras 64–65; of the Swedish representative, ibid, 321, 101st Mtg, paras 42–44; see also the comments of the Swiss representative on the relationship between the retroactivity principle and intertemporality, ibid, 330, 103rd Mtg, paras 7–9.

Without prejudice to the application of any rules set forth in the present Convention to which treaties would be subject under international law independently of the Convention, the Convention applies only to treaties which are concluded by States after the entry into force of the present Convention with regard to such States.

This provision has played no role at all in limiting the use made of provisions of the Vienna Convention to a range of issues even at a stage when the Convention had not yet come into force, the justification being that they represented rules of customary international law.[430] The *Namibia* case has already been mentioned[431] for the role of Article 60 on the ground that it 'may in many respects be considered as a codification of existing customary law on the subject' of termination of a treaty relationship on account of breach.[432] Virtually identical wording was employed by the Court to explain its reliance on Article 62 dealing with the termination or suspension of a treaty as a consequence of a fundamental change of circumstances in the *Fisheries Jurisdiction* case.[433] In more recent years the Court has made regular use of the general rule of interpretation in Article 31 of the Convention on the ground that customary international law is 'reflected' in that provision.[434]

B. *Application to treaties pre-dating the Convention*

The balance achieved by Article 4 between conventional and customary rules was intended to allow for the application of the former from the time of adoption of the Vienna Convention, if they represented existing or crystallised customary international law, even to States which were not parties to the Convention.[435] It is true that, in the *Namibia*

[430] Indeed Articles 31 and 32 which are the main provisions dealt with in this section of the book are generally regarded as codifying 'the *current* international law of treaty interpretation': (Vandevelde, op cit n. 92 at 290 (emphasis supplied)).

[431] Above p 103.

[432] ICJ Rep 1971, 16 at 47; see also the use made of the definition of a material breach in Article 60(3) of the Convention in the *Jurisdiction of the ICAO* case, ICJ Rep 1972, 46 at 67.

[433] ICJ Rep 1973, 3 at 18; see also the Court's reference to Article 52 concerning the invalidity of an agreement concluded under the threat or use of force, ibid at 14.

[434] *Territorial Dispute between Libya and Chad*, ICJ Rep 1994, 6 at 21–22, *Oil Platforms* case, ICJ Rep 1996, 803 at 812; *Kasikili/Sedudu Island* case, Judgment of 13 December 1999, paras 18, 48; reproduced in (2000) ILM 310 at 320, 330.

[435] For a summary of the views expressed at the Vienna Conference, see Rosenne, op cit n. 1 at 5–12. Rosenne seems to have taken a stance similar to that of the text in that he commented (ibid at 23) that 'it would be a rash legal adviser who, on the technical ground that the Vienna Convention is not yet in force . . . for a particular country, failed to have regard for the Vienna Convention at least as regards any international treaty concluded since May 22, 1969.' While initially appearing to emphasise the need to distinguish between rules in the Convention that were *lex lata* and those which were *lex ferenda* (ibid at 3), Rosenne later went on to reject such a 'clear cut polarity . . . between codification and progressive development' (ibid at 17), principally because of the consolidating effect of many of the provisions. Nevertheless, where it was

case,[436] Article 60 had not been adopted at the time of the act of termination of the Mandate agreement by the UN General Assembly, but the Court could at least rely upon the fact that the International Law Commission had regarded the requirement of a material breach as a basis of termination as long established in customary law, and that Article 60 represented a nearly contemporaneous statement of the relevant rule. In two recent cases, however, the Court has employed Article 31 as a statement of customary law, but applied it to the interpretation of treaties that predate the Convention by significant periods. The question arises, therefore, whether this approach is reconcilable with the principle of intertemporality.

1. *The* Libya/Chad *case*

In the *Territorial Dispute between Libya and Chad*,[437] the substance of the case concerned the binding nature and application of the Treaty of Friendship and Good Neighbourliness between France and Libya of 1955, Article 3 of which provided:[438]

> The two High Contracting Parties recognise that the frontiers between the territories of Tunisia, Algeria, French West Africa and French Equatorial Africa on the one hand, and the territory of Libya on the other, are those that result from international instruments in force at the date of the constitution of the United Kingdom of Libya as listed in the attached Exchange of Letters (Annex I).

Annex I listed a series of instruments, commencing with a Franco-British Convention of June 1898 and culminating with a Franco-British Convention of September 1919 and a Franco-Italian Arrangement of four days later in that month.

The rules of interpretation contained in Articles 31 and 32 of the Vienna Convention were relied upon primarily in the context of the initial question of whether the recognition of the frontiers in Article 3 of the 1955 Treaty constituted a legal obligation. In the view of the Court, the 'word "recognise" used in the Treaty indicates that a legal obligation is undertaken. To recognise a frontier is essentially to "accept" that frontier, that is, to draw legal consequences from its existence, to respect it and to

possible to make such a distinction, those rules 'which can be established as being codificatory will be of unlimited temporal application' (ibid at 3), or, in his later words, as 'being timeless' (ibid at 17). It is difficult to accept such a pronouncement at face value. An interpreter should only apply a rule of customary law existing at the time of, and embodied in the Vienna Convention, back in time as far as the inception of the rule. This is expressly the case with regard to Article 52 of the Convention dealing with coercion of the State (see ibid at 13–14 and above p 18), but the principle is of general application.

[436] ICJ Rep 1971, 16.

[437] ICJ Rep 1994, 6.

[438] Ibid at 20–21.

renounce the right to contest it in future.'[439] Hence, by 'entering into the Treaty, the parties recognised the frontiers to which the text of the Treaty referred; the task of the Court is thus to determine the exact content of the undertaking entered into'.[440]

When it turned to the task of determining the frontier in accordance with the instruments listed in Annex I of the 1955 Treaty, which dated between 1898 and 1919, the Court made no reference to any particular rules of treaty interpretation, thus avoiding any problem of intertemporality.[441] As to the employment of the rules of interpretation set out in the Vienna Convention in ascertaining whether the meaning of Article 3 of the 1955 Treaty was to lay down a fixed frontier, this was justifiable on the ground that those rules were based substantially on analyses of the law dating from the period of the 1955 Treaty. The interpretation of treaties was first dealt with by the International Law Commission in Waldock's Third Report of 1964,[442] the draft articles of which took 'their inspiration from the 1956 resolution of the Institute of International Law and from Sir G. Fitzmaurice's formulation of the "major principles" of interpretation in an article ... published in 1957.'[443] There was, therefore, nothing anachronistic in the Court's use of Articles 31 and 32 of the Convention.[444]

[439] Ibid at 22. As the Court continued: 'In the contention of Libya, the parties to the 1955 Treaty intended only to recognise the frontiers that had previously been fixed by the international instruments: where frontiers already existed (as between Tunisia and Libya), they were confirmed by the 1955 Treaty, but where there was no frontier (as in the south), the treaty did not create one. The Court is unable to accept this view; it has no difficulty either in ascertaining the natural and ordinary meaning of the relevant terms of the 1955 Treaty, or in giving effect to them. In the view of the Court, the terms of the Treaty signified that the parties thereby recognised complete frontiers between their respective territories as resulting from the combined effect of all the instruments listed in Annex I; no relevant frontier was to be left undefined and no instrument listed in Annex I was superfluous. It would be incompatible with a recognition couched in such terms to contend that only some of the specified instruments contributed to the definition of the frontier, or that a particular frontier remained unsettled. So to contend would deprive Article 3 of the Treaty and Annex I of their ordinary meaning.'

Subsequently (ibid at 27), the Court observed that it was 'not necessary to refer to the *travaux préparatoires* to elucidate the content of the 1955 Treaty; but, as in previous cases, it finds it possible by reference to the *travaux* to confirm its meaning of the text, namely, that the Treaty constitutes an agreement between the parties which, *inter alia*, defines the frontiers.'

[440] Ibid at 22.

[441] The Court did point out (ibid at 38, 40) that a number of aspects of the law relating to territorial acquisition, including 'the rules of intertemporal law', did not 'come within the ambit of the Court's enquiry'.

[442] YB ILC 1964, vol II, 5 at 52.

[443] Ibid at 55, para 10. The texts quoted appear in *Annuaire de l'Institut de droit international 1956*, 364–365; and Fitzmaurice, 'The Law and Procedure of the International Court of Justice 1951–1954: Treaty Interpretation and Other Treaty Points' (1957) 33 BYIL 203 at 211–212; and are reproduced in Yb ILC 1964, vol II, 55–56.

[444] Similarly, with the Court's use of Articles 31 and 32 of the Vienna Convention to

2. *The* Kasikili/Sedudu Island *case*

More remarkable from the standpoint of what might be described as temporal dislocation was the *Kasikili/Sedudu Island* case between Botswana and Namibia.[445] By a Treaty of 1890, Britain and Germany had defined their respective spheres of influence along a river which, in time, became the boundary between the two parties to the case. According to Article III of the Treaty, the line 'in which the exercise of influence is reserved to Germany . . . runs eastward along [the 18th parallel of south latitude] till it reaches the river Chobe, and descends the centre of the main channel of that river to its junction with the Zambesi, where it terminates'.[446] At that time, neither party had a very clear idea of the topography of the area,[447] and recognised therefore that the situation on the ground might require some adjustment to the line established by the treaty.[448] They were also aware that population movements and activities might affect the extent of the influence which they might be able to exercise. Hence the Treaty also contained provisions designed to protect their rights from such events.[449]

(*a*) *The Court's approach*

As to how the Court should deal with the interpretation of the 1890 Treaty, the Court had no doubt as to the relevance of the provisions of the Vienna Convention:[450]

interpret the Treaty of Amity, Economic Relations and Consular Rights of 1955 between the United States of America and Iran in the *Oil Platforms* case, ICJ Rep 1996, 803 at 812.

[445] Judgment of 13 December 1999, (2000) 39 ILM 310.

[446] Ibid para 21; 39 ILM at 321.

[447] As Lord Salisbury informed the British Ambassador in Berlin in a letter of 14 June 1890: 'The character of this country is very imperfectly known, and the very position of Lake Ngami has been the subject of great uncertainty', quoted by Judge Parra-Aranguren, Dissenting Opinion para 4; 39 ILM at 420; as Lord Salisbury said of this lake in a speech in the House of Lords: 'We have had a fierce conflict over the possession of . . . Lake Ngami . . . our only difficulty being that we do not know where it is. We cannot determine its position within 100 miles, certainly not within 60 miles, and there are great doubts whether it is a lake at all, or only a bed of rushes' (ibid para 6; and at 421).

[448] By Article VI of the Treaty (ibid para 7; and at 421): 'All the lines of demarcation traced in Articles I to IV shall be subject to rectification by agreement between the two Powers, in accordance with local requirements'.

[449] By Article VII (ibid): 'The two Powers engage that neither will interfere with any sphere of influence assigned to the other by Articles I to IV. One Power will not in the sphere of the other make acquisitions, conclude Treaties, accept sovereign rights or Protectorates, nor hinder the extension of influence of the other.

It is understood that no Companies nor individuals subject to one Power can exercise sovereign rights in a sphere assigned to the other, except with the assent of the other.'

[450] Judgment para 18; 39 ILM at 320. At least in the *Beagle Channel* arbitration (1977) 52 ILR 93, the arbitrators, all of whom were at the time or had formerly been judges of the

As regards the interpretation of that Treaty, the Court notes that neither Botswana nor Namibia are parties to the Vienna Convention on the Law of Treaties of 1969, but that both of them consider that Article 31 . . . is applicable inasmuch as it reflects customary international law . . . Article 4 of the Convention, which provides that it 'applies only to treaties which are concluded by States after the entry into force of the . . . Convention with regard to such States' does not, therefore, prevent the Court from interpreting the 1890 Treaty in accordance with the rules reflected in Article 31 of the Convention.

This pronouncement is open to two obvious objections.

In the first place, it is for the Court, and not for the parties, to determine what rules it is to apply to the particular dispute. The Court made its position abundantly clear in the *Nicaragua* case:[451]

The Court notes that there is in fact evidence . . . of a considerable degree of agreement between the Parties as to the content of the customary international law relating to the non-use of force and non-intervention. This concurrence of their views does not however dispense the Court from having itself to ascertain what rules of customary international law are applicable. The mere fact that States declare their recognition of certain rules is not sufficient for the Court to consider these as being part of customary international law, and as applicable as such to those States. Bound as it is by Article 38 of its Statute to apply, *inter alia*, international custom 'as evidence of a general practice accepted as law', the Court may not disregard the essential role played by general practice. Where two States agree to incorporate a particular rule in a treaty, their agreement suffices to make that rule a legal one binding upon them; but in the field of customary international law, the shared view of the Parties as to the content of what they regard as the rule is not enough. The Court must satisfy itself that the existence of the rule in the *opinio juris* of States is confirmed by practice.

(b) Lack of attention to the intertemporality issue

The second objection is the intertemporal one. The only evidence that Articles 31 and 32 constituted customary international law was drawn from the Court's own acceptance of them as having that status on the basis of their adoption in the Convention. While, as already suggested, there is evidence to indicate that a formulation along the lines of those provisions represented the law in the mid-1950s, the position in the period of the Permanent Court was less clear,[452] and no reason was given by the

International Court, justified the invocation of Article 31 of the Vienna Convention with regard to the Boundary Treaty of 1881 between Argentina and Chile on the basis, not just of the parties' wishes (at 124), but also of the fact that it enshrined 'the traditional canons of treaty interpretation' (at 127).

451 ICJ Rep 1986, 3 at 97–98.

452 See, for example, Article 19(a) of the Harvard Draft Convention on the Law of Treaties (1935) 29 AJIL Supp 657 at 937: 'A treaty is to be interpreted in the light of the general purpose which it is intended to serve. The historical background of the treaty, *travaux préparatoires*, the circumstances of the parties at the time the treaty was entered into, the

Court as to why the law set out in Articles 31 and 32 of the Vienna Convention should be regarded as applicable to a treaty from an even earlier time. As Judge Oda observed:[453]

> It appears to me that the Judgment places excessive reliance upon the Vienna Convention . . . for the purpose of the Court's interpretation of the 1890 Anglo-German Treaty . . . Although I am fully aware that the Vienna Convention reflects customary international law, it should, however, be noted, as the Judgment correctly points out in its paragraph 18, that this Convention 'applies only to treaties which are concluded by States after the entry into force of the present Convention with regard to such States' (Art 4). In fact, the Convention came into force in 1980. This case does not appear to me to be one related to the application of the Vienna Convention.

The lack of attention to various aspects of the intertemporality issue was commented upon by several members of the Court. With regard to the interpretation to be placed upon the expression 'main channel' in the 1890 Treaty, Judge Higgins made the point that there was an inevitable balancing between geographical data now available[454] and the task of employing the terms in a way that coincided with the parties' intentions in 1890:[455]

> At the same time, we must never lose sight of the fact that we are seeking to give flesh to the intention of the Parties [as expressed] in generalised terms in 1890. We

change in these circumstances sought to be effected, the subsequent conduct of the parties in applying the provisions of the treaty, and the conditions prevailing at the time the interpretation is being made, are to be considered in connection with the general purpose which the treaty is intended to serve.'

This provision may be disregarded on the ground that it is similar to the US amendment to what became Articles 31 and 32 of the Vienna Convention (Docs of the Conference, 149), which was rejected by 66 votes to eight with 10 abstentions (ibid, 150), though much of the material relied upon by the Harvard project was taken from decisions and pronouncements of the Permanent Court. As already pointed out, in the *Convention on the Employment of Women at Night* case, (1932) PCIJ Ser A/B, No 50, ready use was made of many of the factors referred to in Article 19, though their use was explained by the (bare) majority along the lines later adopted in Articles 31 and 32. A principal difference lay in how the use of subsequent conduct was justified, the Permanent Court allowing it if 'there were any ambiguity' (*Competence of the ILO to Regulate Agricultural Labour* case (1922) PCIJ Ser B, No 2, 39); the Commission ostensibly limiting it to conduct establishing the parties' agreement regarding a treaty's interpretation (though in fact relying upon the latter pronouncement for this purpose, Yb ILC 1966, vol II, 222, para (15)).

453 Separate Opinion para 4; 39 ILM at 358.

454 Declaration para 3; 39 ILM at 355 where the Judge said: 'The Court is indeed, for this particular task, entitled to look at all the criteria which the parties have suggested as relevant. This is not to discover a mythical "ordinary meaning" within the Treaty, but rather because the general terminology chosen long ago falls to be decided today. To use contemporary knowledge and scientific data to assist in fulfilling that task is not at all inconsistent with the intertemporal rule in the *Island of Palmas* Award, which was concerned with the legal rules applicable to title to territory and not with identification, through the legal technique of evaluating evidence, of a chosen term.'

455 Ibid para 4; 39 ILM at 356.

must trace a thread back to this point of departure. We should not, as the Court appears at times to be doing, decide what *in abstracto* the term 'the middle channel' might today mean, by a mechanistic appreciation of relevant indicia. Rather, our task is to decide what general idea the Parties had in mind, and then make reality of that general idea through the use of contemporary knowledge.

However, the more crucial issue concerned the way in which the Court made use of the parties' subsequent conduct in relation to the Treaty. The Court regarded the relevant time span as running from the date of the making of the Treaty until the present, a period which included the disagreements between the Botswana authorities (even prior to independence) and the South African administration of Namibia. As the Court dealt with subsequent conduct in the context of Article 31(3)(b) of the Vienna Convention to the exclusion of Article 32, the evidence from the end of the colonial period demonstrated conclusively that no agreement or understanding had been reached establishing an interpretation of the Treaty in Namibia's favour as to its occupation and use of the disputed island.

This view is open to objection because it pays insufficient attention to a number of factors, indicated by the principle of intertemporality. Judge Parra-Aranguren was able to place an appropriate emphasis on the conduct of the parties in the quarter of a century following the Treaty by selecting 1914 as the critical date and thereby discounting events in more recent times. This is a plausible analysis because, during and after the 1914–18 War, the territory had been occupied by the British army and had then become a Mandate under South African stewardship. Indeed, until Namibia attained independence, it is probably true to say that no conduct on the part of South Africa could have altered the boundaries of the territory.[456] On this approach, the years from 1890 to 1914 constituted a critical period during which the disputed island had been subject to regular occupation and use by residents of German South West Africa, a use which was, in the Judge's view, regulated by its colonial administration, and therefore constituted more than the acts of private individuals.

Judge Weeramantry reached a similar conclusion by a different route, stressing in particular the significance of intertemporality, which he referred to as 'contemporaneity'. As he explained:[457]

[456] Ibid paras 32–43; 39 ILM at 426–429; see also Judge Fleischhauer, Dissenting Opinion para 11; 39 ILM at 419. It could of course be argued that whereas South Africa could not have granted territory to any other State, there is no reason why it could not have acquired territory on behalf of the people of the territory. This was not the view of Judge Fleischhauer, ibid, but the position was so unclear that the British declined to enter into an agreement with South Africa to confirm the entitlement of the Namibians to use and occupy the island, see the Judgment, paras 59–60; 39 ILM at 334–337.

[457] Dissenting Opinion, para 29; 39 ILM at 387. See also ibid, para 18; 39 ILM at 385: 'I may add that contemporaneous conduct in relation to the Treaty is especially important in

This principle of contemporaneity is one of the important principles of treaty interpretation, and is not . . . given its proper effect by taking into account, as the Court has done, the attitude of the Parties more than 50 years later, when political and other circumstances may well have necessitated a change of administrative policy from that which had been evidenced for the half century immediately following the Treaty.

Taking account of the fact that the presence of the persons on the island would have to be 'considered in the context of the particular geographical characteristics of the region and contemporary modes of use and

this case in the light of the fact that observations regarding the various qualities of the river—whether they be breadth or depth or volume of flow—can vary considerably over a period of a hundred years, and could depend very much on the time of observation, be it in the wet season, the dry season or any other. The sense in which the Treaty was understood contemporaneously is the best index to what was actually intended, and any search for clarification of the terms used must focus intensely on this aspect.'

See also ibid, para 22; 39 ILM at 386. This view is entirely consistent with the Court's emphasis upon the importance of material closest in time to the critical event in the *Land, Island and Maritime Dispute*, ICJ Rep 1992, 351 at 395 (above n. 28): 'Such republican titles, particularly those granted in the years immediately following independence, may well provide some evidence of what the position was in 1821, and both Parties have offered them as such.' At around the time of the Anglo-German Treaty (his first edition dated from 1904), Crandall SB, *Treaties Their Making and Enforcement*, 2nd edn (1916), 383, wrote as follows: 'A practical and common construction of the terms of a treaty by the parties through proper representatives shortly after its conclusion is quite conclusive as to their meaning' citing the Opinion of the US members of the Alaskan Boundary Tribunal, see (1903) 15 UNRIAA 481 at 533–534. The divergence between the majority and the minority of the International Court in the *Kasikili/Sedudu* case lay in their differing views as to whether 'proper representatives' had been involved in the conduct attributed by Namibia to the parties. Crandall used as one of his examples the interpretation placed upon the first clause of Article VII of the Treaty of 1795 between Spain and the United States. That provision prohibited embargoes or the detention of the 'vessels or effects' of the subjects or citizens of either of the contracting parties. During the Cuban uprising of 1895–1898 the Spanish authorities had detained property in Cuba, a number of the cases arising out of an order proscribing the export of tobacco leaf from Cuba. It was argued before the Spanish Treaty Claims Commission set up under the Treaty of Peace between Spain and the United States of 1898 (a Commission established under US law to adjudicate 'claims according to the merits . . ., the principles of equity and of international law', see Crandall, 'Principles of International Law applied by the Spanish Treaty Claims Commission' (1910) 4 AJIL 806 at 807) that the expression 'vessels or effects' meant 'vessels or cargoes' and that the words embargo or detention related only to actions directed against vessels or cargoes. Evidence contemporaneous with the 1795 treaty supported such an interpretation, but with 'the outbreak of the Ten Years War, more than seventy years after the treaty was concluded', it was 'then asserted by the American Secretary of State, and thereafter consistently maintained by the Government of the United States . . . that the prohibitions of the article applied to embargoes and detentions of property on land as well as to vessels and their cargoes on the sea. The Spanish Government at first expressly denied the correctness of this instruction, but later acquiesced in it' (Crandall, *Treaties*, loc cit). The Commission accepted that Spanish acquiescence had resulted in the broader prohibition becoming the correct interpretation of the 1795 Treaty (see principle 10 of the Commission's statement of 28 April 1903, Crandall 'Principles of occupation of such territory'[458] and of the absence of protest by the British authorities, the Judge concluded that by 1947, when differences first arose between those authorities and the South African administration, there was already a common understanding that the island was part of South West Africa and that the main channel of the river therefore lay to the south of the island.

Despite his recognition of the importance of the requirements of intertemporality that a treaty should be viewed in the context of the circumstances, including the rules of international law, surrounding its making, even Judge Weeramantry saw nothing wrong in relying upon Article 31 of the Vienna Convention without demanding proof that Article 31 had a contemporary relevance to the 1890 Treaty. The first stage in the discussion of this question will be to consider whether Article 31 can be regarded as representing the customary international law of that time. However, there is the further issue of what consequences intertemporality might have as far as an assessment is concerned of the effect of subsequent changes in the law on the practice of the two States which occurred over an extended period of time after 1890.

(c) *Does Article 31 reflect the law of 1890?*

There can be little doubt that the general rule in Article 31(1) would have been familiar to a lawyer of 1890. The language of Hall's third edition of *A Treatise on International Law* of that year was not dissimilar:[459]

> When the language of a treaty, taken in the ordinary meaning of the words yields a plain and reasonable sense, it must be taken as intended to be read in that sense, subject to the qualifications, that any words which may have a customary meaning in treaties differing from their common signification must be understood to have that meaning, and that a sense cannot be adopted which leads to an absurdity.

Nor could there be any doubt that, at that time, the subsequent conduct of

International Law', at 809). If the Spanish had continued to contest this interpretation, the earlier construction would have held good, a situation which the dissentients in the *Kasikili/Sedudu Island* case would no doubt have regarded as supporting their view of the circumstances surrounding and following the 1890 Treaty between Germany and Britain!

[458] Dissenting Opinion para 31; 39 ILM at 387. As the Judge went on to explain (ibid para 31; 39 ILM at 387–388): 'We must not look for indicia of occupation in terms of settled housing or ordered agriculture, burial sites, or schools, for the very nature of this terrain prevented settled habitation in the manner known to Western jurisprudence and tradition. At best there would have been temporary occupation in makeshift huts from time to time as the rains and the climate determined. Such mud huts as there were would tend to be washed away during flood time, for they were not constructed for permanent occupation. Even agricultural holdings could have been at best a rather haphazard variety as compared with the holdings one is accustomed to in settled societies.'

[459] Op cit, 334; substantially identical words were used by the arbitrator in the *Van Bokkelen* case (1888) Moore, Int. Arb., vol II, 1807 at 1849.

the parties to the treaty was a significant aid to its interpretation.[460] The problem is, however, to identify its precise role in this process.

From one point of view, there is a similarity between the situation then and the position under the Vienna Convention. In draft Article 38, the International Law Commission had accepted that a treaty 'may be modified by subsequent practice in the application of the treaty establishing the agreement of the parties to modify its provisions',[461] in reliance upon the following well-known pronouncement by the arbitrators in the *Air Transport Services Agreement* case:[462]

> This course of conduct may, in fact, be taken into account not merely as a means useful for interpreting the Agreement, but also as something more: that is, as a possible source of a subsequent modification, arising out of certain actions or certain attitudes, having a bearing on the juridical situation of the parties and on the rights that each of them could properly claim.

Following objections from a number of States,[463] this provision was deleted at the Vienna Conference. The objections mainly concentrated on more formal aspects of the problems it would cause: that it would render meaningless the inclusion in treaties of specific provisions for their revision; and that it would raise 'serious constitutional problems for many States'.[464] It was also pointed out that draft Article 38 was either duplicated, or that its role could be performed, by what became Article 31(3)(b) of the Convention, 'under which subsequent practice in the application of

[460] See the *Samoan* claims (1902) 9 UNRIAA 15, arising out of the General Act of Berlin of 1889, in which it was held that the actions of Britain and the United States, without the consent of Germany, were in breach of their obligation to Germany only to proceed with the consent of all three parties. This interpretation of the Act was supported by the apparent understanding of the position by the parties 'in subsequent Agreements supplementary to the General Act made between them in 1892 and 1896 . . . [and] in the instructions issued for the Joint Commission sent to Samoa in 1899' (at 25); see also the Circuit Court of Appeals decision in *US v Eighteen Packages of Dental Instruments* 230 F 564 (1916) in which, in interpreting the US–Germany Postal Convention of 1899, the Court held that its view, 'that each signatory to the . . . convention was in no way to control the customs regulations of the other, is in accord with the subsequent practice of the signatories thereto' (at 569).

[461] Docs of the Conference, 55.

[462] (1963) 38 ILR 182 at 249, citing the *Temple* case, ICJ Rep 1962, 6 at 33, where the International Court had accepted that the subsequent conduct of the parties had 'recognised the line and thereby in effect agreed to regard it as being the frontier line' in substitution for the watershed of the specified range of mountains.

[463] See the comments on behalf of Finland, Japan, Venezuela, Vietnam, France, Spain, Chile, Canada, Soviet Union, United States, Poland, China, Colombia, Turkey, Guinea, Uruguay, Tanzania, Cuba, Philippines, Netherlands, Israel, Czechoslovakia, UN Conf on the Law of Treaties, First Session, 207–214.

[464] De Bresson (France), ibid, 208, para 63; Fijisaki (Japan), ibid, 208, para 58; Martinez Caro (Spain), ibid, 209, para 68; Grishin (Soviet Union), ibid, 210, para 4; Regla (Philippines), ibid, 213, para 43.

the treaty which established the [agreement] of the parties regarding its interpretation was to be taken into account'.[465] Overall, the inclusion of the draft Article might lead to less, rather than greater, flexibility in the attitude of States towards a treaty.[466]

With regard to the position in 1890, there was a similar, though probably stronger, reluctance to admit that the practice of States could informally amend the provisions of a treaty. The reason lay in the parallel regularly drawn in the literature between treaties and the formal contracts of municipal law.[467] The view was that such instruments required the same formalities for their modification as for their formation, and that they could not be altered by the mere conduct of the parties.[468] This perception was reinforced by the fact that international intercourse was not so multifaceted as it is now. The vast majority of international agreements were of the formal kind; there were few informal arrangements of the sort which today give rise to such problems of their legal status and effects.[469]

Where the conduct of the parties diverged from the ostensible meaning of the treaty's text, yet demonstrated an appearance of their common intent, the reaction was to demonstrate from this discrepancy or other sources that the text was ambiguous. This was, of course, the point which

[465] Castren (Finland), ibid, 207–208, para 57; Miras (Turkey), ibid, 212, para 28; Rosenne (Israel), ibid, 213, para 48.

[466] Phan-Van-Thinh (Vietnam), ibid, 208, para 61; De Bresson (France), ibid, 208, para 63.

[467] Wheaton H, *Elements of International Law* (1866), Part III, para 287: 'Public treaties are to be interpreted like other laws and contracts.'; Scott JB, *Cases on International Law principally selected from the English and American Courts* (1922), 452 (a quotation taken from *American and English Encyclopedia of Law*, vol 26, 555): 'In thus giving a construction to the language of treaties, the courts will adopt the same general rules which are applicable to the construction of statutes, contracts and written instruments generally, in order to effectuate the purpose and intention of the makers'; Dickinson E DeW, *A Selection of Cases and other readings on The Law of Nations Chiefly as interpreted and applied by British and American courts* (1929), 1074 (quoting Crandall, *Treaties*, n 456, 377): 'It is a general rule of interpretation of written contracts, applicable to treaties, that prior negotiations are merged in the written instrument, and cannot be resorted to for the purpose of contradicting or explaining its plain provisions.'

[468] At common law, a contract under seal could only be terminated or varied by another contract under seal, see *West v Blakeway* (1841) 133 Eng Rep 940, though, in equity, a written or oral contract of termination or variation was a good defence to an action on the deed, *Berry v Berry* [1929] 2 KB 316. Problems also arose in relation to attempts by oral agreement to terminate or vary contracts which were in written form to satisfy the Statute of Frauds: see *Morris v Baron and Co* [1918] AC 1; *British and Beningtons Ltd v North Western Cachar Tea Co Ltd* [1923] AC 48.

[469] See Schachter, 'The Twilight Existence of Non-Binding International Agreements' (1977) 71 AJIL 296; Widdows, 'What is an Agreement in International Law?' (1979) 50 BYIL 117; Aust, 'The Theory and Practice of Informal International Agreements' (1986) 35 ICLQ 787; McNeil, 'International Agreements: Recent US–UK Practice Concerning the Memorandum of Understanding' (1994) 88 AJIL 821.

Judge Anzilotti made so forcibly in the *Convention on the Employment of Women at Night* case[470] that the meaning of a text could only be regarded as clear if its apparent meaning coincided with the parties' intentions. In the situation now under consideration the guide to those intentions was to be discovered not in the context or negotiating record, but in the parties' later conduct in performing the treaty.

The case which is most illustrative of the international legal position at the end of the nineteenth century and in the early years of the twentieth century was the *Chamizal* arbitration.[471] A change in the course of the Rio Grande river had resulted in the Chamizal tract being separated from other Mexican territory and becoming attached to land abutting El Paso, Texas. In determining whether, as a result, the tract became part of United States territory or remained Mexican, the Award of the arbitrators was careful to demonstrate why the initial two relevant treaties of 1848 and 1853, however strongly they might have 'indicated an intention to establish a fixed line boundary',[472] were in fact not free from doubt so that, as a consequence of their ambiguity, 'the subsequent course of conduct of the parties, and their formal conventions, may be resorted to as aids to construction'.[473] As the Award went on to hold:[474]

> On the whole, it appears to be impossible to come to any other conclusion than that the two nations have, by their subsequent treaties and their consistent course of conduct in connection with all cases arising thereunder, put such an authoritative interpretation upon the language of the Treaties of 1848 and 1853 as to preclude them from now contending that the fluvial portion of the boundary created by those treaties is a fixed line boundary.

The conduct of the parties in the *Chamizal* arbitration, although amounting to an apparent agreement between them as to the meaning to be attributed to the 1848 and 1853 treaties, was nevertheless dealt with in a manner which would have been classified as falling under Article 32, an approach which, as has already been mentioned,[475] coincides with that later adopted by the Permanent Court. What is less easy to ascertain is where the law stood with regard to subsequent conduct of one or more parties to a treaty in a situation where it would have been less easy to suggest that the conduct had been tacitly accepted by the other party or parties. This is not the place to indulge in a detailed discussion of acquiescence and estoppel, but it can be said of the former that its scope is, and was, far from clear. For example, writing in 1954, though basing his

470 (1932) PCIJ Ser A/B, No 50 at 383.

471 Text in (1911) 5 AJIL 782. The Award was prepared by the Presiding Commissioner while the American and Mexican Commissioners submitted 'their opinions on the points in which they dissent' (ibid at 785).

472 Ibid, at 797–798.

473 Ibid, at 798.

474 Ibid, at 805.

475 Above. n 451.

observations on material from earlier times, MacGibbon had this to say:[476]

> Evidence of the inaction of a party, although not conclusive, may be of considerable probative value . . . The failure of one party to a treaty to protest against acts of the other party in which a particular interpretation of the terms of the treaty is clearly asserted affords cogent evidence of the understanding of the parties of their respective rights and obligations under the treaty.

This suggests that the understanding or agreement thus established between the parties will not necessarily be conclusive as to a treaty's interpretation, and is thus in conformity with the current law as expressed in Article 31(3)(b) of the Vienna Convention in that the subsequent practice of the parties establishing their agreement regarding the treaty's interpretation is no more than something to 'be taken into account, together with the context'.

There is, however, a problem with the equation that an agreement or understanding is brought about by the conduct of one party accepted by the conduct of the other, or by that other party's acquiescence in what is taking place. What standard is to be applied to show that acquiescence has occurred and that there is thereby established an agreement or understanding in terms of the conduct of the first party? There is perhaps a parallel to be drawn with the situation under municipal law in relation to the acceptance of offers of a contract. At common law, an offeror could not impose a contractual obligation upon an offeree by stipulating in the offer that, if the latter did not reject the offer, he/she would be taken to have accepted it.[477] Normally, to create a contract, an offer would have to be accepted. On the other hand, there are circumstances in which a duty to reply may be imposed upon an offeree if he/she does not wish his/her silence to be interpreted as an acceptance.[478] At the international level, whether acquiescence has occurred would depend upon the existence of a duty to react to a course of conduct by a party where rights are called in question by the conduct.[479] Whether such a duty has arisen depends upon a variety of

[476] 'The Scope of Acquiescence in International Law' (1954) 31 BYIL 143 at 146. See also that author's later comment (at 163–164) that the 'pleadings in the *Delagoa Bay Arbitration*, the *British-Venezuela Boundary Arbitration*, the *Alaskan Boundary* dispute, and correspondence in the Alaska dispute between Russia and Great Britain, provide further examples of the reliance placed on the notion of acquiescence'.

[477] Greig DW and Davis JLR, *The Law of Contract* (1987), 301.

[478] Ibid, 303. See generally *Empirnall Holdings Pty Ltd v Machon Paull Partners Pty Ltd* (1988) 14 NSWLR 523.

[479] See MacGibbon, op cit, n. 475, 170, citing Anzilotti; *Cours de droit international* (French trans by Gidel, 1929), 344: 'Thus Anzilotti remarked that silence maintained by a State after a situation had been notified or had become generally known could fairly be interpreted as acquiescence and abandonment of claims to the contrary, if, by virtue of special agreements or general practice, the occasion was one on which the State could, or ought to, have protested'.

factors. A reaction would more readily be expected in the context of a specific dispute, or where rights of sovereignty over territory or under a treaty are involved. There is also the issue of knowledge: can a State be expected to react to conduct of which it was unaware?[480]

There is an unfortunate element in this discussion. If a duty to react is not found to have existed, so that no acquiescence can have occurred, and therefore no agreement or understanding can have been established between the parties as to the interpretation of their treaty, what value is to be placed upon the conduct in question? In the *Kasikili/Sedudu Island* case,[481] the International Court's judgment avoided this issue by concentrating upon the parties' (Britain's and South Africa's) later failure to agree and disregarded both the earlier practice and the principle contained in Article 32 of the Vienna Convention. This is rather an extreme view. The existence of an agreement or understanding (the latter presumably being less probative than the former) depends upon the circumstances of and surrounding the conduct in question. But, if the threshold of an agreement or an understanding is not reached, can the conduct simply be ignored? If there is no duty to respond, or if there is an adverse reaction to the conduct, it should not be the case that the conduct (and any reaction to it) can simply be disregarded. As a matter of logic, it would seem that both the conduct and the reaction (if any) are relevant material to an interpreter. It is the circumstances viewed as a whole which establish a gradation in the value of such evidence, rather than determine an artificial cut-off point where the practice ceases to be of relevance because it fails to give rise to an agreement or understanding as to the meaning of the treaty in issue. However, if that is the way that Article 31 is being interpreted, to the total disregard of Article 32 as far as subsequent conduct is concerned, then the effect of the Vienna Convention in this respect is not to codify pre-existing law, but to produce a shift in the law to render it inappropriate for application to treaties of an earlier time.

(d) The significance of Article VI of the 1890 Treaty

Does it follow from these criticisms of the Court's judgment in the *Kasikili/Sedudu Island* case that it was wrongly decided? On a simple issue of intertemporality in relation to the law of treaties, the approaches adopted by the major dissentients to the interpretation of Article III of the

[480] The material relied upon by MacGibbon, op cit, n. 475 at 173–181, suggests that the need to respond is initiated either by actual knowledge or by the notoriety of the conduct in question giving rise to a form of constructive knowledge: see, in particular, the *Anglo–Norwegian Fisheries* case, ICJ Rep 1951, 116 at 139: 'The notoriety of the facts, the general toleration of the international community, Great Britain's position in the North Sea, her own interest in the question, and her prolonged abstention would in any case warrant Norway's enforcement of her system against the United Kingdom.'

[481] Judgment of 13 December 1999; text in (2000) 39 ILM 310.

1890 Treaty seem more persuasive. While preferable to the Court's apparent disregard of the requirements of intertemporality, their versions are equally open to the objection that they took too narrow a view of the Treaty. It was not sufficient to set the practice involved into its relevant timeframe; it was also necessary to place the treaty into context and the circumstances surrounding its creation. Two features in particular stand out. The first concerned the geographical and related uncertainties surrounding its drafting and possible application; and the second related to the context of Article III within the Treaty.

It is not suggested that the fact was ignored that the representatives of the two States had no clear idea of the situation on the ground. What is suggested is that its implications for the interpretation of the Treaty were not fully examined. From the lack of knowledge of the parties to the Treaty, and the context of Article III within the Treaty, it can be said that that provision did not constitute a boundary treaty, designed to determine an international frontier for all time.[482] It is curious, therefore, that Namibia should have been prepared to recognise 'it as the treaty determining the boundary between their territories'.[483] Article III constituted no more than a provisional dividing line between the spheres of influence of the two colonial powers. To preserve the benefits of the Treaty in lessening or preventing possible territorial rivalries between them (the object and purpose of the Treaty), they agreed, in Article VII, 'not to interfere with any sphere of influence assigned to the other by Articles I to IV', nor 'in the sphere of the other make acquisitions, conclude Treaties, accept sovereign rights or Protectorates, nor hinder the extension of influence of the other'.[484] It is clear from the wording of the last part of the provision quoted[485] that the boundary did not relate to an existing, but to a future, sphere of influence in large areas allocated to the State concerned. Indeed, it was because of the geographical and demographic uncertainties of the region that Articles I to IV were qualified by Article VI whereby '[a]ll the lines of demarcation traced in Articles I to IV shall be subject to rectification by agreement between the two Powers, in accordance with local

[482] As Judge Oda asserted (Separate Opinion para 26; 39 ILM at 365): 'The 1890 Treaty is an instrument which determined the respective spheres of influence of the Parties in this region of Africa but which certainly did *not* fix national boundaries there between the territories of Germany and Great Britain. The limit of the German sphere of influence was fixed as the "entre of the main channel of the Chobe River", but in that Treaty no concrete *boundary* line was indicated in this geographically complex area. The determination of the *boundary*, which would certainly have had the effect of determining the *legal status* of Kasikili/Sedudu Island, was at that time a matter far removed from the actual purpose of the Treaty'. See also Judge Weeramantry, Dissenting Opinion paras 94–99; 39 ILM at 402–403.

[483] Judgment, para 43; 39 ILM at 328.

[484] Ibid.

[485] The full text is given above p 112.

requirements'.[486] It would have made more sense from Namibia's point of view, therefore, to have contended that the line drawn in accordance with Article III of the Treaty was only the *de facto* boundary that could be converted into a *de jure* frontier with the due performance by Botswana of its inherited obligation under Article VI.

Given the prohibition in Article VII on subsequent changes affecting the operation of Article III, the 'local requirements' would seem to constitute primarily those existing at the time of the treaty, or perhaps those circumstances becoming subject to regulation by the States concerned in assumed conformity with the Treaty. The evidence would appear to show that the Masubia people from the Caprivi strip of South West Africa had intermittently been using and occupying the Island from at least as far back as 1907,[487] and probably even before the Treaty was made.[488] Moreover, as the Court admitted, the majority of maps from the earlier period 'placed the boundary around Kasikili/Sedudu Island in the southern channel of the Chobe'.[489] Because the thrust of Namibia's case was to demonstrate that the activities constituted either subsequent practice in performance of the Treaty or a basis for acquisitive prescription, the Court was able to determine the case on the ground that these activities had no 'official status'. It rejected the Namibian contention that 'Germany from 1909, then its successors after 1915, incorporated the local institutions of the Masubia into the structure of colonial governance, using them as instruments for exercising their authority'.[490] It was the Court's view that, 'as far as Bechuanaland, and subsequently Botswana, were concerned, the intermittent presence of the Masubia on the Island did not trouble anyone and was tolerated, not least because it did not appear to be connected with

[486] Quoted by Judge Parra-Aranguren, Dissenting Opinion para 7; 39 ILM at 421). The notion that 'rectification' of a boundary denoted its realignment to take account of, and settle, claims conflicting with its previous delineation was current at the time of the 1890 Treaty. The Treaty of Fontainebleau of 1785 prevented a war between the Hapsburg Empire and the Netherlands over the extent of Austrian rights in the Austrian Netherlands. In addition to settling issues relating to the River Scheldt, the Emperor relinquished any claim to Maastricht and its surrounding territory in return for an indemnity of 10 million guilders. After dealing with these matters, Lecky WEH, *A History of England in the Eighteenth Century*, vol V (1893), 355, concluded his description of the 1785 Treaty as follows: 'A few slight rectifications of territory were made, a few small fortresses were dismantled, and the contracting parties formally renounced all further pretensions that either might have against the other.'

[487] There was, of course, a difference between the Court and the dissentients in the way in which the evidence was interpreted as to whether the Trollope–Redman Report of 1948 (see below) should be interpreted as signifying only use of the Island by the Caprivi tribesmen or 'use and occupation' (the expression used by Judge Weeramantry in his Dissenting Opinion, para 33; 39 ILM at 388).

[488] As *Namibia* argued, Judge Weeramantry, Dissenting Opinion, para 35, 39 ILM at 388.

[489] Judgment, para 74; 39 ILM at 343.

[490] The argument as explained by the Court, ibid ; 39 ILM at 342.

interpretation of the terms of the 1890 Treaty'.[491] As to the maps, they could similarly be disregarded because 'none of them officially interpreted the 1890 Treaty'.[492]

This evidence should not have been so readily dismissed as it did show the situation on the ground. As the Court said of those maps, 'the evidence would tend . . . to suggest that the boundary line was shown as following the southern channel as a result of the intermittent presence on the Island of people from the Caprivi Strip'.[493] It was that very evidence which established the need to rectify Article III of the Treaty. There was, accordingly an obligation, imposed upon Britain (and its successors) by virtue of Article VI, to rectify the frontier established by Article III for that stretch of the river Chobe.

(e) Does 'rectification by agreement . . . in accordance with local requirements' amount to a legal obligation?

It has to be admitted that the rectification had to take place 'by agreement between the two Powers'. This raises the issue of whether one party, in this case Britain, was able to prevent a rectification in accordance with local requirements by withholding its agreement, and whether Botswana is entitled to take advantage of the situation thus continued in its favour.

The realisation that there was a genuine reason for departing from the text of Article III occurred when German administrators first moved into the area in 1909. Negotiations took place between the two States and the possibility of arbitration was raised.[494] It was this sequence of events which led the British Government to request the British High Commissioner for Bechuanaland (as Botswana was then called) to provide, for the purposes of a possible arbitration, 'all available information from local sources in support of the view that the north channel is the main channel'.[495] The response came in the form of the Eason Report of 1912 in which two main points were alluded to: in Eason's opinion, 'undoubtedly the North should be claimed as the main channel', but he acknowledged that the 'natives living . . . in German territory are at present growing crops' on the Island.[496] This Report was not passed on to the German authorities, nor did any arbitration take place. If any conclusion can be drawn from this episode, it might be that Britain could not make use of the Report with regard to the identification of the main channel of the Chobe without admitting to the Germans that any claim for rectification of the border around the Island which they might make would be justifiable.

A later attempt was made to achieve such a rectification. In 1947, the

[491] Ibid para 74; 39 ILM at 343.
[492] Ibid.
[493] Ibid.
[494] Judgment, para 53; 39 ILM at 331.
[495] Ibid.
[496] Ibid.

operator of a transport business in Bechuanaland sought the permission of Major Trollope, the South African official responsible for supervising the adjoining area of South West Africa, to bring timber along the northern channel of the Chobe past the Island.[497] As the operator also raised the matter with the Bechuanaland authorities, the ensuing exchanges between the two administrations led to a Report of 1948 prepared by Trollope and Redman, a District Commissioner in Bechuanaland,[498] which largely confirmed the Eason Report of 1912. Having pointed out that 'the "main channel" does not follow the waterway which is usually shown on maps as the boundary between the two Territories', it 'express[ed] the opinion that the "main channel" lies in the waterway which would include the island in question in the Bechuanaland Protectorate', but that, 'since at least 1907, use has been made of the Island by Eastern Caprivi . . . tribesmen and that that position still continues'. The Report also recorded that there was 'no evidence of the Island having been made use of, or claimed by Bechuanaland Tribesmen or Authorities or of any objection to the use thereof by Caprivi Tribesmen being made'; moreover, 'the country on the Bechuanaland side of the boundary is for all practical purposes not tribally occupied by Africans'.[499]

During 1948 and 1949 exchanges took place between the South African Government and the Bechuanaland authorities in which the former ultimately proposed that the latter should recognise the South (West) African claim to the Kasikili/Sedudu Island in return for a general permit for the use of the northern channel for navigational purposes. The Bechuanaland High Commissioner recommended to the Commonwealth Relations Office in London that this offer should be accepted. The proposal was not, however, proceeded with because of British concern about the international ramifications of South Africa's position as a Mandatory. Eventually the two sides agreed to an arrangement whereby the status quo would remain undisturbed.[500]

Apart from the way in which Namibia appears to have presented its case to the Court, it is difficult to understand why Botswana should have been allowed to rely upon the literal application of Article III of the Treaty, augmented by Article VII, to the disregard of the qualification contained in Article VI. It may be that the Namibian approach was influenced by a perception of the Court's Advisory Opinion in the *Status of South West Africa* case[501] that it stood *inter alia* for the proposition that an obligation to perform an act with the agreement of the State under the obligation could not exist as a matter of law. Whether this is in fact so,

[497] Ibid, para 56; 39 ILM at 332.
[498] Ibid, para 57; 39 ILM at 332–333.
[499] Ibid.
[500] Ibid, paras 59–60; 39 ILM at 333–337.
[501] ICJ Rep 1950, 128.

either as an issue of interpretation of the Court's views, or as a question of law, requires further consideration.

Unlike other States the territories supervised by which had not achieved independence in the aftermath of the Second World War, South Africa had refused to transfer South West Africa to the Trusteeship System set up under the UN Charter. One of the questions asked of the International Court by the General Assembly was whether 'the provisions of Chapter XII of the Charter [were] applicable and, if so, in what manner, to the Territory of South West Africa'.[502] It was in this context that the Court considered whether Article 77(1) of the Charter imposed an obligation upon South Africa to transfer the Territory to the new system. Article 77(1) reads in part as follows:

The trusteeship system shall apply to such territories in the following categories as may be placed thereunder by means of trusteeship agreements:
a. territories now held under mandate;
. . .
c. territories voluntarily placed under the system by States responsible for their administration.

The basis of the Court's rejection of the idea of such an obligation was the fact that the process of transfer had to be accomplished by agreement. Indeed, by Article 77(2) of the Charter, it was to be 'a matter for subsequent agreement as to which territories in the foregoing categories will be brought under the trusteeship system and upon what terms'. As the Court said in this context, the 'parties must be free to accept or reject the terms of a contemplated agreement. No party can impose its terms on the other party'.[503]

There were countervailing arguments. As will have been noticed, Article 77(1) opens with the words the 'trusteeship system shall apply', the subsequent reference to 'as may be placed thereunder' being explicable in the case of mandated territories by reference to Article 78 of the Charter whereby the trusteeship system was not to 'apply to territories which have become Members of the United Nations', or at least had achieved independence and were, therefore, as States, in a position to apply for membership of the Organisation. Those who contended that South Africa was under an obligation to place South West Africa under trusteeship reinforced this argument by pointing to the fact that Article 77(1)(c) was expressed to be 'voluntary' on the part of administering powers, whereas this was not the case with regard to mandatories. They also relied upon Article 80(2). Paragraph (1) of Article 80 preserved the *status quo* by providing that, until agreements for placing territories under the trusteeship system had

[502] The text of the Resolution is given ibid at 129.
[503] Ibid at 139.

been concluded, 'nothing in this Chapter shall be construed in or of itself to alter in any manner the rights whatsoever of any States or any peoples or the terms of existing international instruments to which Members of the United Nations may respectively be parties'. However, paragraph (2) made clear that this was to be no more than a provisional measure by stipulating that paragraph (1) 'shall not be interpreted as giving grounds for delay or postponement of the negotiation and conclusion of agreements for placing mandated and other territories under the trusteeship system as provided for in Article 77'.

As the Court started from the standpoint that agreement requires consent and does not signify obligation, it followed that the word 'voluntarily' in category (c) of Article 77(1) could be 'explained as having been used out of an abundance of caution and as an added assurance of freedom of initiative to States having territories falling within that category.'[504] As for Article 80(2), that provision was 'entirely negative in character and cannot be said to create an obligation to negotiate and conclude an agreement. Had the parties to the Charter intended to create an obligation of this kind for a mandatory State, such intention would necessarily have been expressed in positive terms.'[505]

The Court thus shared the view of a significant number of States[506] that, as a transfer from mandate to trusteeship required an agreement with a mandatory, the process of transfer could only be voluntary as far as a mandatory was concerned. As a result of its refusal to render Article 77(1)(a) effective by imposing an obligation to transfer on mandatories in respect of territories not attaining independence, the Court had to render Article 80(1) effective instead, by reading into it a continuing obligation upon the mandatory, not only to abide by the mandate agreement with regard to the territory, but also to accept the supervision of its conduct by the United Nations. If, behind the Court's rejection of the obligatory nature of Article 77(1)(a), was a refusal to write an agreement to impose upon the parties (and more particularly the mandatory), the consequence was a rewriting of the role of the General Assembly. As Article 77(1)(a) did not provide a solution acceptable to the Court, so Article 80(1) was employed to structure an edifice whereby the General Assembly could assume the role of supervisory organ with respect to the mandate over South West Africa, following the demise of the League of Nations. As the Court explained the position:[507]

[504] Ibid.

[505] Ibid at 140.

[506] For the divided opinions on the issue and the gradual shift in favour of the view rejected by the Court, see the present writer's consideration of the relevant material in 'Nicaragua and the United States: Confrontation over the Jurisdiction of the International Court' (1991) 62 BYIL 119 at 147–814.

[507] ICJ Rep 1950 at 136–137.

The necessity for supervision continues to exist despite the disappearance of the supervisory organ under the Mandates System. It cannot be admitted that the obligation to submit to supervision has disappeared merely because the supervisory organ has ceased to exist, when the United Nations has another international organ performing similar, though not identical, supervisory functions.

These general considerations are confirmed by Article 80, paragraph 1, of the Charter . . . It purports to safeguard, not only the rights of States, but also the rights of peoples of mandated territories until Trusteeship Agreements are concluded. The purpose must have been to provide a real protection of those rights; but no such rights of the peoples could be effectively safeguarded without international supervision and a duty to render reports to a supervisory organ.

It has to be said that the Court's opinion was hardly convincing. A conclusion that the Charter provisions did impose an obligation upon South Africa with regard to the Trusteeship System would have involved far less of a departure from those provisions than did its creation for the General Assembly of a role under that instrument as guardian of the mandate over South West Africa. As Judge Dillard said in the *Namibia* case, endorsing the approach of Judge de Visscher in his Dissenting Opinion in the earlier case[508] as having been more 'logically persuasive'.[509]

Although South Africa was under no duty to submit to the trusteeship system or to negotiate a specific trusteeship agreement, yet, as a Member of the United Nations, she was surely under a duty to negotiate in good faith and even, reasonably, with the United Nations concerning a viable alternative either within the trusteeship system or outside it.

This conclusion would seem to be as unsatisfactory as the result prescribed by the Court. If there was no obligation to conclude an agreement on reasonable terms, or on terms which good faith might require, there would still have been a need for the fall-back supervisory functions of the General Assembly over the continuing South West African mandate. An obligation to negotiate without an obligation to agree upon such terms would have been of little value in this context. Indeed, in a rather curious footnote, Judge Dillard came close to admitting as such when he wrote that the 'use of discretion and freedom to bargain which the system may confer does not imply the right to exercise an attitude of uninhibited freedom of action'.[510]

508 Ibid, at 186–190.

509 ICJ Rep 1971, 16 at 159.

510 Ibid, n. 1. The context of which Judge Dillard made this observation was the separate opinion of Judge Klaestad in the *Voting Procedure* case, ICJ Rep 1955, 67 at 88, which the former explained in the following terms: 'Judge Klaestad . . . stated that as a Member of the United Nations South Africa "is in duty bound to consider in good faith" a recommendation by the General Assembly, but concluded that however serious it may be it does not involve a "true legal obligation" ', a conclusion with which Judge Dillard could not 'agree'. The two situations were quite different. Judge Klaestad was making the point that, generally speaking,

There is a parallel to be drawn here with the common law of contract in which it is matter of debate whether, and in what circumstances, an agreement to agree can constitute an effective contract. The basic approach, and one which influenced the Court's thinking in the *Status of South West Africa* case, is that 'there is no concluded contract where an essential or critical term is expressly left to be settled by future agreement of the parties',[512] nor is it the role of a court 'to make a contract for the parties or to go outside the words they have used'.[512] Despite the negative tenor of these judicial pronouncements, it nevertheless remains true that if a court can be persuaded that the 'parties intended to make a contract, it will if possible give effect to their intention no matter what difficulties of construction arise'.[513]

Article VI of the Anglo-German Treaty 1890 raises another issue familiar to the common law. It can be said of that provision that it was designed as an essential element in balancing the superficially strict requirements of Articles III and VII with the reality of local conditions. It certainly appears as if the parties regarded it as creating a legal obligation. However, such an intention would be rendered nugatory if either party could decline to perform the apparent undertaking on the basis that they were free to withhold their agreement. It is certainly arguable under Anglo-Australian law that '[w]here, in a bilateral arrangement, one of the parties is, by the terms of the arrangement, granted an unfettered discretion whether to perform, or how he chooses to perform, . . . no legal relations are created'.[514] In a municipal context, courts will often save such

neither a decision of the League Council, nor that of the General Assembly, despite the fact that its decisions (recommendations) could be adopted by a two-thirds majority vote, would be binding upon South Africa in the absence of its concurrence. Judge Dillard was dealing exclusively with the position of a mandatory power retaining a territory after the dissolution of the League of Nations. This assertion seems to suggest that the discretion implicit in the duty to negotiate is not unfettered: it does not amount to 'an uninhibited freedom of action'. An obligation to negotiate in good faith or reasonably carries with it a duty to accept an offer commensurate with what constitutes reasonable terms for the transfer into, and further supervision of the territory in, the trusteeship system.

[511] Sugerman J of the New South Wales Full Court in a dissenting judgment cited with approval on appeal to the High Court of Australia in the same case by Menzies J: *Thorby v Goldberg* (1964) 112 CLR 597 at 607; see also *May and Butcher Ltd v R* (1929) [1934] 2 KB 17 n at 21 per Viscount Dunedin.

[512] These words of caution were added by Lord Wright to a very broad statement of the law, *inter alia* asserting that it was 'the duty of the court to construe . . . documents fairly and broadly, without being too astute or subtle in finding defects': (*Hillas (WN) and Co Ltd v Arcos Ltd* (1932) 38 Com. Cas. 23 at 36–7).

[513] Williams J in *York Air Conditioning and Refrigeration (A/asia) Pty Ltd v Commonwealth* (1949) 80 CLR 11 at 26.

[514] Greig DW and Davis JLR, *The Law of Contract* (1987), 238, citing *Roberts v Smith* (1859) 157 Eng Rep 861; and *Re Richmond Gate Property Col Ltd* [1965] 1WLR 335; see also *Placer Development Ltd v Commonwealth* (1969) 121 CLR 353.

undertakings from oblivion by fettering the discretion, for instance, by holding that the parties' intentions can be met if the undertaking requires the performer to act 'honestly or honestly and reasonably'.[515]

In relation to the 1890 Treaty, it cannot be supposed that the parties intended to retain for themselves a totally unfettered discretion as to whether or not, under Article VI, they would agree to a rectification of the boundaries prescribed in Articles I to IV. To read it in that way would deprive Article VI of content because, even if no such provision were contained in the Treaty, it would be open to the parties to modify by agreement the boundaries established by the Treaty. However, the issue of agreement apart, the wording of Article VI is that of legal obligation: the expression 'shall be subject to rectification' is a clear undertaking to correct errors. Moreover, the errors are identified as those resulting from 'local requirements' in so far as they differ from the textual requirements of, in this case, Article III.

Nor is it possible to say that this wording is irrelevant to an assessment of the discretion granted to the parties by the reference to rectification 'by agreement'. Although the parties can choose to make more substantial changes if they wish, the only ones which they are obliged to make are those coinciding with local requirements. The discretion available to the parties is limited by that prescription. Indeed, this view of Article VI is reinforced by a different aspect of the way in which the common law deals with such contracts. An agreement including a provision to rectify a situation set out in another provision would be incomplete and ineffective as a contract without some means of identifying the basis upon which the rectification is to take place.[516] In dealing with issues of incompleteness, the courts take the view that where the agreement contains a formula for resolving the difficulty, the contract is complete and enforceable.[517] The reference to local requirements in Article VI is an example of the parties' providing their own formula to identify what had to be rectified.

[515] *Meehan v Jones* (1982) 149 CLR 571 at 589 per Mason J; see also *Greenberg v Meffert* (1985) 18 DLR (4th) 548, a decision of the Ontario Court of Appeal, leave to appeal to the Supreme Court of Canada dismissed (1985) 30 DLR (4th) 768.

[516] As Greig DW and Davis JLR, op cit n. 513, 377, explain the position: 'Where the parties' agreement is incomplete, apparently dependent upon some additional step to be taken by the parties themselves, then prima facie there is no contract. Consequently, if there is no means of ascertaining the true intentions of the parties in resolving the defect, the alleged agreement is of no effect', citing *Scammell (G) and Nephew Ltd v HC and JG Ouston* [1941] AC 251; *King's Motors (Oxford) Ltd v Lax* [1970] 1 WLR 426.

[517] *Brown v Gould* [1972] Ch 53; *Upper Hunter County District Council v Australian Chilling and Freezing Co Ltd* (1968) 118 CLR 429.

(f) *The true significance of the parties' subsequent conduct*

If it is thought that the formula of rectification 'in accordance with local requirements' is itself ambiguous, there is ample evidence, in the form of the parties' subsequent conduct, to identify what that involved in relation to the present dispute. Throughout its long history, the dispute had centred on the relationship between the position on the ground as demonstrated by the activities of the tribesmen of Caprivi and their German and South African promoters, and the boundary as set out in Article III of the 1890 Treaty. The final link in the chain between the rectification required and the agreement of the parties upon which the rectification was to have been based under the Treaty is surely provided by the principle of good faith which was as much part of the law of treaty interpretation and performance in 1890[518] as it is today.[519] It is an important aspect of that principle that, as

[518] Interpretation by reference to the canons of good faith is a primary principle for the interpretation of contracts in civil law systems. Under article 157 of the German Civil Code: 'Agreements shall be interpreted according to the requirements of good faith, ordinary usage being taken into consideration.' Commenting on this provision, Dannemann G, *An Introduction to German Civil and Commercial Law* (1993), 14, observed that it 'had influenced many other European laws'. It has been regarded as constituting a general principle of law and received into international law on this basis: see Lauterpacht, 'Restrictive Interpretation and the Principle of Effectiveness in the Interpretation of Treaties' (1949) 26 BYIL 48 at 56; *Re Italian Special Capital Levy Duties* (1949) 18 ILR 406 at 407: 'By reason of its character as a contractual instrument the Treaty must be interpreted according to the canons of good faith'; *Diverted Cargoes* case (1955) 22 ILR 820 at 825: 'The principles of international law governing the interpretation of international treaties have been evolved by legal writers and more particularly by international case-law in close conformity with the rules for the interpretation of contracts adopted by civilised nations ... [Amongst] those rules of interpretation which must be particularly borne in mind [is] the fundamental principle of good faith which governs both the interpretation and the performance of agreements'; *Lighthouses* Arbitration (Claim No 26) (1956) 23 ILR 342 at 345; *Alsing Trading Co v The Greek State* (1954) 23 ILR 633 at 635, drawing parallels with French and Greek law; *Interpretation of Article 78(7) of the Peace Treaty with Italy 1947 (Franco-Ethiopian Railway* Co claim) (1956) 24 ILR 602 at 626. It had been accepted as part of international law, even by those from a common law background, by the time of the 1890 Treaty, see Kent J, *Commentaries on American Law*, 13rd (1884), 188: 'Treaties of every kind ... are to receive a fair and liberal interpretation, according to the intention of the contracting parties, and to be kept with the most scrupulous good faith'; Taylor H, *A Treatise on International Public Law* (1901), 396: 'A treaty must be so construed as to exclude fraud and to make its operation consistent with good faith'; *Tucker v Alexandroff* 183 US 424 at 437 (1901); Report by the Law Officers dated 27 February 1872, McNair, *The Law of Treaties* (1961), 465: 'the letter of the Board of Trade of the 17th instant raises a totally new point, namely, a question of good faith on the part of Her Majesty's Government in insisting upon our construction, having regard to the intentions of the negotiators of the Treaty, as now stated in that letter.'

[519] Article 31(1) of the Vienna Convention commences by stating that a treaty 'shall be interpreted in good faith'. Indeed the principal requirement of the law of treaties, that, in the words of Article 26, '[e]very treaty in force is binding upon the parties to it and must be performed by them in good faith', can only be carried out if the treaty is also interpreted in good faith, a fact recognised in the Law Officers' Report in n. 517.

far as possible, a treaty should be interpreted in a way that renders it effective. Thus, it has been said that nothing 'is better settled, as a canon of interpretation in all systems of law, than that a clause must be so interpreted as to give it a meaning rather than so as to deprive it of meaning',[520] or indeed of effect.[521]

There is one final factor that should be mentioned. McNair might well have taken a different view of Article VI of the 1890 Treaty. He made the point that '[m]any treaties fail—and rightly fail—in their object by reason of the words used, and tribunals are properly reluctant to step in and modify or supplement the language of the treaty'.[522] He employed as a 'typical instance' of this phenomenon the *Peace Treaties* case,[523] in which Bulgaria, Hungary and Romania were able, on the Court's approach, to avoid having disputes under their respective Treaty arbitrated, by the simple expedient of each refusing to appoint a member of the tribunal to be set up under the Treaty in question. Though this failure to appoint amounted, in the Court's Opinion, to a breach of the Treaty, it did not mean that the Secretary-General could appoint a 'third' member of the tribunal (as was possible once two members were appointed and there was then a failure to agree upon a third member) and the two member panel render a 'majority' judgment by their joint votes in cases in which they were in agreement.

Indirectly, we are brought back to the issue of community values and the question of intertemporality, as they affect matters of interpretation at the time when the interpretation occurs. In terms of effectiveness, the two 1950 cases, *Peace Treaties* and *South West Africa*,[524] stand in striking contrast. With regard to the treaties being considered, no great time had elapsed since the Peace Treaties had been made or the UN Charter adopted. Both contained a significant gap as far as their effectiveness was concerned: in the first case, the possibility of a total lack of co-operation on the part of the former enemy States in relation to the dispute settlement mechanism rendering it nugatory; and, in the second, a lack of co-operation by a mandatory in transferring territory for which it was responsible to the trusteeship system, thus apparently avoiding the supervisory function vested in the United Nations as part of that system.

[520] *Cayuga Indians* case (1926) 20 AJIL at 587; adopted by the ICSID Tribunal in *Asian Agricultural Products Ltd v Republic of Sri Lanka* (1990) 106 ILR 416 at 440.

[521] *German Settlers in Poland* case (1923) PCIJ Ser B, No 6, 23: 'The fact that a question brought before the Court by the Council [of the League of Nations] under Paragraph 2 might conceivably be brought before the Court by a single Power as an international difference under Paragraph 3, cannot be accepted as a reason for preventing the Council from discharging its duties under Paragraph 2 . . . If the Court should refuse to take cognizance of a question presented under either paragraph on the ground that it conceivably might have been or might be presented in a different way under the other, the result might be to make both paragraphs practically ineffective.'

[522] *The Law of Treaties* (1961), 383.

[523] ICJ Rep 1950, 221.

[524] ICJ Rep 1950, 128.

Why was there such a difference in the result? The words of Judge Read in the *Peace Treaties* case could, with minor modification to take account of differing circumstances, be transposed to the alleged obligation to place mandated territories under trusteeship in Article 77 of the Charter. He said:[525]

> It is inconceivable to me that the Allied and Associated Powers would have consented to the setting up of machinery for the settlement of disputes . . . which could be rendered ineffective by the sole will of the three Governments concerned . . . I am, therefore, inclined at the outset to the view that the Disputes Articles must be interpreted in a manner which will ensure their real effectiveness rather than a manner which would deprive them of all effectiveness.

Not that it was applied in that way, because a narrow majority of the Court, including Judge Read, held that no obligation to transfer was imposed under the Charter. Where the difference lay was in the Court's preparedness in the *South West Africa* case, by a large majority, to regard the United Nations as succeeding to the supervisory role formerly exercised by the defunct League of Nations. It was certainly a means of ensuring the continuing effectiveness of the mandate and the overseeing of the performance of its obligations by South Africa.[526]

But the difference is not necessarily, nor solely, attributable to the express provisions of the two sets of documents (the Peace Treaties on the one hand and the Mandate and the UN Charter on the other). There were community values already casting an influence on the results. Within the world community, the need for the clearest evidence of consent on the part of participating States was still viewed as an essential element in all arrangements dependent upon agreement.[527] The *Peace Treaties* case also has to be seen against the background of the Cold War and the unlikelihood of the recalcitrant States abiding by any decision handed down by an

[525] Ibid at 231.

[526] Rather perversely, in view of his advocacy of effectiveness in the *Peace Treaties* case, in which he was in a minority of two, Judge Read took a contrary stance in the *South West Africa* case holding that 'in the absence of an "arrangement agreed between" the United Nations and [South Africa], and in the absence of succession by the United Nations to the political functions of the League, in respect of the Mandates, I am obliged to conclude that . . . [South Africa] is not under any obligation, arising under the Mandate, as regards accountability to, and supervision by, the United Nations' (ICJ Rep 1950 at 173).

[527] Much of the case law dealing with this issue concerned the jurisdiction of the International Court. As the Permanent Court had said in the *Eastern Carelia* case (1923) PCIJ Ser B, No 5 at 27: 'It is well established in international law that no State can, without its consent, be compelled to submit its disputes with other States either to mediation or arbitration, or to any other kind of pacific settlement.'

Certainly, in the early years of its existence, the International Court took a narrow view of what constituted the necessary consent. Compare, for example, the *Aerial Incident* case, ICJ Rep 1960, 146, with the *Barcelona Traction* case, ICJ Rep 1964, 6, and the *Nicaragua* case, ICJ Rep 1984, 391.

arbitral tribunal established in such a fashion.[528] The former aspect of the case would have guaranteed support for the States concerned had the latter situation eventuated. Hence the cause of the peaceful settlement of disputes would not have been advanced by any disregard of the emphasis placed on the consensuality of international jurisdiction.

The position with regard to South West Africa was totally dissimilar. While consensuality was still an element to be weighed in the balance, it was offset by a number of factors. South Africa was already on the way to being regarded as a pariah State. This was so because it was the only mandatory which, in the case of a territory not attaining independence, had refused to bring the territory for which it was responsible into the trusteeship system, which was rejecting any process of international supervision of its administration, and which was, instead, claiming that its obligations under the mandate agreement had come to an end with the dissolution of the League of Nations.

The fact that the transfer of a mandate to the trusteeship system could only take place, on the face of the Charter provisions, with the agreement of the mandatory was only sufficient to give South Africa the barest majority amongst members of the Court in favour of its view that it was under no obligation to effect such a transfer with regard to South West Africa. However, it did not follow from this conclusion that South Africa was released from its obligations under the mandate agreement, nor from international supervision of its performance of those obligations. Indeed, Article 80(1) of the Charter confirmed the continuance in force of existing international instruments, including therefore mandate agreements, until a trusteeship agreement had been concluded. If, through the refusal to co-operate in achieving this outcome, no agreement was made, then the provisional and temporary nature of Article 80(1) was indefinitely extended.

So much was agreed by implication from the Charter. But the doctrine of implied powers was capable of extending the degree of control exercisable by the United Nations. While it was true that 'the supervisory functions of the League with regard to mandated territories not placed under the . . . Trusteeship System were neither expressly transferred to the United Nations nor expressly assumed by that organisation', the 'necessity for supervision continue[d] to exist despite the disappearance of the supervisory organ

[528] The Court's rejection of the 'package deal' approach to the admission of States to membership of the United Nations in the *Admissions* case, ICJ Rep 1948, 57, was ignored in the ultimate resolution of the impasse over membership of the Organisation in the period up to 1955; in the *Competence* case, ICJ Rep 1950, 4, the Court was careful, when asked to approve an alternative solution to that problem, not to disrupt the balance between the General Assembly and the Security Council over the admission of new members under Article 4(2) of the Charter, by rejecting the suggestion that the General Assembly could decide to admit an applicant to membership in the absence of a favourable recommendation by the Security Council.

under the Mandates System'.[529] Moreover, an appropriate vehicle for supervision existed in the form of the General Assembly because, in that body, the United Nations had 'another international organ performing similar, though not identical, supervisory functions'. In this context, too, it was Article 80(1) which provided the essential nexus: the rights of the peoples protected by that provision could not 'be effectively safeguarded without international supervision and a duty to render reports to a supervisory organ', which, in the changed circumstances, was represented by the UN General Assembly.[530]

The refusal by South Africa to transfer South West Africa to the trusteeship system, and the Court's acceptance of its view that there was no obligation under Article 77(1)(a) for it to take such a step, created an ongoing problem, and it is the existence of this problem which brings us back to the question of intertemporality. Intertemporality is not only concerned with setting a treaty issue in the context of the time when the treaty was made. It is inevitable that the circumstances of the time of interpretation will have an influence on how the treaty text is perceived. That perception will also include temporal elements present in the issue to be determined, which, in this case, required a consideration of the prospective nature of the problem to be addressed. The Court's response was to provide an answer, not just affirming the continuation of South Africa's obligations under the Mandate, but also providing the means of ensuring, through the UN General Assembly, South Africa's international accountability in the performance of those obligations.

In the *South West Africa* case, the Court was able to compensate for the narrow view it took of Article 77(1)(a) by imposing an extended interpretation of the Charter and of the United Nations' powers of supervision established under that instrument. There would usually be no such avenue for redress open to a State which is denied the enforceability of an ordinary treaty provision because the implementation of that provision is dependent upon the agreement of the other party. There are strong reasons, therefore, why an interpreter should avoid such a conclusion if it is at all possible to identify objective standards by which to establish appropriate terms for the parties. The reasons are particularly strong in the situation where the provision forms part of the substance of the treaty, rather than dealing with procedures for the settlement of disputes arising out of the treaty.

In the *Kasikili/Sedudu Island* case,[531] the acceptance of a boundary, the implications of which 'on the ground' were entirely unknown to both parties, was conditional on the qualification introduced by Article VI and its implementation in good faith. The conduct of the parties may not have

529 ICJ Rep 1950 at 136.

530 Ibid at 136–137.

531 Judgment of 13 December 1999; (2000) 39 ILM 310.

amounted to their agreement as to the meaning of Article III of the 1890 Treaty. However, it would be difficult to deny that their conduct, throughout the twentieth century, represented an agreement recognising that the Island and the surrounding channels of the Chobe river constituted 'local requirements' within Article VI of the Treaty which the 'agreement between the Powers' needed to address.

The conduct of the parties in fact went further. It was acknowledged on both sides that the Island had been used intermittently, but over most of the century consistently on that time scale, by the tribesmen from Namibia, so that this basis of the need for rectification was clearly established. If Botswana was to refrain from agreeing to such an adjustment, the only possible justification for withholding its consent had also been identified by the Treaty and its surrounding circumstances and by the parties' conduct. In addition to the objective of delimiting as precisely as possible the parties' respective spheres of influence, the other principal reason for the 1890 Treaty was 'to secure for themselves freedom of navigation on the river'.[532] This continued to be a major preoccupation throughout the history of the dispute.[533] Ultimately, in 1992, by the Kasane Communiqué, the Presidents of Botswana and Namibia agreed *inter alia* that 'economic activities such as fishing shall continue on the understanding that fishing nets should not be laid across the river' and that 'navigation should remain unimpeded including free movement of tourists'.[534] The Court concluded, on the basis of its interpretation of Article III of the 1890 Treaty in favour of Botswana, with the following application of the 1992 Communiqué:[535]

> As a result, in the southern channel of Kasikili/Sedudu Island, the nationals of Namibia, and vessels flying its flag, are entitled to, and shall enjoy, a treatment equal to that accorded by Botswana to its own nationals and to vessels flying its own flag. Nations of the two States, and vessels, whether flying the flag of Botswana or of Namibia, shall be subject to the same conditions as regards navigation and environmental protection. In the northern channel, each Party shall likewise accord the nationals of, and vessels flying the flag of, the other, equal national treatment.

It remains to be said that, the only objective justification for Botswana to withhold its consent to a rectification of the boundary to satisfy local

[532] Ibid, para 45; 39 ILM at 329; Dissenting Opinion of Judge Fleischhauer, paras 7, 9; 39 ILM 416, 417.

[533] See the Redman–Trollope letter of 18 December 1947, Judgment, ibid para 56; 39 ILM at 332), and the subsequent proposed agreement whereby the 'Resident Commissioner of the Bechuanaland Protectorate considers that the [South African] proposal to set the boundary in the southern channel need not be resisted, if the use of the northern channel for navigation is guaranteed for the inhabitants and Government of the Bechuanaland Protectorate' (ibid para 59; 39 ILM at 334).

[534] Ibid, para 1202; 39 ILM at 351.

[535] Ibid, para 103; 39 ILM at 351.

requirements having thus been removed, the boundary should have been adjusted to comply with Botswana's obligations under Article VI of the 1890 Treaty. As it was demanding recognition of the (provisional) boundary prescribed by Article III, its failure to abide by Article VI constituted a weighty reason for withholding such recognition pending compliance with Article VI. A decision in favour of Namibia certainly seems more in accordance with the parties' intentions when they entered into the 1890 Treaty.

In terms of intertemporality this view of the dispute has something to commend it. As a first step, intertemporality emphasises the circumstances surrounding the making of a treaty including, but not necessarily limited by, the matters referred to in Articles 31 and 32 of the Vienna Convention. In the *Kasikili/Sedudu Island* case, the Court paid some attention to those circumstances, but the Namibian arguments before the Court do not seem to have relied upon the contextual link involving Article VI of the Treaty as a necessary adjunct to and qualification of Article III. Even under Article 31 of the Vienna Convention, it does not seem possible to ignore that link as a necessary element in interpreting Article III. Intertemporality also recognises that it is difficult, in interpreting an instrument, not to view it from the perspective of the time of interpretation. While it may be that the conduct of the parties closer to the time of a treaty's conclusion is a more significant guide to the makers' intentions than the parties' later conduct, it is rather artificial to suppress, or at least to downplay, that conduct in arriving at the meaning of a treaty. Not that the Court's approach was necessarily preferable. The later evidence certainly showed that the parties did not reach an agreement, though the evidence should nevertheless have been available under Article 32 of the Vienna Convention. In fact, of course, the historical record as a whole was highly relevant, and indeed conclusive, in relation to the significance of Article VI of the 1890 Treaty and how that provision should have operated to resolve the dispute in Namibia's favour.

VIII. CONCLUSION

While it is the thesis of this volume that intertemporality is a crucial element in the operation of the rules of international law in relation to treaties, it has to be admitted that recognition of its significance has been only spasmodic, even with regard to matters of interpretation. Nevertheless, enough has been said to establish that intertemporality is at least a valuable tool by which to assess the existing processes of interpretation and application with respect to the outcomes achieved.

It goes without saying that the starting point of any process of interpretation and application for dealing with a treaty is the situation prevailing at the time the treaty was made. However, the rules contained in Articles 31 and 32 of the Vienna Convention are both technical and restrictive. It is excessively legalistic to attempt to decree that an interpreter is entitled to be placed in the position of the parties at that time, *but only to the extent* that the surrounding circumstances are presented by the context as narrowly defined in Article 31(2), by the rules of international law in accordance with Article 31(3)(c), and by the preparatory work and the circumstances of the treaty's conclusion if, and only if, they, in the words of Article 32, 'confirm the meaning resulting from the application of article 31, or . . . determine the meaning where the interpretation according to article 31:

(a) leaves the meaning ambiguous or obscure; or
(b) leads to a result which is manifestly obscure or unreasonable.'

Fortunately, though paying lip service to the limitation contained in Article 32 with regard to reliance upon preparatory work, the Court has been prepared to bring in a wide range of evidence to place particular treaties in a context, leading up to, and contemporaneous with, their making, broader than that envisaged by Articles 31 and 32 of the Vienna Convention. This is in keeping with what intertemporality would require.

As far as the time of interpretation is concerned, intertemporality has rarely been acknowledged as a specific issue. In the *Namibia* case,[536] the International Court attributed the use of material, postdating the mandate agreement for South West Africa, to the parties' intentions in drafting Article 22 of the Convenant of the League of Nations, the 'sacred trust' being designed as an evolutionary concept. Contemporary community values were clearly influential in that approach and this has generally been true of the Court's interpretation of most constitutional texts.

With regard to the doctrine of implied powers, the Court, in a number of early cases, consistently allowed the United Nations broad scope in carrying out its functions and, in particular, to perform acts which were only reasonably, and not absolutely, necessary for those purposes.[537] While it was generally assumed that a similar approach to its constitutional text was equally available to other international organisations, in the *WHO Nuclear Weapons* case,[538] the Court displayed a much more restrictive attitude towards the powers of that Organisation. It could certainly be said that the regulation of the use of nuclear weapons was not something regarding which it was reasonably necessary for the WHO to recommend measures, given that it was a matter which fell more obviously within the remit of the UN General Assembly or Security Council. It should not have followed that the control of other activities, or of uses of

[536] ICJ Rep 1971, 16, above pp 55–56.
[537] *Reparations* case, ICJ Rep 1949, 174, above p 62; *UN Administrative Tribunal* case, ICJ Rep 1954, 47, above pp 64–66; *Expenses* case, ICJ Rep 1962, 151, above p 63.
[538] ICJ Rep 1996, 66.

materials, hazardous to health, fell outside the Organisation's competence. From the standpoint of intertemporality, the possibility of such regulation could be foreseen as a matter of community need and concern.

The time of interpretation will often constitute a critical date in two other respects. In the first place, whenever the conduct of the parties is claimed to affect the interpretation to be placed on a treaty, or to have achieved the tacit amendment of its provisions, obviously enough the treaty cannot be interpreted or applied exclusively by reference to what appears to have been its original meaning without at least considering the evidence of the conduct in question. It is a moot point whether to consider the time of interpretation as a critical date in order for such evidence to be assessed, irrespective of the outcome of that assessment, or whether it only becomes a critical date if the evidence is persuasive enough to affect the outcome by altering the interpretation to be placed on the treaty or by modifying its terms. The former is the better alternative because it does define a critical period within which the conduct must be examined.

Secondly, the interpretation of a treaty will often be affected by community values current at the time of interpretation. In some cases, the values will be given a legal content, but, in others, they would have to be regarded as extra-legal factors, even if they did affect the outcome of the process. In the former category would be cases like *Namibia*,[539] where the use of the values (the rights of the people of a dependent territory to self-determination and to protection against discrimination) would be ascribed to the original intentions of the parties that the text should be of an evolutionary nature. Values of an on-going nature may also be attributable, as a matter of intention, to the original parties to a treaty. The International Court has consistently taken the view that the fundamental purpose of a boundary treaty is 'the establishment of a precise, complete and definitive frontier'[540] that does not leave 'in suspense and . . . for a subsequent appreciation . . . the determination of the right of one State or the other to the disputed' area(s).[541] This presumption of finality makes it difficult for a State which seeks to rely upon some other explanation of the treaty[542] or upon the subsequent conduct of the parties for this purpose.

With regard to the influence of community values as an extra-legal phenomenon in treaty interpretation, it has to be admitted that illustrations are less readily discernible, except in the various examples of

[539] ICJ Rep 1971, 16.

[540] *Interpretation of the Treaty of Lausanne* case (1925) PCIJ Ser B, No 12, 20.

[541] *Frontier Land* case, ICJ Rep 1959, 209 at 221–222.

[542] *Territorial Dispute between Libya and Chad* case, ICJ Rep 1994, 6, the above two pronouncements being relied upon by the Court at 24.

(mainly) dissenting judges[543] proclaiming the reasons why the Court should have adopted their view in preference to the conclusion it had reached. For the most part, the Court and other international tribunals have been reluctant to acknowledge their influence. Article 31 of the Vienna Convention is based upon, and contributes to, the fiction that the meaning of a text is usually self-evident from the application of the factors referred to in that provision. Nevertheless, it can be said of the *WHO Nuclear Weapons* case[544] that the narrow view taken by the International Court of the implied powers of the Organisation was dictated by its reluctance to become involved in answering the question submitted to it, which it perceived as interference in matters more properly of concern to the United Nations. While this view provided an adequate justification for one of the grounds for deciding that the legality of the use of nuclear weapons lay outside the competence of the WHO,[545] it is difficult to accept that the implied powers of the Organisation did not otherwise extend to matters concerning the legality and regulation of other hazardous activities or the use of other hazardous materials.[546] Moreover, from the standpoint of intertemporality, it is unsatisfactory that attention was not paid to the possible future needs of the WHO to involve itself in such areas.

With respect to the *Kasikili/Sedudu Island* case,[547] the Court's failure to take into account the significance of Article VI of the Anglo-German Treaty of 1890, requiring a rectification of the boundary in accordance with local requirements, resulted in Article III assuming the attributes of the permanence of a boundary delimiting the extent of the territorial sovereignty of two neighbouring States. Namibia's surprising preparedness to concede this point contributed significantly to the transformation of a mere division of the two spheres of influence in colonial times into a modern boundary treaty. The only 'rectification' which occurred was that eventually accomplished by the 1992 Kasane Communiqué,[548] which, in advance of the submission of the dispute to the Court, guaranteed to the two parties equality of access to, and use of, the two channels surrounding the Island. However, the terms of the Communiqué did not effect a rectification of the

[543] Above pp 68–73.

[544] ICJ Rep 1996, 66.

[545] As the Court expressed the position (ibid at 80, and see above pp 77–80): 'There is no doubt that questions concerning the use of force, the regulation of armaments and disarmament are within the competence of the United Nations and lie outside that of the specialised agencies.'

[546] The breadth of the Court's limitation on the scope of WHO activities can be seen from this assertion (ibid at 77): 'The causes of the determination of human health are numerous and varied; and the legal or illegal character of these causes is essentially immaterial to the measures which the WHO must in any case take in an attempt to remedy their effects.'

For the implied powers issue, see above pp 78–79.

[547] Judgment of 13 December 1999; (200) 39 ILM 310.

[548] Ibid, para 102; 39 ILM at 351; above p 137.

boundary as required by Article VI of the 1890 Treaty, so that it in no way satisfied the obligation contained in that provision.

Viewed in the light of intertemporality, the *Kasikili/Sedudu Island* case appears as something of a curiosity. It is distinctly odd to contemplate the interpretation of a Treaty of 1890 in accordance with the rules contained in a Convention of 1969, even if, at that later date, they could be considered as representing customary international law. At least one would have expected some discussion of how Articles 31 and 32 of the Convention could be taken as identical with the law of 1890, whatever the parties may have agreed to be so. In its application of Article 31(3)(b) of the Vienna Convention, the Court largely ignored Article 32, which would not have been in accordance with the legal position during the era of the Permanent Court or earlier. In so far as it is possible to provide an accurate assessment of the law in 1890, it is probable that the conduct would have been judged against a spectrum of value, including that which, in today's terms, might well have been of less than agreement status. But even judged against the apparently stricter standard imposed by the Court in applying Article 31(3)(b), the earlier conduct of the parties could have been regarded as satisfying the requirements of a tacit agreement in the form of action of one side acquiesced in by the other. The mere fact that the later negotiations generated a refusal on the British side to formalise the agreement does not necessarily demonstrate that no previous agreement had been made in that way through the activities of the tribesmen of South West Africa and the conduct of the two administrations in relation thereto.

More unsatisfactory from the point of view of intertemporality was the failure of the Court, a failure resulting primarily from the way in which Namibia presented its case, to deal adequately with the context of Article III of the 1890 Treaty within the background circumstances of the Treaty as a whole. That evidence, basely acknowledged by the Court,[549] pointed unhesitatingly to the parties' ignorance about the position on the ground. From this, the Court, by concentrating upon Article III, deduced that the line drawn in accordance with that provision was to be definitive, as a means of avoiding future disputes regarding the respective spheres of influence of the parties. Those uncertainties should equally have directed the interpreter's attention towards Article VI, which constituted an acknowledgment by the parties that accommodations might have to be made with respect to that line to suit 'local requirements'. The ongoing differences about the Kasikili/Sedudu Island sector of the boundary take on a different significance if related to Article VI, rather than to Article III, of the Treaty. The parties' conduct may not have established the southern channel of the

549 Ibid, para 43; 39 ILM at 328: 'The . . . powers possessed only rudimentary information about Chobe's channels. If they knew that such channels existed, their number, features, navigability, etc., and their relative importance remained unknown.'

river as complying with the description given in Article III, but it undoubtedly demonstrated the need for the rectification provided for in Article VI, and what the rectification should be in order to satisfy that provision.

With regard to the relevant critical dates in the interpretation and application of treaties, these will normally be represented by the time when the treaty was made and by the time when the interpretation and application takes place. As to the former, the need for an interpreter to be made aware of the full circumstances surrounding the making of a treaty has already been restated. However, careful analysis of what constitutes that date can help identify problems in the use of language suggesting that time. The principal examples employed to call attention to the problem were Articles 48, 49 and 52 of the Vienna Convention with their references to 'conclude[d]' and 'conclusion' in relation to the invalidity of treaties. It could be seen from that analysis that, in terms of the presumed intention behind those provisions, if the normal meaning of conclusion as employed in the heading to Part II of the Convention as signifying the negotiation and adoption of the text of a treaty were translocated to those articles from Part V, the results could be unfortunate. It is a difficult matter to supply a more satisfactory interpretation of those provisions. It may be that the only possible solution is to regard the passage in the preamble to the Vienna Convention 'that the rules of customary international law will continue to govern questions not regulated by the provisions of the present Convention' as not preventing the application of such rules to augment those provisions in relation to questions addressed in, but not adequately dealt with by, those articles.

As to whether the time of interpretation constitutes a critical date, its role is not altogether clear. The reason for the uncertainty is that, although present perceptions of a treaty and its relationships, as well as community values where those are relevant, form the inevitable backdrop to how its interpretation is approached, there is a reluctance on the part of interpreters to acknowledge the extent to which they may have been influenced by their contemporary evaluation of a treaty and the circumstances surrounding its application. Where contemporary factors are openly avowed in the interpretative process, they are justified by reference to the proclaimed original intentions of the parties, as in the *Namibia* case,[550] or because the subsequent conduct of the parties demonstrates a later intention to depart from a possible, or even the original, meaning of the text.

Intertemporality in relation to treaties does not concentrate solely upon the law in force at different stages in its life. It emphasises that the process of interpretation and application of a treaty requires an appreciation of its terms in the wider context of the circumstances surrounding their

[550] ICJ Rep 1971, 16, above pp 55–56; *Gabčikovo–Nagymaros Project* case, ICJ Rep 1997, 7, above pp 56–59.

formulation, while also taking account of the significance which changes in those circumstances, both with regard to the treaty and in the wider community, might have for that process. Though particular dates might be critical for individual instruments, they will more likely be critical from the point of view of determining different phases in a treaty's history; only infrequently will a specific date be of determining importance. Ultimately, however, the past cannot be divorced from the present and the perceptions of today will always play a role, though not necessarily disclosed, in interpreting and applying a treaty, of whatever antiquity. The interpreter will inevitably be more comfortable handling what is familiar, hence the attraction of Articles 31 and 32 of the Vienna Convention as comprising the general rules of interpretation in providing the answer to all problems. Whether those solutions are always satisfactory is very much in the eye of the beholder because how those provisions are interpreted is also amongst the problems that have to be faced.